HOSTELS U.K.

"Finally, a hip-shaking, gut-level hostel guide for Britain and points beyond. Bursting with Karr's raw, honest insights, *Hostels U.K.* is an essential pack-item for the hostel hopper of any stripe."

—Ben Corbett, Hostels Editor,
Big World Magazine

"These books are super-useful! What to do, how to get there and what it's like, all rolled into one. You can't get this information all in one place anywhere else!"

—Peter Leblanc, Program Director,
Hostelling International (Seattle)

HELP US KEEP THIS GUIDE UP TO DATE

Every effort has been made by the author and editors to make this guide as accurate and useful as possible. However, many things can change after a guide is published—establishments close, phone numbers change, hiking trails are rerouted, facilities come under new management, etc.

We would love to hear from you concerning your experiences with this guide and how you feel it could be improved and be kept up to date. While we may not be able to respond to all comments and suggestions, we'll take them to heart and we'll also make certain to share them with the authors. Please send your comments and suggestions to the following address:

The Globe Pequot Press
Reader Response/Editorial Department
P.O. Box 833
Old Saybrook, CT 06475

Or you may e-mail us at:

editorial@globe-pequot.com

Thanks for your input, and happy travels!

HOSTELS SERIES

HOSTELS U.K.

The Only Comprehensive, Unofficial, Opinionated Guide

Paul Karr

with Martha Coombs

Old Saybrook, Connecticut

Cover and Text Design: MaryAnn Dubé
Maps: MaryAnn Dubé
Editorial Assistance: Evan Halper
Photography: Paul Karr, Martha Coombs, Hosteling International–Youth Hostel Association (England and Wales) Limited
Contributing Freelancers: Ashlee Arling, Verity Warne
Research Assistance: Rob Fairs, Yuko Masuda, Tomiko Matsumoto

Library of Congress Cataloging-in-Publication Data
Karr, Paul.
Hostels U.K. : the only comprehensive, unofficial, opinionated guide / Paul Karr with Martha Coombs. — 1st ed.
p. cm. — (Hostels Series)
ISBN 0-7627-0396-2
1. Tourist camps, hostels, etc. — Great Britain — Guidebooks.
I. Coombs, Martha. II. Title. III. Series.
TX907.5.G7K37 1999
647.9441'06—dc21 99-13794
CIP

Manufactured in the United States of America
First Edition/First Printing

CONTENTS

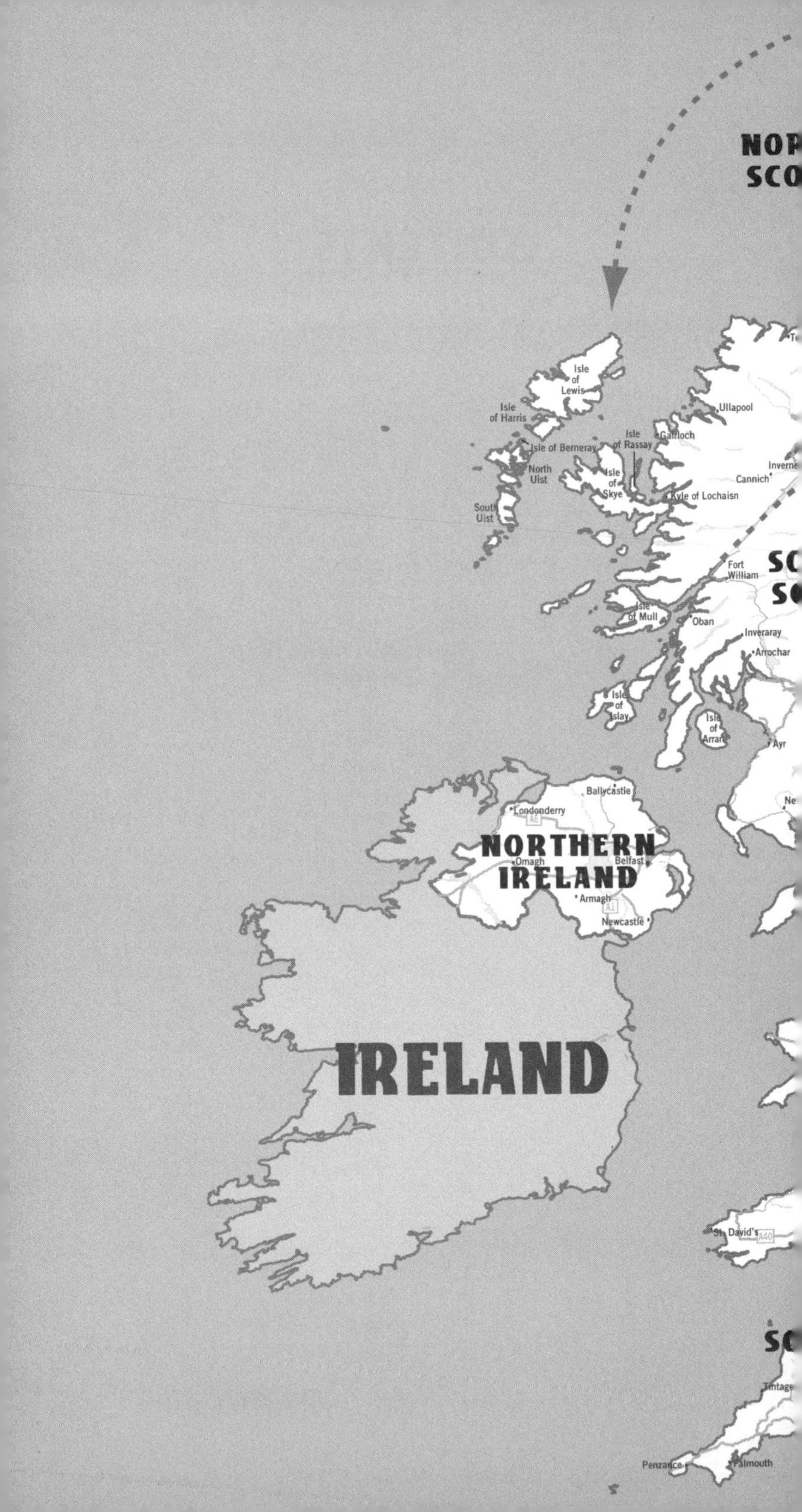

NOR
SCO
Isle of Lewis
Isle of Harris
Isle of Berneray
North Uist
South Uist
Isle of Rassay
Isle of Skye
Ullapool
Gairloch
Cannich
Kyle of Lochaisn
Fort William
Isle of Mull
Oban
Inveraray
Arrochar
Isle of Islay
Isle of Arran
Ayr
Ballycastle
Londonderry
A6
NORTHERN IRELAND
Omagh
Belfast
Armagh
A1
Newcastle
IRELAND
St. David's
A40
Tintage
Penzance
Falmouth

Shetland Islands
Orkney Islands
John o'Groats
A9
UNITED KINGDOM
Aberdeen
Braemar
A90
Perth
Falkland (Fife)
Edinburgh
A1
Newcastle Upon Tyne
Carlisle
Sunderland
A19
Penrith
Barnard Castle
NORTHERN ENGLAND
Kendal
Whitby
Scarborough
York
Leeds
Beverly
M62
Liverpool
Manchester
A55
Chester
M6
Lincoln
CENTRAL ENGLAND AND EAST ANGLIA
Nottingham
Shrewsbury
Birmingham
Norwich
Great Yarmouth
M5
Stratford-upon-Avon
Cambridge
A14
Malvern
M40
M11
A12
Monmouth
Newport
Oxford
Bristol
Bath
LONDON
Gillingham
Margate
M20
Canterbury
Cheddar
M3
Dover
Winchester
SOUTHEASTERN ENGLAND
Portsmouth
Brighton
Hastings
Swanage
Isle of Wight

ACKNOWLEDGMENTS

Paul Karr thanks Martha once again for companionship and editorial assistance. Martha thanks Senja St. John and Richard Coombs for guidance and support.

From both of us, thanks to the following, who went far beyond the call of duty: Ian and Carmen at Cardiff Tourism; Dermot at National Express; and the folks at Invernet, Northern Micro, and MCC for keeping us on-line when it mattered most. Thanks to Evan Halper for his continuing support. And a very special thanks to Mona Marshy in Edinburgh for her friendship and kind hospitality.

Thanks to our tireless freelance contributors, listed on the copyright page. They were our eyes and ears.

Thanks to the good folks at Magellan's for kindly helping sponsor the work a third time around with top-of-the-line travel supplies; to Canada 3000, the lowest-cost airline in North America and staffed by some fine people besides; to Rail Europe for information, assistance and their easy-to-use railpass system; to the London and Paris offices of Eurostar for lots of information and assistance and for making cross-Chunnel travel a real pleasure; to Hostelling International's U.S., Scottish, and English offices for continuous encouragement and assistance; to the independent hostel organizations of the U.K.; and anyone else who provided information, shelter, or a kind word.

And thanks, finally, to a world (literally) of new friends met or made on the road. So many of you have taught us about your corner of the world or otherwise made this work enjoyable and useful.

Thank you all.

The prices and rates listed in this guidebook were confirmed at press time. We recommend, however, that you call establishments before traveling to obtain current information.

HOW TO USE THIS BOOK

What you're holding in your hands is the first-ever attempt of its kind: a comprehensive listing and rating of hostels in England, Scotland, Wales, and Northern Ireland. Dozens of hostellers from countries all over the globe were interviewed in the course of putting this guide together, and their comments and thoughts run throughout its pages. Who knows? You, yourself, might be quoted somewhere inside.

We wrote this guide for two pretty simple reasons: First, we wanted to bring hostelling to a wider audience. Hostels continue to grow in popularity, but many North American travelers still don't think of them as options when planning a trip. We wanted to encourage that because—at its best—the hostelling experience brings people of greatly differing origins, faiths, and points of view together in a convivial setting. You learn about these people, and also about the place in which the hostel is situated, in a very personal way that no textbook could ever provide.

Second, we wanted very much to give people our honest opinions of the hostels. You wouldn't send your best friend to a fleabag, and we don't want readers traveling great distances only to be confronted with filthy kitchens, nasty managers, or dangerous neighborhoods. At least, we thought, we could warn them about unsafe or unpleasant situations ahead of time.

Of course we would also tip our friends off to the truly wonderful hostels—the ones with treehouses, cafes, free breakfasts, and real family spirit. So that's what we've done. Time after time on the road we have heard fellow travelers complaining that the guidebooks they bought simply listed places to stay but didn't rate them. Well, now we've done it—and we haven't pulled a single punch or held back a bit of praise.

How We Wrote This Book

The authors, along with a cadre of assistants, fanned out across England, Scotland, Wales, and Northern Ireland with notebooks and laptops in hand during the spring, summer, and fall of 1998. Sometimes we identified ourselves in advance as authors; sometimes we just popped in for surprise visits. We counted rooms, turned taps, tested beds. And then we talked with managers and staff.

Before we left we also took the time to interview plenty of hostellers in private and got their honest opinions about the places they were staying or had already stayed.

The results are contained within this book: actual hosteller quotes, opinions, ratings—and more.

What Is a Hostel?

If you've picked up this book, you probably know what a hostel is. On the other hand, a surprising number of people interviewed for this book weren't sure at all what it means.

So let's check your knowledge with a little pop quiz. Sharpen up your pencils, put on your thinking caps, then dive in.

1. A hostel is:

A. a hospital.

B. a hospice.

C. a hotel.

D. a drunk tank.

E. none of the above.

(correct answer worth 20 points)

2. A hostel is:

A. a place where international travelers bunk up.

B. a cheap sleep.

C. a place primarily dedicated to bunks.

D. all of the above.

(correct answer worth 20 points)

3. You just turned 30. Word on the street has it that you'll get turned away for being that age. Do you tell the person at the hostel desk the grim news?

A. No, because a hostel is restricted to students under 30.

B. No, because a hostel is restricted to elderly folks over 65.

C. No, because they don't care about your mid-life crisis.

(correct answer worth 10 points)

4. You spy a shelf labeled "Free Food!" in the hostel kitchen. What do you do?

A. b egin stuffing pomegranates in your pockets.

B. ask the manager how food ended up in jail.

C. run for your life.

(correct answer worth 5 points)

5. Essay question. Why do you want to stay in a hostel?

(extra credit; worth up to 45 points)

Done? Great! And the envelope, please. . .

1. None of the above. The word *hostel* is German, and it means "country inn for youngsters" or something like that.
2. All of the above. You got that one, right?
3. C. No age limits or restrictions here!
4. A. Free means free.
5. Give yourself 15 points for every use of the word "friends," "international," or "cool," okay? But don't give yourself more than 45. Yes, we mean it. Don't make us turn this car around right now. We will. We mean it.

What? All you wrote was "It's cheap"? Okay, okay, give yourself 20 points.

So how did you do?

100 points:	Born to be wild
80–100:	Get your motor runnin'
40–80:	Head out on the highway
20–40:	Lookin' for adventure
0–20:	Hope you don't come my way

Don't be embarrassed if you flunked this little quiz, though. Hostel operators get confused and blur the lines, too. You'll sometimes find a campground or retreat center or college setting aside a couple bunks—and calling itself a hostel anyway. In those cases we've used our best judgment about whether a place is or isn't a hostel.

Also, we excluded some joints—no matter how well-meaning—if they (a) exclude men or women, (b) serve primarily as a university residence hall (with a very few special exceptions), or (c) serve you a heavy side of religious doctrine with the eggs in the morning.

In a few cases our visits didn't satisfy us either way; those places were left out, set aside for a future edition, or briefly described here but not rated.

The bottom line? If it's in this book, it probably is a hostel. If it isn't, it's not, and don't let anyone tell you otherwise. There. 'Nuff said.

Understanding the Ratings

All the listings information in this book was current as of press time. Here's the beginning of a sample entry in the book, from a hostel in

Manchester, England. It's a fairly typical entry:

MANCHESTER HOSTEL 

Potato Wharf, Castlefield, Manchester M3 4NB

Phone Number: 0161–839–9960

Fax: 0161–835–2054
Rates: £9.00–£13.00 per HI member (about $13–$20 US)
Beds: 152
Private/family rooms: Yes
Office hours: Twenty-four hours
Affiliation: HI–YHA
Extras: TV, game, laundry, meals ($), lockers, conference rooms

First things first. See those little pictures at the bottom? Those are icons, and they signify something important we wanted you to know about the hostel. We've printed a key to these icons on page 6.

The overall hostel rating consists of those hip-looking thumbs sitting atop each entry. It's pretty simple: Thumbs up means good. Thumbs down means bad.

We've used these thumbs to compare the hostels to one another; only a select number of hostels earned the top rating of one thumb up, and a few were considered unpleasant enough to merit a thumb down. You can use this rating as a general assessment of a hostel.

Often we didn't give any thumbs at all to a hostel that was a mixed-bag experience. Or maybe, for one reason or another—bad weather, bad luck, bad timing, remoteness, an inability to get ahold of the staff, or our own confusion about the place—we just didn't feel we collected enough information to properly rate that hostel for you.

That said, here's a key to what these ratings mean:

 Cream of the crop; recommended

(No Thumbs) Adequate, so-so; or not rated

 Bad news; not recommended

The rest of the information is pretty much self-explanatory:

Address is usually the hostel's street address; occasionally we add the mailing address if that's where the hostel gets mail.

Phone is the primary phone number.

Fax is the primary fax number.

Note that all the phone and fax numbers are written as dialed from *within the U.K.*

E-mail is the staff's e-mail address, for those who want to get free information or book a room by computer.

Web site (this hostel didn't have one) indicates a hostel's World Wide Web page address.

Rates are the cost per person to stay at the hostel—expect to pay somewhere around $10 to $15 per person as a rule, more in cities or popular tourist areas. For private or family rooms, we've listed the total price for two people to stay in the room; usually it's higher than the cost of two singles, sometimes considerably so. Single or triple room rates will vary; ask ahead if you're unsure what you'll pay.

Note that these rates sometimes vary by season, or by membership in a hostelling group such as Hostelling International (HI); we have tried to include a range of prices where applicable. Most HI member hostels, for instance, charge a little extra if you don't belong to one of Hostelling International's worldwide affiliates.

Also, some hostels charge a small amount to supply sheets and towels if you haven't brought your own. (Sleeping bags, no matter how clean *you* think they are, are often frowned upon.) Finally, various local, municipal, or other taxes might also add slightly to the rates quoted here.

Credit cards can be a good way to pay for a bed in a foreign country (you get the fairest exchange rates on your home currency). More and more hostels are taking them. If credit cards are accepted, we have noted this here. That usually means Visa and MasterCard, less often American Express as well. Call the hostel for specific information. If no credit card line appears, that means that none were accepted at the time we did our research, but things may have changed. Again, call ahead and ask if you can use a card.

Office hours indicate the hours when staff are at the front desk and answer the phones, or at least would consider answering the phones. Although European custom is to use military time and all bus and train schedules read that way, most English hostel managers talk like Americans and say 11:30 for 11:30 P.M., not 23:30. We've used "American" time throughout this book.

Keep in mind that nothing is ever fixed in stone; some hostel staffs will happily field calls in the middle of the night if you're reasonable, while others can't stand it. Try to call within the listed hours if possible. A good rule of thumb to follow: The smaller a place, the harder it is for the owner/manager to drag him/herself out of bed at four in the morning just because you lost your way. Big-city hostels, however, frequently operate just like hotels—somebody's always on duty, or at least on call.

Season indicates what part of the year a hostel is open—if it's closed part of the year. (Since this hostel has no "Season" line, that means it's open year-round.) We've made our best effort at listing the seasons of each hostel, but schedules sometimes change according to weather or a manager's vacation plans. Call if you're unsure whether a hostel will be open when you want to stay there.

Private rooms or **family rooms** are rooms for a couple, a family with children, or (sometimes) a single traveler. Sometimes it's nice

KEY TO ICONS

 Attractive natural setting

 Ecologically aware hostel

 Superior kitchen facilities or great cafe/restaurant

 Offbeat or eccentric place

 Superior bathroom facilities

 Romantic private rooms

 Comfortable beds

 A particularly good value

 Wheelchair accessible

 Good for business travelers

 Especially well suited for families

 Good for active travelers

 Visual arts at hostel or nearby

 Music at hostel or nearby

 Great hostel for skiers

 Bar or pub at hostel or nearby

 Editors' choice: among our very favorite hostels

to have your own room on the road: It's more private, more secure, and your snoring won't bother anyone. A good number of U.K. hostels maintain private rooms though simpler places won't have them at all. Private rooms are hard to get; call ahead if you know you want one.

Affiliation indicates whether a hostel is affiliated with Hostelling International or any of several smaller hostel groups. For more information about what these organizations do, see "A Word about Affiliations" (page 10).

Extras list some of the other amenities that come with a stay at the hostel. Some—but not all—will be free; there's an amazing variety of services, and almost as big a variety in managers' willingness to do nice things for free. Laundries, for instance, are almost never free, and there's usually a charge for meals (indicated by dollar sign), lockers, bicycle or other equipment rentals, and other odds and ends. On the other hand, some hostels maintain free information desks. Some give you free meals, too.

Lockout and **Curfew.** Although this hostel has neither, many hostels have hours during which you are locked out of the place, in other words, you're not permitted on the premises. Many also have a curfew; be back inside before this time or you'll be locked out for the night.

With each entry, we've also given you a little more information about the hostel, to make your stay a little more informed—and fun. The sidebar to the right is the last part of the hostel entry that began above.

Best bet for a bite:
Rusholme neighborhood (Indian)

Insiders' tip:
Hacienda dance club nearby

Gestalt:
Manchester united

Hospitality: 

Cleanliness: 

Party index:

What does all this stuff mean?

Best bet for a bite tells you where to find food in the area; usually, we'll direct you to the cheapest and closest supermarket. But sometimes, in the interest of variety—and good eatin'— we'll point you toward a health food store, a place rich with local color, or even a fancy place.

Insiders' tip is a juicy secret about the area, something we didn't know until we got to the hostel ourselves.

What hostellers say relates what hostellers told us about a hostel—or what we imagine they would say.

Gestalt is the general feeling of a place—our (sometimes humorous) way of describing what it's about.

Safety describes urban hostels only; this hostel is not in a big city, so there's no safety rating. If it had been, we would have graded it based on both the quality of the neighborhood and the security precautions taken by the hostel staff, using this scale.

No worries

Keep an eye out

Dial 911

Hospitality rates the hostel staff's friendliness toward hostellers (and travel writers).

Smile city

Grins & growls

Very hostile hostel

Cleanliness rates, what else, the general cleanliness of a place. Bear in mind that this can change—rapidly—depending on the time of year, turnover in staff, and so forth. Use it only as a general guide.

Spic-'n'-span

Could be cleaner. . .

Don't let the bedbugs bite

The **party index** is our way of tipping you off about the general scene at the hostel:

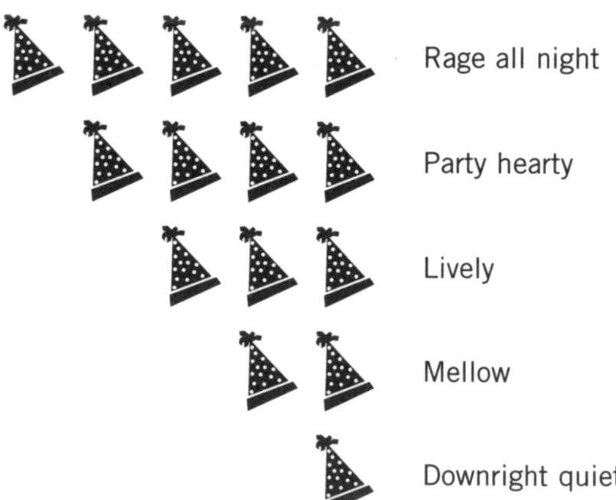

Rage all night

Party hearty

Lively

Mellow

Downright quiet

Finally, **How to get there** includes directions to many hostels—by car, bus, train, plane, or even ferry, in some cases. Subway directions are given in big cities if applicable. Often these directions are complicated, however; in those cases, managers have asked (or we recommend) that you call the hostel itself for more precise directions.

A SHORT HISTORY OF HOSTELLING

Hostelling as we know it started around 1907, when Richard Schirmann, an assistant schoolteacher in Altena, Germany, decided to make one of the empty classrooms a space for visiting students to sleep. That was not a completely unique idea, as Austrian inns and taverns had been offering reduced rates and bunk space to students since 1885. But Schirmann would develop much grander plans. He was about to start a movement.

His idea was to get students out of the industrial cities and into the countryside. Schirmann was a strong believer that walking and bicycling tours in the fresh air were essential to adolescent development and learning. But such excursions were impossible without a place to spend the night. His logic was simple: Since rural schoolhouses were deserted during weekends and holidays, why not make use of those spaces?

The caretakers of the school he chose agreed to serve as houseparents, and some fast ground rules were established. Students were responsible for piling up the tables and benches in the classroom and laying out thin straw sacks on the floor. At some ungodly early-morning hour, the students were to stack the straw mats back up and organize the classroom back as they found it. Boys and girls slept in separate rooms but were treated as equals. Detractors cried scandal, wondering aloud what was going on in these schoolrooms after dark.

The experiment worked, sort of. Altena became a haven for student excursions into the countryside, but finding shelter in other communities proved to be difficult. Sometimes the situation would become dire. Late one night in the summer of 1909, Schirmann decided it was time to expand his movement beyond Altena. His goal was to establish a network of hostels within walking distance of one another; beginning in a schoolhouse with straw mats, Schirmann eventually acquired the use of a castle. It still stands—the Ur-hostel, if you will—in Altena, and it's still used as a hostel.

After World War I the movement really began to spread. By 1928 there were more than 2,000 hostels worldwide. Today tens of thousands of hostellers stay at HI-affiliated hostels each year, hailing from everywhere from Alaska to Zaire; thousands more stay at independent hostels.

Hostels aren't always located within a day's walk of one another, though in parts of England—like the Peaks and Lakes—they are, and many people do indeed walk from hostel to hostel with just a pack on their back. In any case you're quite likely to find a promising brew of cultural exchange and friendship over pots of ramen noodles and instant coffee almost anywhere you go.

In that sense, perhaps, Richard Schirmann's dream has been realized after all.

A Word about Affiliations

A majority of hostels in this book are affiliated with **Hostelling International** (HI); the rest we've labeled independent hostels.

YHA (the Youth Hostel Association of England and Wales) is the English branch of Hostelling International, long the backbone of hostelling worldwide. Run from on office outside London, this organization is part of the International Youth Hostel Federation, which has 5,000 member hostels in seventy countries. Member hostels are held to a number of regulations, such as maximum number of beds per shower, even minimum amount of space that must exist between top bunks and the ceiling.

SYHA (the Scottish Youth Hostel Association) is Scotland's equivalent of YHA. It administrates hostels throughout Scotland from offices in Stirling and holds members to the same strict standards as YHA.

YHANI (the Youth Hostel Assocation of Northern Ireland) is northern Ireland's branch of Hostelling International, handling fewer than ten hostels out of a Belfast office.

Overall, the HI hostels tend to earn higher marks from our reviewers than independent hostels. They regularly own the nicest buildings and keep the floors cleanest. On the other hand, the organization's mission statement trumpets its contribution to "the education of young people," so be warned that some of its most popular hostels attract youth groups like molasses does flies. Families and senior travelers are also attracted to the Hostelling International network in increasing numbers. Bottom line: They're cleaner and nicer but can be extremely boring. Like going back to school—or, in the worst cases, prison.

Back to the rules. Liquor is supposed to be off-limits at most of these places, and guests tend to be an orderly bunch. Many of the giant urban hostels are purpose-built facilities owned by the organization itself, often resembling well-equipped college dormitories. Some of these HI-owned hostels have developed impressive educational programs that incorporate volunteers from the local community and so forth.

INDEPENDENTS (no affiliation) are what we call all the others, though they might belong to small chains called Scotland's Top Hostels or the like. Some owners opt not to join any organization. Membership costs are high, and they feel the return on such an investment isn't enough. Such a decision—in and of itself—does not reflect on the quality of the hostel. It would be foolish to write a hostel off simply because it is not affiliated.

On the other hand, there's no guarantee of quality, and the standards, upkeep, noise level, and beer flow tend to vary wildly from place to place.

HOW TO HOSTEL

Hostelling is, generally speaking, easy as pie. Plan ahead a bit and use a little common sense, and you'll find check-in goes pretty smoothly.

Reserving a Bed

Getting a good bunk will often be your first and biggest challenge, especially if it's high season. Hostellers often have an amazingly laissez-faire attitude about reservations; many simply waltz in at midnight expecting a bed will be available.

Sometimes it is. Sometimes it isn't.

Most every Hostelling International abode takes advance reservations of some form or another, so if you know where you're going to be, use this service. Increasingly, the popular English hostels make you confirm your booking the day before if you didn't hold the bed with a credit-card deposit. Make sure you call! Or you'll lose that bunk.

Some HI hostels are also affiliated with the worldwide International Booking Network; check with a big HI hostel and you might be able to book future dates at smaller ones.

Independent hostels are sometimes more lax about taking solid reservations, though they're also a lot more willing to find extra couch space or a spare mattress in case you're squeezed out. Calling a few days ahead to feel the situation out is always a good idea.

If you can't or won't reserve, the best thing to do is get there super-early. Office opens at 8 A.M.? Get there at 7:00. No room, but check-out ends at 11:00? Be back at 11:05 in case of cancellations or unexpected check-outs. The doors are closed again til 4:30 in the afternoon? No problem. Come back around 4:00 with a paperback and camp out on the porch. That's your only shot if you couldn't or wouldn't reserve ahead, and hostellers are pretty respectful of the pecking order: It really is first come, first served. So come first.

Paying the Piper

Once you're in, be prepared to pay for your night's stay immediately—before you're even assigned a bunk. Take note ahead of time which hostels take credit cards, checks, and so forth. Think you're being cheated with the bill? Remember that most hostels charge $1.00 or so per night for linens if you haven't brought your own. (You always have the option of bringing your own, however, and we recommend it. See below.)

Other charges could include a surcharge for a private room and charges for phone calls from your room, if a phone is included (very unusual).

You might also need to leave a small deposit for your room key—usually about $5.00, sometimes more—which you'll get back when you check out, unless you lost the key in the meantime. Sometimes you will also be required to show some form of photo identification to check in. Very occasionally, you'll even be forced to leave a passport or driver's license with the front desk. This is annoying and possibly illegal, but a few hostels still get away with it. Scream bloody murder; threaten to sue—but you might still get shut out unless you play along.

Remember to pay ahead if you want a weekly stay. Often you can get deep discounts, though the down side is that you'll almost never get a partial refund if you decide you can't stand it and leave before the week is up.

If you're paying by the day, rebook promptly each morning; hostel managers are very busy during the morning hours, keeping track of check-ins, check-outs, cleaning duties, and cash. You'll make a friend if you're early about notifying them of your plans for the next day. On the other hand, managers hate bugging guests all morning or all day about whether they'll be staying on. Don't put the staff through this.

Some hostel managers have the curiously softhearted habit of letting the rent slide a few days. We can't figure why; when managers do this, a day often becomes a week or a month. Even if this courtesy is extended to you, don't use it except in an emergency. You never know who'll they hire to get that money out of you later.

All right, so you've secured a bed and paid up. Now you have to get to it. This may be no easy task at some hostels, where staff and customers look and act like one and the same. A kindly manager will probably notice you bumbling around and take pity. As you're being shown to your room, you're also likely get a short tour of the facilities and a briefing on the ground rules.

Knowing the Ground Rules

There's one universal ground rule at every hostel: You are responsible for serving and cleaning up after yourself. And there's a corollary rule: Be courteous. So while you're welcome to use all the kitchen facilities, share the space with your fellow guests—don't spread your five-course meal all over the counter space and rangetop burners if other hungry folks are hanging around waiting. And never, ever, leave a sink full of dirty pots and pans behind. That's bad form.

Hostel guests are almost always asked to mark their name and check-in date on all the food they put in the refrigerator. Only the shelf marked FREE FOOD is up for grabs; everything else belongs to other hostellers, so don't touch it. (Hostellers get very touchy about people stealing their grub.) Some of the better-run hostels have a spice rack and other kitchen essentials on hand. If you're not sure whether something is communal, ask. But don't assume anything is up for grabs unless it is clearly marked as such.

Alcohol is still a major issue at some hostels. Hostelling International rules officially forbid it on the premises of HI hostels. We were not surprised to see this rule bent or broken in some places, but inquire with a smile on your face before you bring that brew inside. Independent hostels are a lot more forgiving; some even have bars.

Then there's the lockout, a source of bitter contention among hostel factions. A few rural and small-city Hostelling International hostels throw everybody out in the morning and don't let them back in until the early evening. Lockouts tend to run from around 10 A.M. to 4 P.M., during which time your bags might be inside your room—but *you* won't be.

The practice has its pros and cons; managers usually justify a lockout by noting that it forces travelers to interact with the locals. The real reason is usually that the hostel can't or won't pay staff to hang around and baby-sit you all day. On the other hand, some hostels become semiresidential situations stuffed with couch potatoes. A lockout sure solves that problem.

In the reviews we've identified those hostels that enforce lockouts. Usually you wouldn't want to be hanging out in the hostel in the middle of the day anyway, but after several sleepless nights of travel—or when you're under the weather—daytime downtime sure is appreciated. So beware.

Some hostels also enforce a maximum limit on your stay—anywhere from three days, if the hostel is really popular, to about two weeks. You will know if such a policy is in effect the moment you walk into a place. If there are lots of cigarette butts, slackers, or dirty clothes hanging around, it's the curse of the dreaded long-termers: folks who came for a day and stay for a lifetime just to avoid finding work. So a maximum-stay rule can be a very good thing. On the other hand, you might find yourself wanting to spend more than three days in some great place—and be shown the door instead.

Savvy budget travelers have learned how to get around this unfortunate situation, of course: They simply suck it up and spend a night at the "Y" or a convenient motel—then check back into the cheaper hostel first thing in the morning. But *we* didn't tell you to do that. Uh-uh.

Etiquette and Smarts

Again, to put it simply, use common sense. Hostellers are a refreshingly flexible bunch. All these people are able to make this system work by looking after one another; remember, in a hostel you're a community member first and a consumer second. With that in mind, here are some guidelines for how to act:

- The first thing you should do after check-in is get your bed made. When you're assigned a bed, stick to it. Don't spread your stuff out on nearby bunks, even if they are empty. Someone's going to be coming in late-night for one of them—you can bet the backpack on it.

- Be sure to lock your valuables in a locker or the trunk of your car. Good hostels offer lockers as a service; it might cost a little, but it's worth it.

- Set toiletries and anything else you need in a place where they are easily accessible. This avoids your having to paw through your bag late at night, potentially disturbing other guests from their slumber. The same goes for early-morning departures: If you're taking off at the crack of dawn, take precautions not to wake the whole place.

- If you're leaving early in the morning, try to make all arrangements with the manager before going to bed the night before. Retrieve your key deposit before the desk closes if possible, and settle up any other debts. Managers are usually accommodating and pleasant folks, but guests are expected to respect their privacy and peace of mind by not pushing things too far. Dragging a manager out of bed at four in the morning to check out—or for some other trivial matter—is really pushing it.
- Be sure to mind the bathroom. A quick wiping of the shower floor with a paper towel after you use it is common courtesy.
- Finally, be sure to mind the quiet hours. Some hostels have curfews, but very few force lights-out. If you are up after hours, be respectful. Don't crank the television or radio too loud. (Save that for the beach—and for annoying people staying in much nicer digs.)

Packing

Those dainty hand towels and dapper shaving kits and free soaps you get at a hotel won't be anywhere in sight at the hostel. In fact, even some of the base essentials may not be available; you're on your own, so bring everything you need to be comfortable.

There are only a few things you can expect the hostel to supply:

- a bed frame with a mattress and pillow
- shower and toilet facilities
- a communal kitchen with pots, pans, and stove
- a common room with some spartan furniture
- maybe a few heavy blankets

Some of the more chic hostels we've identified in this guide may be full-service. Heck, we've stayed in hostels that provide the food for you to cook—not to mention generous spice racks. But they are the exception to the rule.

Bring this stuff to keep your journey through hostel territory comfortable:

- If you're traveling abroad from the United States, you obviously need a passport. Unlike U.S. hostels, a Euro-hostel will often take your passport when you check in as collateral. Don't get nervous; this is extremely common. It's the European equivalent of taking down your driver's license number when you write a check. However, in the unlikely event that someone loses your passport, make sure you've got backup copies of the issuing office, date, and passport number with you and also back home.
- Hostelling International membership cards are a good thing to have on hand. They can be purchased at many member HI hos-

tels on the road or back home before you go. This card identifies you as a certified super-hosteller and gets you the very cheapest rate for your bed in all HI (and also some unaffiliated) hostels. With discounts of $2.00 to $4.00 per night, the savings can add up fast. Cost of membership is $25 for adults ages 18 to 54 and $15 if you're over age 54. Kids under age 18 are members for free.

Sometimes that membership card also gets you deals at local restaurants, bike shops, and tours. Again, it will be easier to deal with the front desk at some of the more cautious hostels (even nonmember ones) if you can flash one of these cards.

- Red Alert! Do not plan on using a sleeping bag in all hostels. A good number of places simply won't allow it—problems with ticks and other creatures dragged in from the great outdoors have propelled this prohibition. The alternative is a sleepsack, which is basically two sheets sewn together with a makeshift pillowcase.

You can find them at most budget travel stores, or make your own. Personally we hate these confining wraps, and we rarely get through the night in one without having it twist around our bodies so tight that we wake up wanting to charge it with attempted manslaughter. Our preferred method is to bring our own set of sheets, though that might be too much extra stuff to pack if you're backpacking.

Some hostels give you free linen; most that don't will rent sheets for about $1.00 to $2.00 per night. You don't get charged for use of the standard army surplus blankets or the musty charm that comes with them.

- Some people bring their own pillows, as those supplied tend to be on the frumpy side. This is a good idea if you're traveling by car and can afford the space.

- We definitely suggest earplugs for light sleepers, especially for urban hostels—but also in case you get caught in a room with a heavy snorer.

- A small flashlight is a must. Not only for late-night reading, but also to find your bed without waking up the entire dorm.

- A little bit of spice is always nice, especially when you have had one too many plates of pasta. You'll find the cost of basil, oregano, and the like in convenience stores way too high to stomach once you're on the road. Buy it cheap before you leave and pack it in jars or small plastic bags.

- Check which hostels have laundry facilities. It's much easier to do the wash while making dinner than to waste a day sitting around with the cast of *The Shining* at a local laundromat.

- Wearing flip-flops or other plastic sandals in the shower might help you avoid a dreaded case of athlete's foot.

- Be sure your towel is a quick-drying type. Otherwise you'll wind up with mildew in your pack—and your food.

TRAVELING IN THE U.K.

GETTING THERE

By Plane

The airline business is crazy: Deals and rip-off fares come and go with a regularity that is frightening to behold—supply, demand, season, the stock market, and random acts of cruelty or kindness all appear to contribute to the quixotic nature of fares.

As a result, there is no one piece of simple advice we can give you, other than this one: Find a darned good travel agent who cares about budget travelers, and trust him/her with all the planning. You can cruise the Internet if you like, and you might find an occasional great deal your agent doesn't know about. Just make sure the sellers are reputable before giving out that credit-card number.

Cheap-ticket brokers (also called consolidators or bucket shops) are a great bet for saving money, but you have to be fast on your feet to keep up as the deals appear and disappear literally daily. London and New York are major centers for bucket shops.

Flying as a courier comes highly recommended by some folks who've tried it. Others are nervous about it. It works this way: You agree to carry items for a company in exchange for a very cheap round-trip ticket abroad. You must be flexible about your departure and return dates, you can't change those dates once assigned to you—and you usually can only bring carry-on luggage. London is pretty much the only place you can go this way, but it is always in big demand. Check out *The Courier Air Travel Handbook* by Mark Field (Perpetual Press: Seattle, 1996) for courier company listings.

Also check out the Web site www.courier.org.

It's very easy to get from North America to London—just about every major airline goes there from the east and west coasts, and in summertime charter companies fire up, offering still more choice.

Some of the best bets? British Airways probably offers the best and most comfortable flight on a coach ticket, though you'll pay extra for the privilege unless you score tickets from a consolidator. Another advantage is that BA flies from lots of different airports around the United States. Fares on the larger U.S. airlines, such as Delta, TWA, Continental, and American, all fluctuate and bear close watching. Keep in mind that an advance booking is always better—not only because summer is often booked solid, but because you can also save quite a bit on the ticket price with an APEX (advance purchase) fare.

From Canada, Canada 3000's charter fares are unbeatably low and fly to a lot of places besides London—Glasgow, Manchester, Ireland, Newcastle—sometimes direct. That's handy if you want to dive right into the U.K. experience without hitting hectic London first on your itinerary. You can fly out of Toronto, Halifax, and sometimes Montreal; factor in the exchange rate for Canadian dollars, and you've got one sweet deal here.

By Train

There's only one way to get to England from the continent by train: **Eurostar.** They've got a monopoly on the sub-Chunnel service that takes you from England to France in three hours, but they run it well. You'll never get onto a faster or more efficiently run train. Eurostar likes to advertise that you can have breakfast in Westminster and lunch in Montmartre, and you really can—without the delays of airport check-in and check-out and with pretty minimal customs and immigration formalities.

Of course, you pay extra for the privilege. Tickets tend to run from as little as 99 pounds (about $180 U.S.) off-season, booking in advance, up to much more if you book on short notice or travel during a summer weekend. And—bummer—buying a single one-way ticket isn't any cheaper than purchasing a round-tripper. So you might as well go whole hog. Always check ahead for price information. Book ahead by fifteen days and you might save as much as 50 percent! It's easiest to book ahead through your travel agent at home, but Eurostar also has offices in Paris's Gare du Nord and London's Waterloo Station. Call the central information number (0345–303030) for full timetables or fares, or check at any Paris, Brussels, or London train station.

By Ferry

You can still take ferries from France, Holland, and even Scandinavia to the U.K. The most popular routes seem to be Norway to Newcastle, northern France to southern England, and Cherbourg to Cork (free with a Eurail pass).

A ferry is a whole lot cheaper way to cross the English Channel than taking the train, but it also takes a lot longer. Figure the better part of a day to get from Paris to London, counting transit, dockings, sailings, and so on.

By Car

It's possible and quite legal to drive a French or other Continental car to England, but we don't recommend it. Why? Simple—the steering wheel's in the wrong place to drive on the other side of the road. This makes corners awfully tricky if someone's passing on the curve. And, shudder to think, people sometimes forget and drive on the wrong side of the road.

GETTING AROUND THE U.K.

Take a careful look at your transportation options when planning a hostel journey. You should be able to hop from city to city by bus or train without a problem, but you could have trouble getting to rural hostels without a car.

By Train

Trains are still king in Europe. Sure, the car dominates everyday life for locals, but when you're a tourist you just can't beat the iron horse.

In our experience, BritRail passes (800–677–8585 or 888–274–7245) are a fantastic deal. They're not cheap, but they're superconvenient if you're going to be traveling a lot within the U.K. during a short period of time.

You've gotta play by the rules, though: Wait until the first day you're gonna use the pass, then go to the station early and have it validated (stamped) by a ticket agent. Write the current date into the first square (it should have a "1" beneath it)—and remember to put the day first (on top), European-style.

Now it gets easier. Just show your pass to ticket agents when you want to reserve a seat on a train (which is crucial in summer season, on weekends, and during rush hours); that smiling person will hand you a seat reservation, which you show to the conductor. You must reserve seats two hours before the train leaves its first station, and since you'll have no idea where or when that was, it's best to reserve a day or two ahead as you're getting off the train.

If you can't or won't get a reservation, just show your pass to the conductor.

Finally, don't fold, bend, or otherwise mangle the long cardboard pass (and that can be difficult to achieve while fumbling for your money belt at the station as the train whips in). For some reason, that might invalidate the whole bloody thing.

Anyway, the cost of these passes depends on a few things, including how many days you're traveling and how much comfort you want. More days obviously cost more dough. And first-class passes, which few hostellers buy, cost 50 percent more and give you a little more legroom. At press time the range was from $215 (for eight consecutive days, under age twenty-six, second class) all the way up to $900 (thirty consecutive days of riding first class). A BritRail Flexipass, which allows the holder to pick which days he or she will use it, now lasts you two months instead of one—but it costs more as a result. Depending on your age and comfort level, four rail days in a two-month period now cost from $185 to $350; eight days in two months cost from $240 to $510; and fifteen days cost you between $360 and $770. Call BritRail for the latest fare information, and remember the key fact: You have to buy the pass *before* you get to Britain. Occasionally you can find one at a train station, but don't risk it.

The pass now includes free passage on the Heathrow Express, a handy commuter train that zips from Heathrow airport to a Tube stop in downtown London three times hourly; no word at press time, however, on whether this ride will cost you a full rail day or not. Probably it will.

Train schedules can be accessed anywhere in the U.K. by calling the national info number (0345–484950). It's a toll call, but it's well worth it; these pros can plan any rail journey for you.

By Bus

Buses are by far a cheaper ride than trains, and in the U.K. and Scotland they're a fine way to go—reasonably on time, scenic, with lots of locals riding alongside you happy to give advice, opinions, or soccer scores. They're probably going to be your main mode of transport in the U.K., so get used to riding and waiting. The main problem: figuring out what seem like hundreds of local bus lines and their changing schedules.

The good news is that there's usually a bus going wherever you're going in England, as long as you don't travel on Sundays or certain Mondays, when some lines run less frequently. It might take you all day to make connections, but most bus drivers in the U.K. are among the most helpful human beings on earth, so you'll get there eventually.

Between-city buses run constantly, too, and even in the sticks you'll be amazed when a double-decker pulls up in the middle of nowhere to whisk you away to East Twee or somewhere. Look for "coach" in the phone directories.

National Express (01990–808080) is England's huge, Greyhound-like company; it runs tons of scheduled daily lines along major routes and some weird ones too—if you're seriously wanting to get from Aberdeen to, say, Stratford-upon-Avon, give 'em a call to see if they go there. They well might. Buses are less expensive than the train, but not a lot cheaper with the Express. In return you get a few perks like on-time buses, helpful drivers, toilets, and sometimes, an attendant walking down the aisle with snacks for sale.

Local buses fill the rest of the gaps, and these can range from incredibly efficient lines to laughable ones. You'll know what we mean once you try to get across the Peaks District or Cotswold Hills in a hurry.

There are literally hundreds of small bus companies in England, sometimes a half-dozen in one town or city, so there's no central way to contact them. Just ask at the hostel or bus station when you arrive, or study the posted schedules at the bus stop where you're dropped off.

In Scotland, Scottish Citylink (0199–050–5050) brings you from big city to big city efficiently; on the Isle of Skye, call Skye-Ways (0159–94328) for starters.

To get to *really* remote places in Scotland, the **postbus** system is one more potential ally. These buses or station wagons, which really do carry the mail, will carry you, too, for a slight charge. However, they sometimes run as infrequently as once a day or week, so be sure you know the return schedule before you commit. (They don't run at night.) Usually it's no trouble.

By Plane

Planes within Europe used to be fantastically expensive. However, times are changing: A raft of cut-rate short-hop airlines have sprung up recently and can make a trip from places like Edinburgh or central England to Milan, Copenhagen, or Lisbon incredibly quick and cheap—much more so than the trains.

The question right now is whether the fierce competition among these upstarts will weed some of them out.

Go (01279–666333) is British Airways' cut-rate airline, and it's been mighty aggressive about promoting its good and cheap services. We'd try them first.

British Midland (01345–554554), which makes you buy a book of tickets for at least three one-way trips around the Continent before you can begin traveling, is another option if you'll be hopping around for a while.

EasyJet (01990–292929) flies from Luton around Europe for competitively low prices.

Virgin Express and **Ryanair** are two more cut-rate airlines worth checking out.

By Car

Renting a car is definitely the most expensive way to see Europe, and yet it has advantages: You can cover the hamlets a whole lot quicker, you have complete freedom of movement, and you get that cool feeling of the wind and rain rushing past your ears.

Just bring your wallet: Rentals in England go for a good $60 US a day, and that might or might not include heavy taxes and insurance. Rent or lease long-term through a company like Kemwel (800–678–0678), which does short- and long-term rentals for a fraction of the normal European daily rate if you book ahead from your home country. AutoEurope (800–223–5555) is another good service.

You won't use as much gas as in the United States because it's a smaller car, but it'll cost—something like $3.00 a gallon at last check. (Want a bike yet?)

If you're still going to do it, remember this cardinal rule. YOU GOTTA DRIVE ON THE LEFT. Sound simple? Not exactly. Our tip? Keep your body in the middle of the road. The other tricky part is shifting with your left hand instead of your right, while your feet continue to do the same clutch-gas dance they do on an American car. It's a bit like learning a new hokey-pokey—clumsy as heck at first, and you don't want to make a mistake with a busload of tourists screaming toward you at 60 miles an hour. So practice in a parking lot first.

Next issue: numbers. Confusingly, speeds and distances in the U.K. are measured in both miles and kilometers, depending apparently on local custom—and miles actually seem to be winning the battle. Make sure you know which one's being used on your road sign, map, or speed limit sign.

Just to remind you, 1 mile is about 1⁶⁄₁₀ kilometers; 100 miles is roughly 160 kilometers. Basically, to convert miles to kilometers, multiply by 1.6. To convert kilometers to miles, multiply by .6.

Stop signs are rare, but when present they're round and red. More often, you'll slow down at a dotted line, then merge with traffic. Before long you'll hit one of the infamous roundabouts, rotary intersections where you must keep to the left at all costs until you exit.

Gas is measured in liters, and there are roughly four liters to the U.S. gallon. Gas prices are listed per liter, so multiply by four and then convert into home currency to estimate the price per gallon you'd pay back home—you'll be shocked.

By Minibus

The most popular kind of backpacker travel these days, however, is none of the above; it's the "JOJO" (jump on, jump off) minibus service that circles the British Isles like sharks, scooping up backpackers in faraway train stations and depositing them safely in remote, beautiful places. It's also known as "HOHO," which is hop on and hop off.

The Stray Travel Network (+44–0171–373–7737 in London, (+353–01–679–2884 in Dublin) was the first in the U.K.—under its previous name of Slow Coach—to do this circular route, and it offers the greatest variety. Their tours explore various combinations of England, Scotland, and Ireland under a variety of price structures. Call for an update of the latest offerings.

In Scotland, the JOJO/HOHO craze has really exploded; besides Stray Travel, three more companies offer the same service to difference places.

Go Blue Banana (0131–556–2000 or 0131–220–6868), Scotland's original "jump-on, jump-off" service, is pretty decent; it offers three-, six-, and nine-day tours of the country for £75 to £199 (about $112 to $300 U.S.). The hostel you have to stay in are mostly party joints, which can be good or bad.

Haggis Backpackers (0131–557–9393) has an equally weird name. Started by a couple of brothers, it's just as fun-loving (sometimes too much so) as the other guys.

MacBackpackers (0131–558–9900), a newer company started up by an independent hostel chain, offers one-, four-, and five-day tours of a similar ilk for £12 to £89 (about $18 to $135 U.S.). As with Blue Banana, you've gotta stay in their hostels, like 'em or not. But their drivers are pretty knowledgeable.

Finally, **Leapin' Leprechaun** (015047–42655) runs minibuses from Belfast to Dublin and back daily for £30 (about $45 U.S.) total. But they don't do the same fun stuff as these other services; it's mostly just a convenient shuttle.

By Ferry

You probably won't be using ferries much, unless you're visiting Scotland—in which case you almost certainly will, to see the islands. **Caledonian MacBrayne** (01475–650–100) runs most of the ferries in Scotland; **P&O** (01224–572–615) runs most of the rest. Other ferries in England, Wales, and Scotland are locally run; consult the local tourism office for information on getting to places like the Orkneys and such.

To get to Northern Ireland by ferry, you'll go from Wales or Scotland by regular boat or, maybe, the lurching fast ferries known as HoverCats. Some of these services are covered by BritRail passes, and some aren't. Call **Irish Ferries** (01990–171717), **Sealink** (01776–702262) or **Seacat** (01345–523523) for the correct information.

MONEY

You'll need it, that's for sure. Everything in the U.K. is expensive, whether it's good or not. That includes fruit, gas, clothes, everything. Why? Simple. Most of it's been shipped to these wee little islands from somewhere else in the world. Deal with it, and remember—when you get back home, everything from hummus to walking shoes will seem that much cheaper.

One English pound equals, at this writing, about $1.80 US. (*Note:* The pound fluctuated between $1.60 and $1.80 during the writing of this book, so prices expressed in U.S. dollars are approximate—but they're pretty darn close. Check the current exchange rates before your departure for the U.K.) To get a rough idea of what something in English pounds would cost you in the United States, double the price and subtract a little. Ouch! Yeah, you just paid thirty bucks for that pub meal purchased in that oh-so-cute little seaside village.

Look over the change, because bigger isn't always better. A copper pence is just like an American penny. Two-pence coins are also copper but bigger. Ten-pence coins are like dimes, except larger. Twenty-pence coins look funny, like small stop signs; fifty-pence coins look like bigger stop signs. A pound is a very small but thick coin that's worth a lot—don't tip people with them unless you mean to tip $1.80 US each time you toss one down. Two-pound coins are kind of rare; they're two-colored, a gold outside and a silver inside.

Bills (or "notes") are more obvious, but look sharp: The number of pounds is printed lightly in the upper-left-hand corner. A five-pound bill is worth about $9.00 U.S. A ten-pound bill is worth about $18 U.S., and so on. In Scotland you'll sometimes get unusual one-pound bills. Exchange them for coins or larger bills before you get to France because they might be suspicious of these. Honest.

In Ireland, the unit of currency is the Irish pound—which they actually call a "punt" almost all the time—and it's worth roughly the same as a British sterling pound. That's about $1.80 American.

In Northern Ireland you'll get a slightly different kind of cash from the ATM or the change bureau. They're actually British pounds sterling (known simply as pounds), but they look a little different because they're printed by banks in Northern Ireland. They're worth exactly the same as pounds in England and almost the same as Irish pounds.

If you're going to England afterward, note that you can't spend Northern Ireland–printed pounds there, so change them all before you leave, if possible. (You can use British or even Scottish pound notes in Northern Ireland with no trouble at all, however.)

Coming from Ireland? Irish pounds aren't good in Northern Ireland, needless to say, except in some border towns, where the merchants might accept 'em.

PHONES

All of the phone and fax numbers listed in the book are written as dialed from *within the U.K.* (and that includes all of England, Wales, Scotland, and Northern Ireland). So when calling hostels from anywhere in the U.K., dial the number *exactly as listed in the book.*

If you're calling from the United States, first dial 011–44 and then dial the number as printed but *drop the first zero* from the number listed in the interior of the book *or the call won't go through.*

From other European countries, dial the correct long-distance code (usually 00), add 44 for England or Northern Ireland, and then tack on the listed number—but again, remember to *drop the first zero* from the phone number listed in the interior of the book or the call won't go through.

SPEAKING BRITISH

British English is not the same as American English, but that's no reason to knock it; in fact, it's wildly colorful, much better than the food. Better still, there are distinct accents and vocabularies for Scotland, Ireland, York, Cornwall . . . heck, just about everywhere. Not to mention Gaelic, spoken in pockets of Ireland and a bit of Scotland, or Welsh, which is making a comeback in Wales.

Hereforth, a short primer. Cheers!

WHAT THEY SAY	WHAT THEY MEAN
pound	a one-pound coin, size of a penny but worth about $1.80 US
quid	same thing (we've no idea why)
fiver	five-pound note, worth about $9.00 US
tenner	ten-pound note, worth about $18 US
tens	ten-pence coins, size of an American quarter, worth about 18 cents US
bloody	very
dear	expensive
wee	a little or a lot
fresh	cold, bracing or naughty
telly	television
rail	train
football	soccer
footballers	soccer players
tabs	daily tabloid newspapers
knackered	beat, exhausted
shattered	ditto
carriageway	highway
dual carriageway	divided highway
roundabout	rotary intersection
boot	trunk of a car
torch	flashlight
brilliant	Great! (northern England)
Cheers!	Thanks! Goodbye! Great! (northern England)
aye	yes (Scotland)
lass, lassie	girl (Scotland)
lad	guy (Scotland)
heya	hello (Scotland)

OTHER RESOURCES

The best place to get information about the U.K. is from the respective tourist offices; Wales, Scotland, and Britain all maintain friendly and efficient information offices that can supply you with plenty of advance skinny and advice. They're sensitive to the needs of backpackers, too—a nice switch from the North American way of doing things.

Haven't got time? Hit the Web running then, starting perhaps at YHA's official site (*yha-england-wales.org.uk*—nothing special, but it does contain news updates and some hostel info—or a tourism site such as londontown.com or visitbritain.co.uk.

Finally, there are regional councils of Hostelling International-U.K. to steer you on your way:

YHA London (Headquarters)
8 St. Stephen's Hill
St. Albans, Hertfordshire AL1 2DY
ENGLAND
01727–855215
Fax: 01727–844126

YHA Northern England Region
P.O. Box 11
Matlock, Derbyshire DE4 2XA
ENGLAND
01629–82850
Fax: 01629–825471

YHA Southern England Region
11B York Road
Salisbury, Wiltshire SP2 7AP
ENGLAND
01722–337515
Fax: 01722–414027

YHA Wales
1 Cathedral Road
Cardiff CF1 9HA
WALES
01222–396766
Fax: 01222–237817

SYHA Aberdeen District
11 Ashvale Place
Aberdeen AB1 6QD
SCOTLAND
01224–588156

SYHA Dundee District
8 Bell Place
Dundee DD1 1JG
SCOTLAND
01382–322150

SYHA Edinburgh District
161 Warrender Park Road
Edinburgh EH9 1EQ
SCOTLAND
0131–229–8660

SYHA Glasgow District
12 Renfield Street
Glasgow G2 5AL
SCOTLAND
0141–226–3976

Final Advice

There's surprisingly little out there about hostelling and hostels—that's why you're reading this, right?—but we did find a few sources. Most simply list phone numbers and addresses.

Just remember that we've done our best, but hostels are constantly opening, closing, renovating, being sold and changing their policies. So not everything written in a guidebook will always still be true by the time you read it. Be smart and call ahead to confirm prices, availability, and directions, rather than rolling into town depending on a bed—and getting a nasty surprise like a vacant lot instead. We know; it has happened to us.

Good luck!

The Hostels

LONDON

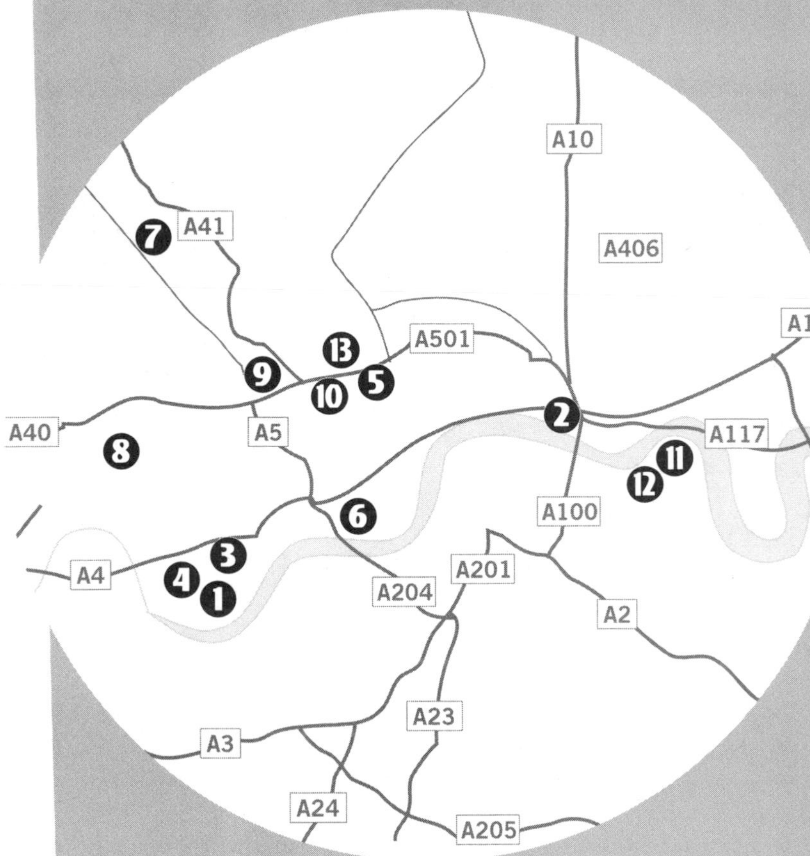

Numbers on map refer to hostels numbered below.

1. Chelsea Hotel Hostel
2. City of London Hostel
3. Curzon House Hostel
4. Earl's Court Hostel
5. Generator Hostel
6. Granada Hotel Hostel
7. Hampstead Heath Hostel
8. Holland House (King George VI Memorial Hostel)
9. International Student House
10. Oxford Street Hostel
11. Rotherhithe Hostel
12. St. Christopher's Inn Hostel
13. St. Pancras International Hostel

LONDON

London's one happenin' place these days. A melting pot since forever, it seems, the city has only improved in recent years: the incredible selection of ethnic food options, the all-night dance scene, the history staring you in the face everywhere you go—it's almost enough to make you forget the dreary weather and air pollution so bad that it still leaves you coughing up black stuff.

The hostels here are strange—some come and go each summer (mostly run by skanky hotels trying to make a fast buck off the desperate budget travelers), but the legitimate ones are pretty good. Especially considering the way student types storm London by force so reliably each summer that hostels could charge fifty bucks for a sleeping bag on the floor and probably get away with it. Instead, most of them pass the minimum test for cleanliness,

LONDON HOSTELS at a glance

	RATING	COST	IN A WORD
International Student House	👍	£12.35-£23.40	popular
City of London Hostel	👍	£17.90-£21.30	downtown
St. Pancras Hostel	👍	£17.90-£21.30	nice
Rotherhithe Hostel	👍	£19.90-£21.30	remote
Earl's Court Hostel	👍	£16.45-£18.70	okay
Oxford Street Hostel	👍	£15.25-£18.70	central
Holland House Hostel	👍	£16.45-£18.70	quiet
Hampstead Heath Hostel	👍	£13.35-£17.10	creaky
Curzon House Hostel	👍	£13.00-£26.00	decent
Generator Hostel		£17.50-£37.00	hip
St. Christopher's Inn		£12.00-£15.00	hoppin'
Granada Hotel Hostel		£16.50	new
Chelsea Hotel Hostel		£10.00-£16.00	scruffy

friendliness, and fun; they're also mostly well located, almost all close to some cool neighborhood or a train station.

The exceptions are some of Hostelling International's seven London joints (they run more here than they do in any other city in the world); some of them are quite a long way from the center of London, though they can be nice as green suburban getaways. YHA's hostels are as humdrum as they are elsewhere, but the Oxford Street and Earl's Court joints are two very welcome exceptions to the usual rule.

For maximum transit value, order a London Visitor Travelcard ahead of time. This handy-dandy pass—good for three, four, or seven consecutive days—gets you unlimited travel on the Tube, the city bus system, most regional British Rail trains, and the Docklands Light Railway (as if you needed that).

At press time, the pass cost $29 to $59 for adults; for kids, only $12 to $22. Just remember that you've gotta buy the pass *before* you get to England. Call BritRail at (888) 274–7245 for more information.

If you forget, buy regular Travelcards in London at any Tube station as soon as you get to town. A one-day pass costs around £3.80 (about $6.00 US) for four zones, a bit less if you're staying downtown and don't need to get out to the 'burbs. Weekend passes are even cheaper, about £5.40 ($9.00 US) for four zones, less for a central pass. A weekly pass is cheaper still; all quickly pay for themselves if you make at least three hops per day, which you're guaranteed to do unless you're a total couch potato.

One final note: Though England is generally quite safe, certain parts of London—such as the King's Cross/St. Pancras area, the docks, and Brixton—need to be treated with caution. Really, so does anywhere that's deserted at night. So be careful, especially if traveling alone or venturing out after dark.

CHELSEA HOTEL HOSTEL

33-41 Earl's Court Square, London SW5

Phone Number: 0171–236–6892 or 236–4965

Fax: 0171–244–6891
Rates: £10–£16 per person (about $15–$24 US), doubles £25–£27 (about $38–$40 US)
Beds: 300
Office hours: Twenty-four hours
Affiliation: None
Extras: Breakfast, meals ($), laundry, TV, bar, pool table, shuttle

People love this place, though it's no great shakes—just a very cheap bed in London, basically.

Occupying a bunch of intertwined town houses, this huge complex is superrelaxed on rules and therefore not the tidiest hostel in town. Rooms are small, bare, and cluttered, though bathrooms are pretty decent and the attached restaurant serves good food. They also include a bit of continental breakfast here and run a free shuttle to and from nearby Victoria Station. Aha! That's why it's so popular—because you won't spend much money staying.

Chelsea, as an area, is a mixed bag—near some tony squares and buildings, but a little too boho for our taste.

How to get there:

By Tube: Take Tube to Earl's Court, then walk south on Earl's Court Road 3 blocks to Earl's Court Square; turn right.

What hostellers say: "Can't we do better than this?"

Gestalt: Chelsea morning

Safety:

Hospitality:

Cleanliness: 

Party index:

CITY OF LONDON HOSTEL 

36-38 Carter Lane, London EC4V 5AD

Phone Number: 0171–236–4965

Fax: 0171–236–7681
Rates: £17.90-£21.30 (about $27-$38 US) per HI member, £44 (about $66 US) doubles
Credit cards: Yes
Beds: 193
Single rooms: Yes
Private/family rooms: Yes
Office hours: 7:00 A.M. to 11:00 P.M.
Affiliation: HI-YHA
Extras: TV, laundry, breakfast, meals ($), bureau de change, shop, video games

Once a choir school for beautiful St. Paul's Cathedral, this place would seem to have the best location of any hostel in London Town—it's right smack in the financial district, and during the daytime this area hops with bankers, museum-goers and bridge-gawkers, plus people looking up at tremendously inspiring St. Paul's Cathedral. (That's where Charles and Di got married, in case you've been living under a rock for the past hundred years.)

However, keep in mind that this part of town becomes a ghost town at night because nobody actually lives here; everyone heads

City of London Hostel

London

(photo by Paul Karr)

home or to Bloomsbury or the West End, so you'll be hard pressed to find excitement after hours.

Not surprisingly, the place tends to draw families and elderly travelers who pile into dorm rooms that range from four to fifteen beds. Quad rooms are slightly more expensive; "economy dorms," with fifteen beds, are cheaper. There's

Best bet for a bite:
The Rising Sun (Thai)

Insiders' tip:
St. Paul's dome climb (375 steps)

the usual kitchen and TV lounge—heck, some rooms even have TVs! No breakfast is included with your night's sleep, but upper-floor rooms are blessed with great views of downtown London. There's a decent restaurant here, plus video games and a friendly, fairly hip front desk.

All in all, this hostel grades out as decent and quiet, if boring. Hey, at least you're almost on top of that cathedral and a few pubs.

What hostellers say:
"London bridge is falling down..."

Gestalt:
Saint in the city

Safety:

Hospitality:

Cleanliness:

Party index:

How to get there:

By Tube: Take Tube to St. Paul's or Blackfriars stops. From Blackfriars, walk 2 blocks north on New Bridge, then make a right onto Carter Lane; from St. Paul's, walk down Godliman Street, then right onto Carter Lane.

CURZON HOUSE HOSTEL

58 Courtfield Gardens, London SW5

Phone Number: 0171–581–2216 or 0171–373–6745

Fax: 0171–835–1319
Rates: £13–£28 per person (about $20–$42 US); doubles £38-£42 (about $57–$63 US)
Credit cards: Yes
Beds: 62
Extras: Breakfast, TV

Good views and decent rooms characterize this place, which is pretty popular with your rucksacking set—those types who blow into London with a smile and not much else, fresh from a junket to Tasmania.

Rooms have nice windows and just four to six beds—that's beds, not bunks—each. Some have views of a local church; some look out onto the quiet square known as Courtfield Gardens. Continental breakfast is also included here, plus access to a small kitchen; all things considered, including the so-so state of London hostels, this place is a good value.

Gestalt:
Courtfield of dreams

Safety:

Hospitality:

Cleanliness:

Party index:

How to get there:

By Tube: Take Tube to Gloucester Road stop. From station, turn right onto Courtfield Road, then right again on Courtfield Gardens.

EARL'S COURT HOSTEL

38 Bolton Gardens, London SW5 0AQ

Phone Number: 0171–373–7083

Fax: 0171–835–2034
E-mail: 106170.760@compuserve.com
Rates: £16.45–£18.70 (about $25–$27 US) per HI member
Credit cards: Yes
Office hours: 7:00 A.M. to 11:00 P.M.
Private/family rooms: None
Affiliation: HI-YHA
Extras: Breakfast, laundry, bureau de change, meals ($), TV, garden, bike storage, video games

Handy and well placed, this joint looks like a good deal to us, if plain—and predictably stuffed to the gills in high summer season. It's a town house located in a quiet and pretty neighborhood, safe and very near all sorts of other good things—nightlife, sights, and so forth.

Dorms come with four to twelve beds per bunkroom, most of them more in the six to twelve-bed range. Things get tight as a tick sometimes, as this is a pretty popular location. They've even resorted to using triple bunkbeds—three bunks on one frame! Needless to say, this can be a major pain if you're on the bottom and one or two inebriated bunkmates show up late-night.

We liked the exceptionally nice kitchen and courtyard garden, not to mention the access to airport buses and great Kensington museums. However, those triple bunks aren't much fun.

Best bet for a bite: Shish kebab stands

What hostellers say: "Cool, man."

Gestalt: Duke of Earl's

Safety:

Hospitality: 

Cleanliness: 

Party index:

How to get there:

By Tube: Take Tube to Earl's Court stop, then exit right onto Earl's Court and make a left onto Bolton Gardens.

GENERATOR HOSTEL

MacNaghten House, Compton Place, London WC1H

Phone Number: 0171–388–7666

Rates: £17.50–£37.00 per person (about $26–$55 US); doubles £44 (about $66 US)
Credit cards: Yes
Beds: 800

Private/family rooms: Yes
Affiliation: None
Extras: Restaurant ($), bar

This is definitely one of the weirder joints in England. It's a huge, monstrous brick building on a sidestreet just off Russell Square—which, itself, is practically on top of the world-famous (and free!) British Museum—in a quiet neighborhood of Camden. And the hostel logo is a guy with a cyber-helmet on. Or is that a cyber-face? Who knows?

Best bet for a bite: Safeway

Insiders' tip: Nice park nearby

What hostellers say: "Moooo."

Gestalt: Big Generator

Safety: 

Hospitality: 

Cleanliness: 

Party index: 

Anyway, this enormous hostel packs in 800 beds. Yes, 800. Some are occupied by long-termers—you know, people living here while they look for a job or dodge the visa police—and others are taken up by huge tour groups. It's a basic place, to be sure, but fun and reasonably well equipped. It is what it is, a place to get hip with Generation X'ers from all over Europe. Definitely not the place to choose if you don't like dyed hair, rave clothing, tattoos, piercings, trust-fund hippies, guys with ties . . . hey, who let them in here?

On the other hand, if you don't feel comfortable with all that other stuff, we've got just one question: Why the heck are you in London in the first place??

The bar and cafeteria here seem to focus the socializing, and rooms are decently maintained. There's a serious herd feeling, but if you can stand that, it's an okay bunk.

How to get there:

By Tube: Take Tube to Russell Square stop, then walk down Bernard Street to Marchmont, turn left, and continue to Tavistock Place; turn left at Compton Place shortly afterward. Hostel is at end of short street.

GRANADA HOTEL HOSTEL

73 Belgrave Road, Victoria, London SW1V 2BG

Phone Number: 0171–821–7611

Fax: 0171–976–6261
E-mail: repton@lhghotels.demon.co.uk
Web site: smoothhound.co.uk/a44207.html
Rates: £16.50 (about $25 US) per person; doubles £33 (about $48 US)

Private rooms: None
Office hours: Call hostel for hours
Affiliation: None
Extras: TV, breakfast

We learned about this new place right before press time, and hostellers we talked with seem to like it so far. Dorms contain from four to six beds apiece, and all come with en-suite bathrooms. A maid apparently cleans the rooms each day fairly well, as it is also a hotel, and the place is quite central to the Victoria and Belgravia area—the place you'll probably arrive if you've come by bus, and close to one of London's most expensive residential areas.

Oh, yeah, and you're quite close to Buckingham Palace, too, where you-know-Herness lives. Lots of good restaurants and pubs circle the area, which does empty out and get a bit sketchy after dark. Definitely an option, though not fancy at all.

Best bet for a bite: Tandoori houses

Insiders' tip: Café Internet for e-mailing

What hostellers say: "Hmmm. Maybe."

Gestalt: Camp Granada

Safety: 

Party index:

How to get there:

By bus or train: From Victoria Station go left onto Buckingham Palace Road, then left onto Belgrave Road. Hostel is on left.

By Tube: Take Tube to Victoria stop. Turn onto Buckingham Palace Road.

HAMPSTEAD HEATH HOSTEL 

4 Wellgarth Road, Hampstead, London NW11 7HR

Phone Number: 0181–4589054

Fax: 0181–2090546
Rates: £13.35–£17.10 per HI member (about \$20–\$23 US); doubles £38.50 (about \$58 US)
Credit cards: Yes
Beds: 200
Private/family rooms: Yes
Office hours: 7:00 A.M. to 11:30 P.M.
Affiliation: HI-YHA
Extras: Bureau de change, laundry, meals (\$), TV, garden

This blah-looking brick hostel way up in north London's suburbs is fairly well maintained, yet quiet (except when subways rumble beneath), so good luck snagging a room in high season. Why's this place so popular? Two words: school groups. Lots of 'em.

The hostel's mostly made up of good and fairly small dorm rooms—just two to six beds, except in the case of one huge dorm—and each room has its very own sink. Some rooms, especially the doubles, even overlook a quiet back garden. The place has a tiny kitchen, smoky common room with blaring telly, and a front desk that sells Travelcards and a whole lot more. If you rent a family room, you pay for it and get a so-so breakfast.

Out here in the green suburbs of Hampstead Heath, there's not a lot to do except poke around the ethnic restaurants, hunt for Karl Marx's former home (not far away), check out a nice view of the city from a hilltop, and simply chill out if you're tired of the human circus of the Tube and the public markets. All in all, definitely a good deal here—one of London's best, although you're going to sacrifice a little access to London's hippest sights.

Even that problem can be easily remedied, however, by buying a Travelcard (see Introduction) and hopping the Tube every chance you get. You're only ten minutes by subway from Camden, Bloomsbury, Soho, and the rest of what you really want to see, anyway. So what if you're tripping over German schoolkids?

Best bet for a bite: Japan Café

Insiders' tip: Parliament Hill view

What hostellers say: "Where's the action?"

Gestalt: Heath bore

Safety: 

Cleanliness:

Hospitality:

Party index:

How to get there:

By bus: From downtown, take 210 bus or 268 bus to first stop, or N13 bus to hostel at night. Or take 13, 139 or 82 bus to Golders Green area and walk along North End Road to Wellgarth; turn left and walk 50 yards to hostel on right. Entrance is just past parking lot.

By train: From Euston Station, take Northern Tube line north to Golders Green stop. From station, turn left and walk down North End Road to Wellgarth; turn left and walk 50 yards to hostel on right. Entrance is just past parking lot. From Paddington Station, take Tube to Golders Green and follow directions above.

By Tube: Take Tube to Golders Green. From station, turn left and walk down North End Road to Wellgarth; turn left and walk 50 yards to hostel on right. Entrance is just past parking lot.

KEY TO ICONS

- Attractive natural setting
- Ecologically aware hostel
- Superior kitchen facilities or cafe
- Offbeat or eccentric place
- Superior bathroom facilities
- Romantic private rooms
- Comfortable beds
- Editors' choice: among our very favorite hostels
- A particularly good value
- Wheelchair accessible
- Good for business travelers
- Especially well suited for families
- Good for active travelers
- Visual arts at hostel or nearby
- Music at hostel or nearby
- Great hostel for skiers
- Bar or pub at hostel or nearby

HOLLAND HOUSE (KING GEORGE VI MEMORIAL HOSTEL)

Holland Walk, Kensington, London W8 7QU

Phone Number: 0171–9370748

Fax: 0171–3760667
Rates: £16.45–£18.70 (about $25–$28 US) per HI member
Credit cards: Yes
Beds: 201
Office hours: 7:00 A.M. to 11:30 P.M.
Affiliation: HI-YHA
Extras: Laundry, lockers, breakfast, TV, bureau de change, dinner ($)

The biggest advantage to this Hostelling International joint is its very quiet location: It's stuck smack in the middle of gorgeous Holland Park, and not too far from Kensington's artsy offerings and upscale shopping. We liked that, but some hostellers found it boring to have to hike to the fun stuff—and noticed that some guests tend to stay here a looooong time. Ah, well. It's still just fine, and there's no lockout either.

Best bet for a bite: Marks & Spencer

What hostellers say: "Zzzzzz."

Gestalt: Dutch treat

Safety:

Hospitality:

Cleanliness:

Party index:

Half the place is a roomy Jacobean mansion (as YHA will remind you again and again), though take note: When you get there, you could well get put in the newer concrete annex across the outdoor walkway instead—and that's more like a barracks than a palace, definitely a little less glamorous than what you might have been expecting. Dorms vary wildly in size from four to twenty beds per room (most contain at least a dozen bunks), and they can be a tight squeeze; that's one drawback here. A handful of private rooms are possible but almost never available, as group leaders get first dibs on 'em.

The kitchen here is good, dinners aren't bad at all, and they give you a sizable breakfast, too. Front desk staff are super at orienting you; they will also sell guidebooks (though not *this* one for some reason!), useful Travelcards for the Tube, and other stuff. A separate laundry building is also a bonus.

While we didn't have any problems, the friendly staff recommends you be careful walking through the park if you're arriving by night. There are two ways to come by Tube. At night get off at the High Street Kensington stop. In daytime, use the Holland Park stop instead, though you'll need to look sharp for the sign marking the entrance to the park on your right.

A good security system requires everyone to be buzzed in by a security guard after 4:30 in the afternoon, a bit annoying, but a good idea nevertheless. Why so early? It's already dark by then in winter, that's why.

How to get there:

By Tube: At night, take Tube to High Street Kensington. Exit station, cross street and turn left. Walk several blocks to Holland Park entrance on right, turn right onto Holland Walk; pass field, enter park on left, then take a right to hostel. In daytime, you can also take the Tube to Holland Park. Exit station, cross street, and turn left. Walk down street away from convenience store, turn right into park entrance, and walk down pathway to hostel entrance on right.

INTERNATIONAL STUDENT HOUSE

229 Great Portland Street, London W1 5HD

Phone Number: 0171–631–3223 or 0171–631–8300

Fax: 0171–636–5565
E-mail: accom@ish.org.uk
Web site: ish.org.uk
Rates: £12.35–£23.40 per person (about $19–$40 US); doubles £40 (about $60 US)
Credit cards: Yes
Beds: 600
Affiliation: None
Extras: Laundry, breakfast, restaurant ($), bar, gym, Internet access

This hostel's well equipped and caters to students (duh), hence it's very, very popular—full, in other words—most of the time. You'll certainly need to book in advance, especially during the summer.

The hostel actually consists of three separate facilities: two buildings here on Great Portland Street, a university residence hall that opens its door to travelers during the summer, and an annex nearby. Among the recently added goodies are an Internet cafe, a gym/fitness center, a bar, a restaurant, and a laundry. Breakfast comes with your bed almost all the time, and the staff runs a potpourri of activities and events.

Only drawback? All this luxury costs a lot of quid: This is perhaps the most expensive hostel in London, unless you're an ISIC card holder (a student, in other words), and then you get a discount.

Best bet for a bite: Covent Garden area

What hostellers say: "Bonjour!"

Gestalt: International house of pancakes

Hospitality: 

Cleanliness: 

Party index:

How to get there:

By bus: Call hostel for transit route.
By car: Call hostel for directions.
By plane: Two airports outside London; take A2 Airbus to hostel.
By train: Call hostel for transit route.
By Tube: Take Tube to Great Portland Street stop; walk across street to hostel.

OXFORD STREET HOSTEL 

14-18 Noel Street, London W1 1PD

Phone Number: 0171–7341618

Fax: 0171–7341657
Rates: £15.25–£18.70 per HI member (about $23–$28 US)
Credit cards: Yes
Beds: 75
Private/family rooms: Sometimes
Office hours: 7:00 A.M. to 11:00 P.M.
Affiliation: HI-YHA
Extras: TV, lockers, bureau de change, breakfast ($), laundry

How on Earth did YHA snag such a primo hostel location? You're smack in the heart of London's hippest addresses, SoHo and Covent Garden and the West End—incredible. The pub, club, and schmooze scene here rivals any in the world.

Best bet for a bite: Mildred's

Insiders' tip: Hostel pay phones useless

What hostellers say: "This neighborhood is SO cool."

Gestalt: West End Girls

Safety: 

Hospitality: 

Cleanliness: 

Party index:

And the hostel's okay, considering how many folks want to squeeze in here. Be forewarned that this is a really small hostel (in a bland building) with smallish dorm rooms; expect a bit of a squeeze plus lots of stairs to hike up first. Cleaning also suffers sometimes. Your reward for the hike? Rooms that mostly contain just two to four beds each.

Management and staff are usually friendly (lots of Aussies!) and should make your stay a pleasure; if not, tell us and we'll fix 'em up good. The kitchen's small but pretty good and clean, actually. And the new laundry is an extremely welcome addition in a town where just finding a place to wash your clothes can be a chore.

Hostellers come here for the extremely hip location, so you've got to book very

Oxford Street Hostel

London

(photo by Paul Karr)

early. Some hostellers hang out in the enormous television room. One thing this place ain't is quiet—with all the clubbing at hand, you're sure to be sandwiched between an Aussie and a brewski, but that's all right.

How to get there:

By Tube: Take Tube to Oxford Circus. Walk east on Oxford Street, turn right on Poland and then turn left on Noel.

ROTHERHITHE HOSTEL 

Island Yard, Salter Road, London SE16 1PP

Phone Number: 0171–2322114

Fax: 0171–2372919
Rates: £19.90–£21.30 per HI member (about $30–$32 US)
Credit cards: Yes
Beds: 320
Private/family rooms: Yes
Office hours: 7:00 A.M. to 11:00 P.M.
Affiliation: HI-YHA
Extras: Laundry, bureau de change, breakfast ($), travel shop, TV

Best bet for a bite:
Elsewhere

What hostellers say:
"Pass the Geritol."

Gestalt:
Dry dock

Safety:

Hospitality:

Cleanliness:

Party index:

You'll hear this well-equipped place touted as being just a mile from the Tower Bridge, but truth be told we're a bit skeptical about the location. It's in the Docklands, distant from most attractions —and not heavily foot-trafficked at night, either. The twenty-four hour desk security made us feel better once we'd arrived, though.

Otherwise, this purpose-built hostel is great. Rooms are nice and small—lots of doubles here—and all contain en-suite bathrooms. The private rooms reminded us of a hotel, and there's a travel shop for stocking up on supplies. Just allow lots of time to get to this not-exactly-perfect location, which isn't so much seedy as blah.

KEY TO ICONS

 Attractive natural setting

 Ecologically aware hostel

 Superior kitchen facilities or cafe

 Offbeat or eccentric place

 Superior bathroom facilities

 Romantic private rooms

 Comfortable beds

 Editors' choice: among our very favorite hostels

 A particularly good value

 Wheelchair accessible

Good for business travelers

 Especially well suited for families

 Good for active travelers

 Visual arts at hostel or nearby

 Music at hostel or nearby

 Great hostel for skiers

Bar or pub at hostel or nearby

How to get there:

By bus: Take East London Tube line to Rotherhithe. From station, walk along Brunel Road to Salter or take taxi to hostel. From Waterloo Station, take P11 bus to hostel.

By Tube: Take East London Tube line to Rotherhithe. From station, walk along Brunel Road to Salter or take taxi to hostel.

ST. CHRISTOPHER'S INN HOSTEL

121 Borough High Street, London SE1 1NP

Phone Number: 0171–407–1856

E-mail: st.christophers@interpub.co.uk
Web site: interpub.co.uk/st.christophers
Rates: £10–£12 per person (about $15–$18 US)
Private/family rooms: Yes
Extras: Laundry, bar, TV, roof patio, job board, breakfast, meals ($), pinball

$

The name says it all: The Hostel With Attitude. And let's face it: The reason most hostellers rolled in here was (a) the cheap price and (b) the attached pub.

Yes, a pub. And what a deal! For half what some hostels in London charge, you get a free continental breakfast, meal discounts, and access to a good private lounge.

Dorms come four to eight beds per room, but you won't spend much time there. You'll likely be in the pub, shooting free pool on Monday or trying out your karaoke. Noise can be a problem when rock bands play late in the club, though; best to bring your earplugs. Also, smoke from the bar curls upward inevitably to the dorm rooms. If it bugs you, this might not be the place to stay.

The staff here seems to go the extra mile, though, with advice on getting through the hoops of money changing, visas, and so forth—it seems to attract people who've landed in London to work for a while. They also do wake-up calls. Other amenities include a laundry; that private hostellers' lounge with bar, pinball machine, and forty-channel TV (yippee); a job

Best bet for a bite:
On-site pub grub

What hostellers say:
"Fill 'er up!"

Gestalt:
Brew hotel

Safety:

Hospitality: 

Cleanliness: 

Party index:

board; and a mail-forwarding service. We were also impressed with security measures: Each room here is accessed with a key card.

Just 200 yards from London Bridge, the hostel straddles a blue-collar area and sparkly sights. Keep in mind that it's on the much-less-nice South Bank of the Thames, but there are fewer crowds here. Try a dance club like The Ministry of Sound for something different.

How to get there:

By Tube: Call hostel for directions.

ST. PANCRAS INTERNATIONAL HOSTEL

79-81 Euston Road, London NW1 2QS

Phone Number: 0171–388–9998

Fax: 0171–388–6766
Rates: £17.90–£21.30 (about $27–$32 US) per HI member; doubles £44 (about $66 US)
Beds: 150
Private rooms: Yes
Affiliation: HI-YHA
Extras: TV, bike storage, laundry, dinner ($), breakfast

London's newest Hostelling International joint isn't in the greatest neighborhood, but it's close to a number of fine attractions and extremely well equipped.

Best bet for a bite: Drummond Street, near Euston Square

What hostellers say: "No, I don't wanna buy any drugs."

Gestalt: St. Pancreas

Safety: 

Hospitality: 

Cleanliness:

Party index: 

Placed near St. Pancras train station, it gets seedy at night and isn't recommended for the solitary female traveler. On the other hand, facilities are pretty nice. Dorm rooms contain just two to five beds, and everything's new, of course. The outside and inside are decked out in modern touches like chrome trim.

The train station couldn't be closer, and you're an incredibly short walk from the British Library as well as several Tube stops. The Camden Town area hops despite the sleaze factor, offering bargain shops by day and lots of live music and pubbing by night.

How to get there:

By train: From St. Pancras station, turn right onto Euston Road, cross Judd Street; hostel is second building on right after crossroad.

By Tube: Take Tube to King's Cross Station. Turn right onto Euston Road and cross Judd Street; hostel is second building on right after crossroad.

SOUTHEASTERN ENGLAND

Numbers on map refer to towns and islands numbered below.

1. Alfriston
2. Arundel
3. Bradenham
4. Brighton
5. Broadstairs
6. Canterbury
7. Dover
8. Eastbourne
9. Gillingham
10. Hastings
11. Hindhead
12. Holmbury St. Mary
13. Isle of Wight
14. Jordans
15. Kemsing
16. Loughton
17. Margate
18. Portsmouth
19. Shoreham-by-Sea
20. Streatley
21. Tanners Hatch
22. Telscombe
23. Uckfield
24. Wantage
25. Winchester
26. Windsor

SOUTHEASTERN ENGLAND

The Southeast of England's a very historic region, but it's one that travelers often blast through without a look en route to the bright lights of Paris or London. Still, some of these old towns are worth a look—places like Canterbury and Windsor continue to beguile. The hostels around here are pretty basic, though.

ALFRISTON HOSTEL

Frog Firle, Alfriston, Polegate, East Sussex BN26 5TT

Phone Number: 01323–870423

Fax: 01323–870615
Rates: £5.95–£8.80 per HI member (about $9.00–$13.00 US)
Beds: 68
Private/family rooms: Sometimes
Affiliation: HI-YHA
Extras: Bike storage, dinner ($)

This sixteenth-century stone home is pretty basic, offering a garden and a splendid view of the Cuckmore Valley and quaint (read rural) surroundings. Most folks hit the South Downs Way—the crowd here always includes at least a few hikers doing the ten-day hike—or explore the tiny village of Alfriston; this hostel also isn't far from the ocean at all.

Party index:

Dorms have two to ten beds, and a cycle shop on premises makes repairs a snap. For fun, seek out the Long Man, a prehistoric figure incised into the chalk. Or stare into the big eyes of the cows next door.

How to get there:

By bus: Bus stop at Seaford, 2 miles away; follow footpath

By car: Call hostel for directions.

By foot: From South Downs Way, follow riverbank to Litlington footbridge; take path west 400 yards.

By train: Train stop at Seaford, 2 miles away.

ARUNDEL HOSTEL

Warningcamp Hostel, Arundel, West Sussex BN18 9QY

Phone Number: 01903–882204

Rates: £5.95–£8.80 (about $9.00–$13.00 US) per HI member
Beds: 60
Private/family rooms: None
Affiliation: HI-YHA
Extras: TV, bike storage, campground
Lockout: 10:00 A.M.–5:00 P.M.
Curfew: 11:00 P.M.

People tell us this place runs hot and cold: It's mighty friendly and sometimes packed with day-trippers and trail walkers, but it can get uncomfortable as the building isn't heated or well ventilated. It's also a little farther from town than it should be.

In any case, it's cheap and quiet, with beds in dorms of four to eight beds; you decide if it's worth the trek. Other amenities include the oh-so-quaint location amongst a river, fields, and animals. Camping is also available.

Gestalt: Early warning

Party index:

Arundel itself has nice sights in a compact area, including the requisite cathedral and castle. You can also walk a mile and take a free tour of the home offices of The Body Shop in Littlehampton or grab a list of good hikes from the hostel front desk.

How to get there:

By bus: From Arundel station, walk 1 mile north.

By car: Take A27 just east of Arundel train station; turn north, make left at crossroads, and two lefts.

By train: From Arundel station, walk 1 mile north.

BRADENHAM HOSTEL

Village Hall, Bradenham, High Wycombe, Buckinghamshire

HP14 4HF

Phone Number: 01494–562929

Rates: £4.45–£6.50 per HI member (about $6.00–$10.00 US)
Beds: 18
Private/family rooms: None
Season: Call ahead for open days
Affiliation: HI-YHA
Extras: Bike storage

An amazing little village in the Chiltern Hills, Bradenham is protected by the National Trust. The hostel here is quite simple; you have to walk to get to the bathrooms, for instance, but at least you walk along a garden path. There are three dorm rooms, with four, six, and eight beds, plus a dining room, lounge, and kitchen.

Tremendous opportunities for hiking and biking abound in the area, offsetting somewhat the plainess of the hostel. A cycle shop allows for patching tires and fixing chains.

Insiders' tip: Hughenden Manor nearby

Party index:

How to get there:

By car: Take A4010 to Bradenham; hostel is next to Red Lion pub.

By train: Saunderton Station. Walk 1 mile down A4010 to village; hostel is next to Red Lion pub.

BRIGHTON BACKPACKERS

75-76 Middle Street, Brighton, Sussex BN1 8YD

Phone Number: 01273–777717

Fax: 01273–887778
E-mail: backpackers@fastnet.co.uk
Beds: 80
Rates: £9.00–£12.50 (about $14–$19 US) per person; doubles £25 (about $38 US)
Private/family rooms: Yes
Office hours: 9:00 A.M. to 11:00 P.M.
Affiliation: None
Extras: Laundry, bar, TV, cafe, pool table

This place, housed in two buildings, is laid back—check out the murals and lots of fun stuff like a bar and poolroom.

Besides the usual spartan dorms, they've got double rooms with en-suite bathrooms in an annex around the corner. Things can get cramped, but at least it's fairly hip here. You're also near The Lanes shopping area.

Insiders' tip: Nude beach nearby

Gestalt: Brighton blast

Cleanliness: 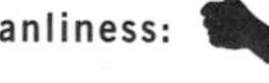

Party index:

How to get there:

By bus: Call hostel for transit route.

By car: Call hostel for directions.

By train: From Brighton station, walk down Queen's Road to waterfront, turn left on King's Road, then turn left again on Middle Street.

PATCHAM PLACE HOSTEL

London Road, Brighton, Sussex BN1 8YD

Phone Number: 01273–556–196

Fax: 01509–366
Rates: £6.55–£9.75 per HI member (about $10–$14 US)
Beds: 84
Private/family rooms: None
Affiliation: HI-YHA
Extras: TV, laundry, dinner ($), bicycle storage
Lockout: 10:00 A.M.–1:00 P.M.
Curfew: 11:00 P.M.

This sixteenth century mansion is quite a ways outside town—around 3 miles, in fact—and as prim as English hostels always seem to be. Not exactly oceanside, if you know what we mean, and not the place for a good time, either, as they lock you out before midnight if you're not back by then.

Party index:

The place tries to compensate with its sylvan location, however. The hostel building is in a pleasant enough park; some of the dorms are pretty large, though, with upwards of a dozen beds apiece.

How to get there:

By bus: From downtown, take 5 or 5A bus to near hostel.

By car: A27 to A23. Hostel is on west side of A23 (London Road), across from Black Lion hotel.

By train: From Preston Park Station, walk down hill and walk 1½ miles along London Road.

THISTLE LODGE

3 Osborne Road, Broadstairs, Isle-of-Thanet, Kent CT10 2AE

Phone Number: 01843–604121

Fax: 01843–604121
Rates: £5.95–£8.80 per HI member (about $9.00–$13.00 US)
Beds: 34
Private/family rooms: Sometimes
Season: Open March 28 to September 30
Affiliation: HI-YHA
Extras: TV, VCR, laundry, grill, garden, bike storage

Thistle Lodge is a Victorian villa in a residential neighborhood, with medium-sized dorms (six to seven beds) and smaller ones, too. We noticed that the hostel garden was popular with solitary hostellers, as was the grill with sociable ones.

History-minded hostellers know this is Dickens country, and the others hit the good sandy beach in town or hop ferries to Dunkirk or Ostend.

Gestalt:
Thistle Stop

Party index:

How to get there:

By car: Call hostel for directions.

By train: From Broadstairs station, go under bridge and along Broadway, then left onto Osborne.

ELLERSLIE HOSTEL

54 New Dover Road, Canterbury, Kent CT1 3DT

Phone Number: 01227–462911

Fax: 01227–470752
Rates: £6.55–£9.85 per HI member ($10–$14 US)
Credit cards: Yes
Beds: 86
Private/family rooms: 1
Office hours: 7:30 to 10:00 A.M.; 1:00 to 11:00 P.M.
Season: February 1 to December 31
Affiliation: HI-YHA
Extras: Restaurant ($), TV, bike storage, lockers, bureau de change, laundry, garden
Lockout: 10:00 A.M.–1:00 P.M.
Curfew: 11:00 P.M.

Canterbury's "official" hostel, in a Victorian building, is superpopular and pretty well equipped. Dorms come in six to twelve beds (though six is most common); the single family room includes a pair of sinks and all of six beds. There's also a small kitchen and on-site cafeteria. Other fun amenities include the garden, a bike storage, and a bureau de change. Staff will gladly sell you ferry tickets, too.

This is very close to the historic downtown, with Chaucer stuff everywhere; frankly, we think it's gotten way-y-y-y-y-y-y out of hand and we're sick of it, but that's just us. Chaucerites, knock yourselves out.

Insiders' tip:
Skip the castle

Gestalt:
Canterbury tale

Party index:

How to get there:

By bus: From terminal, go left on Upper Bridge Street, then right onto St. Georgia's place to New Dover Road. Walk 1 mile to hostel on right.

By car: From London, take A2 toward Dover. Hostel in on right, south of city, on the A2.

By train: From Canterbury East Station, turn right, follow road past fire station, go right at second roundabout, continue along New Dover road 1 mile; hostel is on right.

KIPPS HOSTEL

40 Nunnery Fields, Canterbury, Kent CT1 3JT

Phone Number: 01227–786121

Fax: 01227–766992
E-mail: S.P.P.Harman@ukc.ac.uk
Rates: £10 per person (about $15 US)
Credit cards: Yes
Beds: 36
Family/private rooms: Yes
Affiliation: None
Extras: Laundry, store

Yes, it's another option in the tiny walled city of Chaucer. Accommodations here come in many sizes, including singles, doubles, and coed dorms. There's the usual kitchen and common space, as well as a laundry and small hostel store.

Party index:

How to get there:

By bus: Call hostel for transit route.

By car: From A28, take B2068 to Hythe. Turn right at first light by church; hostel is on left.

By train: Call hostel for transit route.

CHARLTON HOUSE HOSTEL

306 London Road, Dover, Kent CT17 0SY

Phone Number: 01304–201–314

Fax: 01304–202–236
Rates: £6.55–£9.75 per HI member (about $10–$15 US); doubles £21 (about $32 US)
Credit cards: Yes
Beds: 133
Private/family rooms: Yes
Affiliation: HI-YHA
Extras: TV, garden, bike storage, lockers
Lockout: 11:00 A.M.–5:00 P.M.
Curfew: 11:00 P.M.

$

This bland but surprisingly cheap hostel spreads over two buildings with roughly an equal number of beds. Most of the dorm rooms contain eight bunks apiece, though there are a few private rooms as well. A cycle shop and lounge add slight appeal to the place, but we wouldn't mark it tops on our list.

Well-worn? Yeah. (Some of the hostellers seem as archaic as the furniture—even the young ones.) At least the multilingual staff offers help sorting through the chaos.

In town, the chalky White Cliffs are the obvious top sight-seeing pick here—you've just gotta see 'em to believe 'em—but Dover Castle and St. Augustine's Abbey aren't bad either. Both the North Downs Way and the neat Pilgrim's Way walking tracks pass nearby, too.

Gestalt: Chalk Dust

Party index:

How to get there:

By car: Call hostel for directions.

By train: From Priory Station, take first left; walk 1 mile up High Street.

EASTBOURNE HOSTEL

East Dean Road, Eastbourne, East Sussex BN20 8ES

Phone Number: 01323–721081

Fax: 01323–721081
Rates: £5.40–£8.00 per HI member (about $8.00–$12.00 US); double £19 (about $29 US)
Beds: 30
Private/family rooms: Yes
Season: March 1 to September 28
Affiliation: HI-YHA
Extras: Bike storage, porch, campground

This former clubhouse for a golf course—how English—has plenty of small dorm rooms and one family room. A porch allows dry relaxation during the daytime lockouts.

This is the very start of the South Downs Way, so the hostel is especially well positioned for walkers. Rooms aren't great, just simple bunkbeds is all.

Gestalt: Fore on the Floor

Party index:

How to get there:

By car: Take A259 to Eastbourne; hostel is near new golf club.

By train: Eastbourne station. Walk along A259 1½ miles to hostel, just past new golf club.

CAPSTONE FARM HOSTEL

Capstone Road, Gillingham, Kent ME7 3JE

Phone Number: 01634–400788

Fax: 01634–400794
Rates: £5.95–£8.80 per HI member (about $9.00–$13.00 US), doubles £21 (about $32 US)

Beds: 41
Private/family rooms: Yes
Season: Call ahead for open days
Affiliation: HI-YHA
Extras: TV, laundry, bike storage, lockers, dinner ($)

About 5 miles from Rochester and even closer to Chatham, this "oast house" so typical of old Kent delivers Mother Nature in the form of trails, a lake, and more in an adjacent park. There are nice family rooms here, plus a shop for bike rentals and the usual lounge and kitchen setup.

In close-by Chatham, hostellers tend to explore a Napoleonic fortress; in Rochester, folks usually hit the Norman castle.

Gestalt: Nightcap

Party index:

How to get there:

By car: Call hostel for directions.

GUESTLING HALL HOSTEL

Rye Road, Guestling, Hastings, East Sussex TN35 4LP

Phone Number: 01424–812373

Fax: 01424–814273
Rates: £5.95–£8.80 per HI member (about $9.00–$13.00 US)
Beds: 50
Private/family rooms: Yes
Season: Call ahead for open days
Affiliation: HI-YHA
Extras: Breakfast, dinner ($), Ping-Pong, bike storage, camping

Composed of five dorm rooms of various sizes, this Victorian manor house hostel is set on four acres of grounds that include a murky lake and wooded footpaths—incredibly pretty English scenery here, though quite a ramble from any population centers. It's furnished with a kitchen, Ping-Pong table, and lounge: in short, the most basic stuff you've come to expect of a decent hostel. Rooms contain four to twelve bunkbeds, a couple of private rooms are available, too.

Some hostellers come here because it's the nearest hostel to Rye, which is a quieter English Channel resort town. All in all, this is actually a happenin' area—in a relaxing way. Here's a sample: Within a couple miles of the hostel lie a nudist colony (sorry, we're duty-bound to report it), good beaches, tacky but fun amusement parks, gardens, and a pond.

Insiders' tip: Street theatre

Gestalt: Rye bed

Party index:

How to get there:

By bus: From Rye, take 11 or 12 bus to White Hart pub; walk 300 yards to hostel.

By car: Take A259 into Eastbourne; hostel is near White Hart pub, north of highway.

By train: Call hostel for transit route.

HINDHEAD HOSTEL

Devil's Punchbowl, Hindhead, Thursley, Surrey GU8 6NS

Phone Number: 0142860–4285

Fax: 01428–604285
Rates: £4.45–£6.50 per HI member (about $7.00–$10.00 US)
Beds: 16
Season: April 6 to August 31
Affiliation: HI-YHA
Extras: fireplace, woodstove

These three refurbished cottages, located in a geographical formation known as the Devil's Punchbowl, are protected by the National Trust and make up a summer-only hostel off the beaten track. It's mighty simple here: Since water's scarce there is no shower. It's certainly pretty country, though, with lots of nature at hand and the Pilgrim's Way for walking.

Party index:

How to get there:

By bus: Call hostel for transit route.

By car: Take A3 to just north of Hindhead; turn east carefully, park at turnout, walk ¾ mile to hostel.

By train: Call hostel for transit route.

KEY TO ICONS

Attractive natural setting
Ecologically aware hostel
Superior kitchen facilities or cafe
Offbeat or eccentric place
Superior bathroom facilities
Romantic private rooms
Comfortable beds
Editors' choice: among our very favorite hostels
A particularly good value
Wheelchair accessible
Good for business travelers
Especially well suited for families
Good for active travelers
Visual arts at hostel or nearby
Music at hostel or nearby
Great hostel for skiers
Bar or pub at hostel or nearby

HOLMBURY ST. MARY HOSTEL

Radnor Lane, Holmbury St. Mary, Dorking, Surrey RH5 6NW

Phone Number: 01306–730777

Rates: £5.95–£8.80 per HI member (about $9.00–$13.00 US)
Beds: 52
Family/private rooms: Sometimes
Season: Call ahead for open days.
Affiliation: HI-YHA
Extras: Camping, bike storage

Visiting this hostel, set in 4,000 acres of woodlands, is like going to Oz. There's an orienteering course, treasure hunt, and mountain biking on the grounds, among other stuff to do. All rooms here are small—there are two doubles and twelve quads—ensuring privacy.

Gestalt:
Home sweet Holmbury

Party index:

How to get there:

By bus: Call hostel for directions.

By car: Take A25 to Abinger Hammer, then B2126 to Radnor Lane; make a right.

By train: Gomshall station, 2 miles away.

SANDOWN HOSTEL

The Firs, Fitzroy Street, Sandown, Isle of Wight PO36 8JH

Phone Number: 01983–402651

Fax: 01983–493565
Rates: £5.95–£8.80 per HI member (about $9.00–$13.00 US)
Beds: 46
Affiliation: HI-YHA
Extras: TV, garden, bike storage, dinner ($)
Lockout: 10:00 A.M.–5:00 P.M.
Curfew: 11:00 P.M.

Despite the good location—we like parts of Wight, despite its critics—both the food and the dorm rooms in this place get consistently poor reviews from our hostelling snoops. There are way too few bathrooms for such a popular place, for instance.

The island itself is a mixture of nature and tackiness, with a Coney Island–like amusement park and loads of tourists on one side and quiet beaches on another. Sandown itself is hardly worth a glance; truck instead to the other joint on the island in Totland Bay.

Insiders' tip:
Try island railroad

Gestalt:
Wight wash

Party index:

How to get there:

By bus: Call hostel for transit route.

By car: Take A3055 to Sandown, turn onto Melville Street and then onto Fitzwilliam Street.

By train: From Sandown Station, walk down Station Avenue to Fitzroy, turn right. Hostel is on left.

TOTLAND BAY HOSTEL

Hurst Hill, Totland Bay, Isle of Wight PO39 0HD

Phone Number: 01983–752165

Fax: 01983–756443
Rates: £6.55–£9.75 per HI member (about $10–$14 US)
Beds: 74
Private/family rooms: None
Affiliation: HI-YHA
Extras: dinner ($)
Lockout: 10:00 A.M.–5:00 P.M.
Curfew: 11:00 P.M.

This hostel has a great location on the nicer, western side of the popular Isle of Wight and has a sense of whimsy about it: The rooms are actually named for people! Dorm rooms aren't too big, and sometimes contain simple furniture that make 'em feel like our bedrooms back home. We give the kitchen kudos for neatness and organization, too.

This is a great area for cycling or walking about: You'll avoid the crowds that sometimes make Wight life not so fun.

Insiders' tip:
Check out Colwell Bay Inn

Gestalt:
Wight stuff

Party index:

How to get there:

By bus: Call hostel for transit route.

By car: Take ferry from Lymington Pier to Yarmouth. Follow A3054 to Totland Bay; from roundabout in center of village, make left onto Weston Road, then take second left up Hurst Hill.

By train: From London's Waterloo Station, take train to Brockenhurst; change trains to Lymington Pier. Then take ferry to Yarmouth. Walk 3 miles to Totland Bay, or take 42 bus.

JORDANS HOSTEL

Welders Lane, Jordans, Beaconsfield, Buckinghamshire HP9 2SN

Phone Number: 01494–873135

Fax: 01494–875907
Rates: £4.95–£7.20 per HI member (about $7.00–$11.00 US)
Beds: 20
Season: March 1 to November 1
Affiliation: HI-YHA
Extras: Porch, bike storage, camping

Quite small, the Jordans hostel places bathrooms outdoors. So it's rustic. But there's central heating to keep things toasty and decent beds in four rooms—two with quad beds, two with six bunks apiece.

Milton's Cottage nearby is a frequent stop on the tourist itinerary. Interestingly, though, the area also has a close tie to Pennsylvania and the Quaker movement: William Penn's grave is close by. There's a meetinghouse and a barn nearby, too.

Party index:

How to get there:

By car: From London, take A40 past Gerrards Cross to near Beaconsfields; make a right onto Pot Kiln Lane, then right again on Welders Lane at Quaker meetinghouse. Hostel is on left.

By train: From Seer Green Station, walk ¾ mile to Jordans. Hostel is on Welders Lane, just past Quaker meetinghouse.

KEMSING HOSTEL

Church Lane, Kemsing, Sevenoaks, Kent TN15 6LU

Phone Number: 01732–761341

Fax: 01732–763044
Rates: £5.95–£8.80 per HI member (about $9.00–$13.00 US)
Beds: 50
Season: Call ahead for open days
Affiliation: HI-YHA
Extras: Porch, camping, TV, bike storage

This Victorian home on big green grounds is just 25 miles outside London, good for day-tripping. Dorms have four to ten beds, while a lounge and a quiet room provide opportunities for hanging out during rain showers or lockouts.

Party index:

How to get there:

By bus: From Sevenoaks, take 425, 426, or 433 bus to Kemsing.

By car: From London, take A25 to Seal, turn north through Seal and continue to Kemsing

Village; make right on West End and left on Church Lane. Hostel is behind church.

By train: From Kemsing station, walk 1½ miles to hostel.

EPPING FOREST HOSTEL

Wellington Hall, High Beach, Loughton, Essex IG10 4AG

Phone Number: 0181–5085161

Fax: 0181–5085161
Rates: £5.40–£8.00 per HI member (about $8.00–$12.00 US)
Beds: 36
Season: March 29 to November 8
Affiliation: HI-YHA
Extras: Garden, bike storage, camping

This one-story building is just 10 miles from downtown London. In fact you can get here just by taking the Tube subway, but it seems a world away. Tucked in 6,000 acres of forest, it features eight dorm rooms of roughly equal size.

They've got a garden and a campground, which already sets it apart in quality from other YHA joints. Give it a look if you need to chill out from London for a few days and don't want to spend a lot of dough getting to John O' Groats or somewhere.

Insiders' tip:
Duke of Wellington pub

Gestalt:
Forest bunk

Party index:

How to get there:

By car: Take M25 to Junction 26; get onto Epping/Loughton Road, turn right at Volunteer Inn, then make next right. Go left and up Wellington Hill; hostel is on right.

By Tube: Loughton. Take cab (£3, about $5.00 US) or walk 2 miles; call hostel for directions.

BEACHCOMBER HOSTEL

3-4 Royal Esplanade, Westbrook Bay, Margate, Kent CT9 5DL

Phone Number: 01843–221616

Fax: 01843–221616
Rates: £6.55–£9.75 per HI member (about $10–$15 US); doubles £22 (about $33 US)
Beds: 46
Private/family rooms: Yes
Season: March 1 to November 1
Affiliation: HI-YHA
Extras: Laundry, bike storage

This brand-new hostel is basically a beach house retrofitted for hostelling hordes. You're practically planted in the sand, and the fun little village is around you as well. Rooms here are small, which is good, and we hear the couples' rooms are nice, too.

Gestalt:
Beach blanket

Party index:

How to get here:

By bus: Call hostel for transit route.

By car: From Canterbury, take A28 to Margate; turn onto Westbrook Gardens by water, continue to Royal Esplanade.

By train: From Margate station, go west on Promenade ⅓ mile to Westbrook Bay.

WYMERING MANOR HOSTEL

Old Wymering Lane, Cosham, Portsmouth, Hampshire
PO6 3NL

Phone Number: 01705–375661

Fax: 01705–214177
Rates: £5.95–£8.80 per HI member (about $9.00–$13.00 US)
Beds: 64
Season: February 1 to December 31
Affiliation: HI-YHA
Lockout: 10:00 A.M.– 5:00 P.M.
Curfew: 11:00 P.M.

Located too far outside town, Wymering Manor is a great building in fine Tudor style with interesting little touches like recurving stairways and secret passages. It's also one of the oldest houses in the area. (Could ya tell? Sure ya could.) However, the consid-

erable hike out here makes it unattractive as a layover unless you're just passing through.

The dorm room situation here isn't great, though; some rooms have as many as twenty-two beds, giving you that cattle-like feeling, and it's frequently booked to the gills. Portsmouth itself—a working-class port town since time immemorial, it seems—doesn't so much offer up resorts and shops as it does fish, diesel fuel, and anchors. The old town is moderately interesting, but we wouldn't spend a BritRail pass day just to get here. (Unless we were taking the ferry to France.) Get our drift?

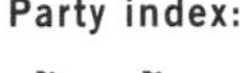

Party index:

How to get there:

By bus: Take #12 bus from center of town.

By car: From London, take A3 into Portsmouth; at Medina Road roundabout, turn right and continue to seventh right. Go right on Old Wymering Lane, just after church.

By train: Cosham station, ½ mile away.

TOTTINGTON BARN HOSTEL

Truleigh Hill, Shoreham-by-Sea, West Sussex BN43 5FB

Phone Number: 01903–813419

Fax: 01903–812016
Rates: £5.95–£8.80 per HI member (about $9.00–$13.00 US); doubles £21 (about $32 US)
Beds: 56
Private/family rooms: Yes
Season: March 30 to October 3
Affiliation: HI-YHA
Extras: Garden, bike storage, dinner ($)
Lockout: 10:00 A.M.–5:00 P.M.
Curfew: 11:00 P.M.

This Truleigh Hill hostel was purpose-built not far from Shoreham-by-the-Sea, a coastal resort offering the usual surf fun. Its position upon the South Downs Way gives it good views of the Downs, and there are family rooms available—unusual in small hostels. It's not actually a barn, though, but rather a new, spartan building with a garden and meal service.

Gestalt:
Shoreham leave

Party index:

How to get there:

By car: From Shoreham, take Upper Shoreham Road to Erringham Road; continue to Mill Hill.

By train: From Shoreham station, walk 2 miles to hostel.

STREATLEY-ON-THAMES HOSTEL

Hill House, Reading Road, Streatley, Reading, Berkshire RG8 9JJ

Phone Number: 01491–872278

Fax: 01491–873056
Rates: £6.55–£9.75 per HI member (about $10–$15 US); doubles £22 (about $33 US)
Beds: 51
Season: Call ahead for open days
Affiliation: HI-YHA
Extras: TV, dinner ($)

This Victorian house isn't exactly on the beaten path, but it does get some visitors. A popular diversion in this sleepy area is to watch boats dock at Goring, just a hop away. A bit of advice: Grab one of the few family rooms, and you won't get locked out during the day.

Best bet for a bite: The Bull for pub grub

Gestalt: High Thames

Party index:

How to get there:

By bus: Call hostel for transit route.

By car: Take A329 to Streatley. Hostel is just south of traffic lights, on west side of street.

By train: From Goring and Stanley Station, walk west 1 mile to Streatley village center. Hostel is just south of lights on A329.

TANNERS HATCH HOSTEL

Tanners Hatch, Polesden Lacey, Dorking, Surrey RH5 6BE

Phone Number: 01372–52528

Fax: 01372–452528
Rates: £4.45–£6.50 per HI member (about $7.00–$10.00 US)
Beds: 28
Affiliation: HI-YHA
Extras: Bike storage, camping

This hostel's a cottage, plain and simple, in the Surrey Hills—and it's for walkers only! You actually need a compass, good treaded boots, and a flashlight (at night) to hike ¾ mile into the place along a muddy path; talk about earning your bed. That explains the incredibly low rent.

Once there, you'll rough it some more, sharing a single unisex shower and catching your Z's in triple bunks. Thrillsville, we know.

Tanners Hatch Hostel
Tanners Hatch, England
(photo courtesy of HI-YHA)

Actually, though, this is more what hostelling is supposed to be, so enjoy it while you can.

Gestalt:
Escape hatch

Party index:

How to get there:

By bus: Bus stops in West Humble, 2 miles away.

By car: Call hostel for directions.

By train: Dorking West Station, 2½ miles away.

TELSCOMBE HOSTEL

Bank Cottages, Telscombe, Lewes, East Sussex BN7 3HZ

Phone Number: 01273–301357

Fax: 01273–301357
Rates: £4.95–£7.20 (about $7.00–$11.00 US) per HI member
Beds: 22
Season: April 9 to September 5
Affiliation: HI-YHA
Extras: Bike storage
Lockout: 10:00 A.M.–5:00 P.M.
Curfew: 11:00 P.M.

A set of three 200-year-old cottages constructed in the roaring 1700s, this hostel's only open during summertime (groups can rent the place out in winter); it's quiet and simple, with simple scenery such as the local chalk downs nearby.

Party index:

Some folks also hustle over to Lewes, a bigger town where Virginia Woolf and Thomas More both once lived—though not together, we'll hasten to add. Hmm. Might have been interesting. Ah, well.

How to get there:

By car: Call hostel for directions.

By foot: From Lewes, walk Kingston Road for 4 miles; turn right at sign for Telscombe Village.

By train: Call hostel for directions.

BLACKBOYS HOSTEL

Uckfield, East Sussex TN22 5HU

Phone Number: 01825–890607

Fax: 01494–56473
Rates: £4.45–£6.50 per HI member (about $7.00–$10.00 US)
Beds: 18
Affiliation: HI-YHA
Extras: Camping, bike storage, fireplace

A wood cabin placed 4 miles outside already-small Uckfield, this place is quite plain—just four dorm rooms, a lounge, a kitchen, and some grounds. You can camp, too, though the price is already dirt-cheap. Local attractions include author Rudyard Kipling's former home and a steam railway.

Party index:

How to get there:

By bus: From Eastbourne take 217, 218, or 728 bus to Uckfield.

By car: Take A 272 or B2102 to Gunn Road, turn; hostel is on Gunn Road.

By train: Buxted station, 2½ miles from hostel.

RIDGEWAY HOSTEL

Courthill, Wantage, Oxfordshire OX12 9NE

Phone Number: 012357–60253

Fax: 01235–768865
Rates: £5.40–£8.00 per HI member (about $8.00–$12.00 US)
Beds: 59
Season: Call ahead for open days

Affiliation: HI-YHA
Extras: TV, laundry, bike storage, grill, dinner ($)

This is a real oddity, although—this being Old England—we shouldn't be so surprised. But we were. Why?

Because of the horse. Of course.

It's a rare hostel indeed where horses are stabled up in the countryside along with hostellers, but that's just what you get at Ridgeway. The hostel is composed of a set of converted barns arranged around a courtyard, and you might start to feel kinship with one of those equines after a while, as all ten dorm rooms here are big. This is definitely not a great place for privacy-seekers; we noted rooms with as many as thirteen bunks packed in. Not that it'll be fully booked, though; this is too far off the track to get very full, unless a school group has arrived en masse.

Gestalt: Horsin' around

Party index:

Attractions in the area include mountain biking, hiking trails, and the general lushness of the Oxfordshire countryside.

How to get there:

By car: Take A420 or M4 to A338 in Wantage; hostel is on the A338.

By train: From Didcot Parkway Station take Thames Transit 32A, 35A, or 36A bus to Wantage. Walk 2 miles south on A338 to hostel.

CITY MILL HOSTEL 

1 Water Lane, Winchester, Hampshire SO23 8EJ

Phone Number: 01962–853723

Fax: 01962–855524

Rates: £5.95–£8.80 per HI member (about $9.00–$13.00 US)
Beds: 31
Season: Call ahead for open days
Affiliation: HI-YHA
Extras: Dinner ($), garden, bike storage, dollar
Lockout: 10:00 A.M.–5:00 P.M.
Curfew: 11:00 P.M.

This great place, tucked on a little lane right smack in historic Winchester, is tops. You've got atmosphere: It's an eighteenth-century mill sitting on a little island in the River Itchen. You've got views of the river and ancient buildings. There's a good garden. And it's quite a deal for the dollar—er, pound.

All right, so it isn't the Hilton. Dorm rooms here range from okay (quads) to enormous (the big one contains eighteen bunks); in shoulder seasons, we've heard, that big honker can get a little nippy. Also, the facilities are rather plain, and the staff enforces rules a little too fervently.

Insiders' tip:
Jane Austen's House in nearby Chawton

Gestalt:
Thanks-a-mill

Party index:

Still, we like being so dang close to Winchester Cathedral and other hot spots in this old, old city. This might be the crown jewel of England's sights—the realm's first king, after all, got his crown here back in the ninth century. Local friars penned the *Domesday Book,* too.

Our pick of the feast of sights? The cathedral, of course, with its ancient bibles and famous remains. Really, this is the seat of much of Western History—Vikings, Saxons, the whole nine yards—as we know it; London came later.

How to get there:

By bus: From station walk along Broadway over Eastgate Bridge; take first left onto Water Lane. Hostel is third door on left.

By car: No parking on site. Call hostel for directions.

By train: Winchester station is 1 mile away. From station walk downtown to Broadway and over Eastgate Bridge; take first left onto Water Lane. Hostel is third door on left.

EDGEWORTH HOUSE HOSTEL

Mill Lane, Windsor, Berkshire SL4 5JE

Phone Number: 01753–861710

Fax: 01753–832100
Rates: £6.55–£9.75 per HI member (about $10–$14 US)
Beds: 76
Private/family rooms: Sometimes
Affiliation: HI-YHA
Extras: Dinner ($), laundry

A surprisingly big place packing in seventy-six beds, this joint might stick you in a larger room than you want: Two of the dorms have more than fifteen beds each.

Gestalt:
Windsor palace

Party index:

But, hey, there's a laundry, and you're just a mile from Windsor's fabulous attractions. It's convenient to Heathrow and London, too, if you're not quite ready to tackle the big city without a dose of quieter life first.

How to get there:

By car: Drive M6 to Junction 6. From roundabout turn toward Windsor. Make first exit; at next roundabout take third right onto A308. At smaller roundabout turn into Mill Lane; hostel is on right.

By train: Windsor & Eton Central Station, 1 mile away.

SOUTHWESTERN ENGLAND

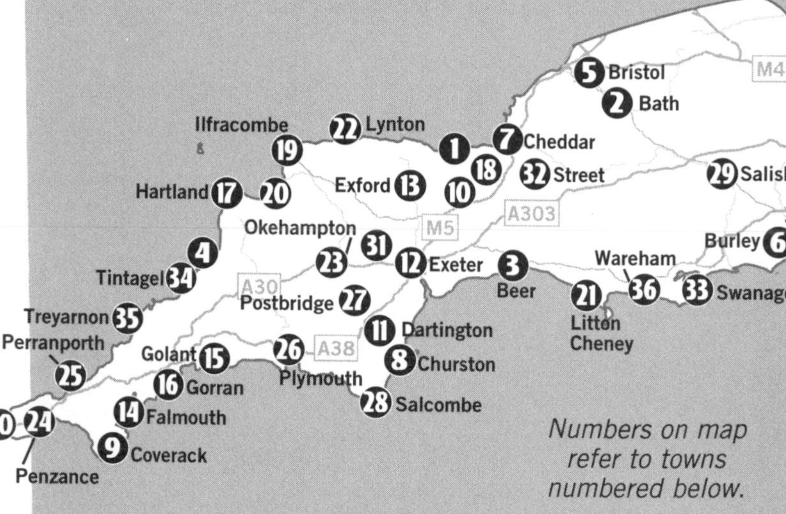

Numbers on map refer to towns numbered below.

1. Alcombe Combe
2. Bath
3. Beer
4. Boscastle Harbour
5. Bristol
6. Burley
7. Cheddar
8. Churston
9. Coverack
10. Crowcombe Heathfield
11. Dartington
12. Exeter
13. Exford
14. Falmouth
15. Golant
16. Gorran
17. Hartland
18. Holford
19. Ilfracombe
20. Instow
21. Litton Cheney
22. Lynton
23. Okehampton
24. Penzance
25. Perranporth
26. Plymouth
27. Postbridge
28. Salcombe
29. Salisbury
30. St. Just-in-Penwith
31. Steps Bridge
32. Street
33. Swanage
34. Tintagel
35. Treyarnon
36. Wareham

SOUTHWESTERN ENGLAND

Much of England is pastoral, but in southwestern England the superlatives—awe, amazement—begin to crowd out the usual fuzzy feelings. This is perhaps England's most beautiful countryside, a landscape where rolling green hills run up to towering sea cliffs. In addition, this is a surprisingly inexpensive place to rest your head—well, not any more expensive than the rest of England, let's put it that way.

Unfortunately, everybody and their mother has begun to figure this out. As a result, England's most beautiful corner is rapidly becoming its tackiest, as well. You can't possibly miss the billboards in Cornwall hawking attractions that, trust us, aren't worth the detours. (Kinda reminds us of the America Midwest, in fact. Sign-wise.)

To get away from it all, there are a goodly number of hostels located in towns that aren't overhyped. Some of the country's most amazing hostels are here, clinging to cliffs or tucked deep in the moors.

Transit here is sometimes good, sometimes not so good. You can readily get all the way out to Penzance from London by rail (though it takes a good five hours to make the trip). That's the good news. Bad news? If you want to get out and beat the bushes, you need to climb off that one train line somewhere near the end, then depend on the tenuous network of local bus systems branching out into the countryside. It could take you a whole day just to get to the hostel from London, and that's a shame in such a small country.

But take heart. Once you stare out at the sea view, you just won't care anymore.

MINEHEAD HOSTEL

Alcombe Combe, Minehead, Somerset TA24 6EW

Phone Number: 01643–702595

Fax: 01643–703016
Rates: £5.95–£8.80 per HI member (about $9.00–$14.00 US)
Beds: 36
Season: Call ahead for open days.
Affiliation: HI-YHA
Extras: Dinner ($), bike storage

Pretty sparse, hostellers tell us, though nicely located in hilly woods above the ocean with lots of room to ramble around. Six dorm rooms here offer a variety of accommodation.

You can get directly to Exmoor National Park's extensive footpaths from here; in fact, Minehead's perhaps the best base before shoving off into Round Table turf.

Gestalt: Trailhead

Party index:

How to get there:

By bus: From Taunton or Minehead take 28 bus to Alcombe; walk 1 mile down Brook Street to Manor, make sharp left to hostel.

By car: Take A39 to Alcombe, then turn south on Brook Street to Britannia Inn. Continue to Manor Road (a private road) and make sharp left up to hostel. *Note:* The hostel is very hard to find after dark.

By train: Dunster Station, 2 miles away; walk northwest on A39 to Brook Street, turn left, walk up Brook to Manor, make a sharp left to hostel.

BATH BACKPACKERS HOSTEL

13 Pierrepont Street, Bath, Avon BA2 6JZ

Phone Number: 01225–446787

Fax: 01225–446305

Rates: £11 per person (about $16 US)

Affiliation: None

Extras: Breakfast

Just what you'd expect from the name: a laid-back joint near the center of town. This hostel's much closer to the transit stations and downtown architecture than the HI joint, which is a big plus; it's also tons more fun.

It isn't as clean, though, but what'd you expect? Bunkrooms contain six to ten beds each, a bit of breakfast is included—not the English fry, thank goodness—and you're within walking distance of everything you need to see here.

Insiders' tip: Driving's tricky

Gestalt: Bath beads

Hospitality: 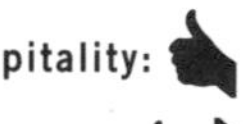

Cleanliness: 

Party index:

How to get there:

By bus: Call hostel for transit route.

By car: Call hostel for directions.

By train: From Bath Spa Station walk 3 blocks to hostel on Pierrepont Street.

BATHWICK HILL HOSTEL 

Bath, Avon BA2 6JZ

Phone Number: 01225–465674

Fax: 01225–482947
Rates: £6.55–£9.75 per HI member (about $10–$14 US)
Beds: 117
Family/private rooms: Sometimes
Office Hours: 7:15 A.M. to 11:00 P.M.
Affiliation: HI-YHA
Extras: TV, lockers, laundry, bike storage, meals ($), garden

An Italianate mansion 1 breath-sapping mile above Bath's downtown, this hostel features nice gardens and some stunning local views of the area. Dorm rooms too big, say some, but the friendly staff and clientele keep things fresh. You won't be spending much time here anyway, we'd wager.

That's because Bath itself is an incredible place, if heavily touristed. There's a good reason. Few cities in England compare for architecture. Check out The Circus or The Crescent, for example, two uniquely designed streets—one's circular, one's semicircular, duh—composed of attractive, connected town houses. Or poke around in the Roman baths that gave this city its name. This is also a great first-night jumping-off point for southwest England.

Gestalt:
Bathtaking

Hospitality: 

Party index:

How to get there:

By bus: From station take Badgerline 18 bus to hostel.

By car: A4 to Bath. Turn off at Pulteney Road, continue north. At roundabout ascend Bathwick Hill to hostel.

By train: From Bath Spa Station take Badgerline 18 bus to hostel.

KEY TO ICONS

- Attractive natural setting
- Ecologically aware hostel
- Superior kitchen facilities or cafe
- Offbeat or eccentric place
- Superior bathroom facilities
- Romantic private rooms
- Comfortable beds
- Editors' choice: among our very favorite hostels
- A particularly good value
- Wheelchair accessible
- Good for business travelers
- Especially well suited for families
- Good for active travelers
- Visual arts at hostel or nearby
- Music at hostel or nearby
- Great hostel for skiers
- Bar or pub at hostel or nearby

BEER HOSTEL

Bovey Combe Townsend, Beer, Seaton, Devon EX12 3LL

Phone Number: 01297–20296

Fax: 01297–23690
Rates: £5.95–£8.80 per HI member (about $9.00–$13.00 US)
Beds: 40
Private/family rooms: Sometimes
Season: April 6 to November 1
Affiliation: HI-YHA
Extras: Dinner ($), garden, bike storage

You know you wanna come here. You know you're gonna snap photos of the town sign, giggling, and send 'em back to your less fortunate buds. But what's the scoop on the hostel? Plain Jane, it turns out—not the beer-soaked orgy you might've imagined but, instead, a nice quiet place for chillin' out.

Beer's hostel, aptly described as a peaceful country house, features nice family quad rooms for just £32 (about $48 US). Rooms are medium-sized, not tiny and not humungous.

What to do? Well, obviously, Beer is quite well stocked with pubs. Would you expect anything less? These people know a marketing opportunity when they see one. There's also oh-so-quaint shopping, a pebbly beach, and a steam train to hop on.

Insiders' tip:
Surprise 'em—order wine instead

Gestalt:
Lite Beer

Party index:

How to get there:

By bus: From Seaton take bus to Axminster and change to Beer bus.

By car: Take B3052 to B3174. In Beer, go up Fore Street to Townsend, then turn right at sign.

By train: Axminster Station, closest one, is 7 miles away.

PALACE STABLES HOSTEL

Boscastle Harbour, Cornwall PL35 OHD

Phone Number: 01840–250287

Fax: 01840–250615
Rates: £5.95–£8.80 per HI member (about $9.00–$13.00 US)
Beds: 25
Affiliation: HI-YHA
Extras: Dinner ($), bike storage, fireplace

You won't find too many other folks landing at this pretty little hostel by a harbor that was—in a former life—a stable. But come, because it's great.

Palace Stables Hostel

Boscastle Harbour, England

(photo courtesy of HI-YHA)

Four tiny rooms contain between four and nine single beds apiece, and the hayloft still retains its original beams. And, hey, where else are you gonna eat a home-cooked meal before a roaring fire for only a few bucks? Don't miss the super surroundings, either, which include hills, dales, and a babbling river.

Insiders' tip:
Colwell pub

Gestalt:
Say hay

Party index:

How to get there:

By bus: From Bodmin Parkway take 52B bus; from Bude, take X4 bus.

By car: Take B3263 to Boscastle Harbour; hostel is at river.

By train: From Bodmin Parkway Station take 52B bus.

BRISTOL INTERNATIONAL HOSTEL

Hayman House, 14 Narrow Quay, Bristol BS1 4QA

Phone Number: 010117–9273789

Fax: 010117–9273789
Rates: £8.00–£11.65 per HI member (about $12–$18 US); doubles £24 (about $36 US)
Beds: 124

Family/private rooms: Yes
Affiliation: HI-YHA
Extras: Laundry, store, TV, dinner ($), coffeeshop, pool table

Everybody wants to go to Bristol these days: The town is up and comin', that's for sure. The hostel, once a warehouse, serves capably and is certainly well located if you're hanging out downtown by the Bristol Channel.

There's a cafeteria, modern and pretty small dorm rooms—a nice surprise—and lots of extras such as a laundry, TV lounge, and game room including a pool table. Family rooms include breakfast with the deal.

Insiders' tip: Arts center next door

Gestalt: Bristol cream

Party index:

Once here, you'll want to check out the cathedral, which is almost across the street, or maybe the city's suspension bridge and gorge, or maybe all those galleries and museums. Heck, we don't care. Just get out and stay out.

How to get there:

By bus: Station in town, call hostel for transit route.

By car: From London take M4 to Junction 19; switch to M32; from Birmingham, take M5 to Junction 18, then switch to A4. Call hostel for directions from town.

By train: From Bristol Temple Meads Station, walk ¾ mile along Redcliffe Way. Make left onto Narrow Quay.

COTTESMORE HOUSE HOSTEL

Cott Lane, Burley, Ringwood, Hampshire BH24 4BB

Phone Number: 01425–403233

Fax: 01425–403233
Rates: £5.95–£8.80 per HI member (about $9.00–$13.00 US)
Beds: 36
Season: March 1 to October 31
Affiliation: HI-YHA
Extras: Dinner ($), bike storage

Located in a forest, this hostel gives you access to all those English-style outings you've heard so much about: horseback riding, water sports, mountain biking, hiking, and golf—all in the "New Forest," which is part forest and part, well, developed towns. There's a beach at Bournemouth, not so far away.

Most of the dorm rooms here are big, eight-to-ten-bed affairs. Camping's also an option, though, if you've got a tent, and might be a better way to get into the green spirit of the place.

Party index:

How to get there:

By bus: From Southampton take X1 bus to Burley.

By car: Call hostel for directions.

By train: Nearest train station in Sway, 5½ miles away; call hostel for transit route.

CHEDDAR HOSTEL

Hillfield, Cheddar, Somerset BS27 3HN

Phone Number: 01934–742494

Fax: 01934–744724
Rates: £5.95–£8.80 per HI member (about $9.00–$13.00 US); doubles £21 (about $32 US)
Beds: 53
Private/family rooms: Yes
Season: Call ahead for open days
Affiliation: HI-YHA
Extras: Dinner ($), laundry, bike storage

Okay, here we go again. We're in the southwest of England, we look at our map, and all of a sudden we realize we can get some Cheddar to go with our Beer. Are you kiddin'? You *knew* we'd end up here.

This stone Victorian house, bigger than you'd expect, is smack across from the village of Cheddar's fire station. So we felt safe, at least. Most dorm rooms are surprisingly private, just two or four beds apiece.

Some people come for the cheese, of course. Some come for the Mendip Hills, a good hiking area. But the real draw is that this is the closest hostel to Glastonbury—England's hip, hippie center, a place of magical and mystical energies (they say) and lovely mountain views. Come at the end of June and you won't be alone, either: Tens of thousands of Euros pour into the area, booking up the hostel for England's biggest and wildest music festival.

Gestalt:
Cheesy

Party index:

Consider yourself warned.

How to get there:

By bus: Call hostel for transit route.

By car: Take A371 to Cheddar; in village turn north onto The Hayes and left again past school at Hillfield.

By train: Nearest station is Weston Milton, 10 miles away; call hostel for transit route.

MAYPOOL HOUSE (CHURSTON) HOSTEL

Galmpton, Brixham, Devon TQ5 0ET

Phone Number: 01803–842444

Fax: 01803–845939
Rates: £5.40–£8.00 per HI member (about $8.00–$12.00 US)
Beds: 93
Affiliation: HI-YHA
Extras: TV, bike storage, game room, meeting room, science room, fireplace

A simple hostel, yes, but it's one that really uses its location to advantage. This former shipbuilder's home is set near the River Dart, with good views of the area, and the facilities include an environmental discovery room where you can learn more about the local nature. Bravo! Lotsa beds here, too, in thirteen (count 'em; *we* did) different rooms. Just for fun, sleep a night in each. Just kiddin'.

Party index:

Bigger than you'd expect, it's also very likely to be overrun with schoolkids come summertime. Yikes.

How to get there:

By bus: Take 12 bus to Churston; walk 2 miles up Manor Vale Road to hostel.

By car: Take A38 to A380 to A3022, then merge with A379 and go south. Make second right onto Manor Vale Road, continue 1 mile to hostel.

By train: From Dart Valley Rly (Churston) Station, walk 2 miles up Manor Vale Road to hostel.

COVERACK PARK BEHAN HOSTEL 

School Hill, Coverack, Heltson, Cornwall TR12 6SA

Phone Number: 01326–280687

Fax: 01326–280119
Rates: £5.95–£8.80 per HI member (about $9.00–$13.00 US)
Beds: 38
Season: April 1 to October 31
Affiliation: HI-YHA
Extras: Dinner ($), camping, game room

This summer-only hostel overlooks the little bay on which the quiet little fishing village of Coverack is situated. It wasn't always this way: The town was once a notorious haven for smugglers, though those times are gone now. We think.

It's the usual here: a lounge and game room to dawdle away the hours. But staff is good and views are, well, superb. Windsurfing classes are even available sometimes from a school in town—cool!

Hospitality: 

Party index:

How to get there:

By bus: Call hostel for transit route.
By car: Call hostel for directions.
By train: Call hostel for transit route.

DENZEL HOUSE HOSTEL

Crowcombe Heathfield, Taunton, Somerset TA4 4BT

Phone Number: 019847–249

Fax: 01984–667429
Rates: £4.95–£7.20 per HI member (about $7.00–$11.00 US)
Beds: 45
Season: April 3 to September 9
Affiliation: HI-YHA
Extras: Laundry, TV, garden, camping

This rustic house stuck amongst trees in the countryside has lots of space, good if you're wanting to stretch out. Dorm rooms mostly contain four to six bunk beds apiece, but there are a couple family rooms open sometimes, too.

Party index:

How to get there:

By bus: Call hostel for transit route.
By car: Take 358 from Taunton 10 miles; make left at crossroads cottage, head toward Crowcombe Station. Go ¾ mile; hostel is on right.
By train: Crowcombe Station nearby. Hostel is after railway bridge.

DARTINGTON HOSTEL

Lownard, Dartington, Totnes, Devon TQ9 6JJ

Phone Number: 01803–862303

Fax: 01803–865171
Rates: £5.40–£8.00 per HI member (about $8.00–$12.00 US)
Beds: 30
Season: April 7 to October 31

Affiliation: HI-YHA
Extras: Garden, bike storage

Yep, you've arrived in England all right: a sixteenth-century cottage with burbling brook and plenty of gardens and green grass. A wooden cabin contains the bunks, which are spaced out among five bunkrooms, and there are—get this—two kitchens in the joint; you'll never wait in line for the gas range again.

Party index:

We recommend tramping 2 miles over to Totnes to check out the medieval castle, plus the bulk of the shops and better food options.

How to get there:

By bus: From Torquay or Plymouth, take X80 bus to Shinners Bridge roundabout; walk west on A385 ¼ mile to narrow lane, turn right, walk 200 yards.

By car: Take A385 and pass through the Shinners Bridge roundabout in the center of village. Just west of center, turn north onto narrow lane. Hostel is 200 yards farther.

By train: Totnes Station, 2 miles away; walk along A385 through center of town. Just east of roundabout, turn right on narrow lane and walk 200 yards.

EXETER HOSTEL

47 Countess Wear Road, Exeter, Devon EX2 6LR

Phone Number: 01392–873329

Fax: 01392–876939
Rates: £6.55–£9.75 per HI member (about $10–$15 US); doubles £21.50 (about $33 US)
Beds: 88
Season: January 2 to December 28
Affiliation: HI-YHA
Extras: Meals ($), TV, laundry, lockers, garden, camping
Lockout: 10:00 A.M.–5:00 P.M.

This hostel—in a quaint location with great views—isn't central to Exeter at all; instead, it's quite east of town, almost in another village. Luckily, you can hoof it along a riverside path or a canal to get to the big town. Buses run pretty regularly. Just be prepared to take some time getting there.

There are two hug-g-g-ge dorm rooms here, with at least twenty beds apiece; we didn't like those, but nice smaller rooms were also available. Private rooms, too—a rarity in Britain.

Most folks head downtown, although hanging out in the garden gazing on the views of local sheep is also an option. Exeter's charm includes St. Peter's Cathedral, reputedly the longest church in Europe. (Just a thought: Who keeps track of this stuff, anyway? Some monk in tennis shoes with a really long tape measure?) Narrow streets also beckon.

Gestalt: Generation Exeter

Party index:

How to get there:

By bus: Take J, K, T, or 57 bus to hostel.

By car: Take A379 to Topsham, then make a left at Countess Wear roundabout; take another left onto School Lane. From downtown, follow signs to Topsham and go right on School Lane at post office.

By train: Topsham Station, 2 miles away.

EXFORD HOSTEL

Exe Mead, Exford, Minehead, Somerset TA24 7PU

Phone Number: 01643–831288

Fax: 01643–831650
Rates: £5.95–£8.80 per HI member (about $9.00–$13.00 US); doubles £21 (about $32 US)
Beds: 51
Season: February 16 to November 1
Affiliation: HI-YHA
Extras: Dinner ($), bike storage

Yet another roomy Victorian house: That's what this hostel is, plus an attached cedar annex right in little Exford village. You're directly in the green heart of Exmoor National Park, so you might not mind the rather simple fixings here.

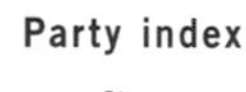

Party index:

At least the dorm rooms are small enough to ensure privacy. Nearby lie some impressive hills if you're up to them, or some close-to-the-earth country villages if you're not.

How to get there:

By bus: From Taunton or Lynton take L4 or L5 bus to Exford (runs certain days only). From Minehead take 38 bus to Porlock, 7 miles away.

By car: Take B3223 or B3224 to Exford; hostel is beside bridge.

By train: Nearest stop is West Somerset Rly Station, 13 miles away; call hostel for transit route.

PENDENNIS CASTLE HOSTEL 

Falmouth, Cornwall TR11 4LP

Phone Number: 01326–311435

Fax: 01326–315473
Rates: £5.95–£8.80 per HI member (about $9.00–$13.00 US); doubles £21 (about $32 US)
Credit cards: Yes
Beds: 76
Private/family rooms: Yes
Affiliation: HI-YHA
Extras: TV, laundry, dinner
Lockout: 10:00 A.M.–5:00 P.M.
Curfew: 11:00 P.M.

Ah, here we have it: one of the most famous hostels in England, set in an impressive seaside castle that ole Henry VIII built back in the sixteenth century. What could be finer? This is livin' right up top of the hog.

Party index:

We-l-l-l-l, not exactly. Actually, you sleep in an army barracks. But you are technically still in the castle, yeah, and it's a sixteenth-century army barracks. Feeling better? There are some awesome views of the ocean from here, too. You've got your pick of private rooms, quad rooms, and (summer only) a huge sixteen-bedder if you're really desperate for new friends.

The castle's floodlit at night, so be sure to step outside and take a look around; during daytime, lie on the good local sand beaches, or hit the Maritime Museum. (Skip the interior castle tour, though, which is tackier and less interesting than it could be.) On second thought, hit the South West Coastal Footpath instead: Stay in town and you might be trampled by the pack of local art students.

KEY TO ICONS

- Attractive natural setting
- Ecologically aware hostel
- Superior kitchen facilities or cafe
- Offbeat or eccentric place
- Superior bathroom facilities
- Romantic private rooms
- Comfortable beds
- Editors' choice: among our very favorite hostels
- A particularly good value
- Wheelchair accessible
- Good for business travelers
- Especially well suited for families
- Good for active travelers
- Visual arts at hostel or nearby
- Music at hostel or nearby
- Great hostel for skiers
- Bar or pub at hostel or nearby

How to get there:

By car: Take A39, going around Falmouth town center toward docks and beaches; from roundabout outside Falmouth Docks, follow signs 100 yards uphill to ocean. Hostel is inside castle.

By train: From Falmouth or Falmouth Docks Station, walk ¾ mile down Castle Drive to castle on ocean.

PENQUITE HOUSE HOSTEL

Golant, Fowey, Cornwall PL231LA

Phone Number: 01726–833507

Fax: 01726–832947
Rates: £6.55–£9.75 per HI member (about $10–$15 US)
Beds: 94
Affiliation: HI-YHA
Extras: Dinner ($), TV, game room, laundry, bike storage

Set in a tiny village beside a little river, big Penquite House features big grounds with plenty of woods. Dorms come in several shapes and sizes.

There's not much to do here except cruise around on a mountain bike, perhaps checking out the port town of Fowey just downriver. Mostly, though, this is just a quiet place for the kids and family to get away for a holiday, and you're unlikely to meet tons of hip young folks here.

Best bet for a bite: Local pub

Party index:

How to get there:

By bus: From St. Austell or Fowley, take 24 bus to Castle Dore Crossroads; walk 1½ miles, following signs.

By car: Take A390 to B3269, and make left at Castle Dore Crossroads. Continue 1½ miles to hostel, following signs.

By train: Par Station, 3 miles away.

BOSWINGER HOSTEL

Boswinger, Gorran, St. Austell, Cornwall PL26 6LL

Phone Number: 01726–843234

Fax: 01726–843234
Rates: £5.40–£8.00 per HI member (about $8.00–$12.00 US)
Beds: 38
Private/family rooms: Yes
Season: April 5 to October 31
Affiliation: HI-YHA

Extras: Laundry, grill, camping, dinner ($), bike storage

This former farmhouse in the Cornish countryside was better equipped than we'd had any reason to expect it would be: grill, laundry, camping area, dinner—even a new set of four family rooms in an annex facility for around £30 (about $45 US) per quad. It's only half a mile from little Hemmick Beach, too.

Party index:

How to get there:

By bus: From St. Austell take 26A bus to Mevagissey; sometimes you can change to local bus for Gorran, otherwise you must walk 4½ miles to hostel.

By car: From St. Austell take B3273 for 5 miles; turn right and follow signs for Boswinger to hostel.

By train: From St. Austell Station take 26A bus to Mevagissey; sometimes you can change to local bus for Gorran, otherwise you must walk 4½ miles to hostel.

ELMSCOTT HOSTEL

Elmscott, Hartland, Bideford, Devon EX39 6ES

Phone Number: 01237–441367

Fax: 01237–441910
Rates: £4.95–£7.20 per HI member (about $7.00–$11.00 US)
Beds: 38
Season: April 10 to October 2
Affiliation: HI-YHA
Extras: Bike storage

Elmscott, a former schoolhouse, certainly has great location: It's only 2 miles south of already well-placed Hartland village, which kisses the coast near superquaint Clovelly. However, getting here's a bit of a chore. The country roads can be darned confusing, so make sure you've got good directions.

The actual hostel's rather bare-bones in point of fact, as befits a former English school: just a bunch of dorms in an annex and a kitchen. Can't beat such splendid views of the sea, though.

Party index:

How to get there:

By bus: From Barnstaple or Bude take 119 bus to Hartland; walk to west end of High Street, then follow footpath 3 miles to hostel.

By car: Take A39 to just south of Hartland; at West Country Inn, turn west (toward the ocean) and follow signs to hostel.

By train: Closest station is Barnstaple, 25 miles away; from Barnstaple, take 119 bus to Hartland; then walk to west end of High Street and follow footpath 3 miles to hostel.

QUANTOCK HILLS HOSTEL

Sevenacres, Holford, Bridgwater, Somerset TA5 1SQ

Phone Number: 01278–741224

Fax: 01278–741224
Rates: £4.95–£7.20 per HI member (about $7.00–$11.00 US)
Beds: 28
Affiliation: HI-YHA
Extras: Camping, bike storage

This simple hostel—and how many times have we said that?—offers proximity to nice walking trails and a super view of a bay and beach speckled with good fossils. That's it. Six dorm rooms compete for your sterling, and there's a kitchen and lounge. The bike shop's open all day for gearheads.

What else to do? Well, you're in Coleridge country—he was born and lived near here—so find out more about the guy who penned *Kubla Khan.* And, as a bonus (if you care), there's a stable nearby that rents horses for riding.

Party index:

How to get there:

By bus: From Bridgwater or Minehead take 15 bus to Holford; walk 1½ miles through Alfoxton Park Hotel; cross second cattle gate, go uphill to sharp bend, go right. Follow path to hostel.

By car: Take A39 to Kilve, turn south onto Pardlestone Lane across from post office, and go 1 mile. Make a left and follow path to hostel.

By train: Nearest station at Bridgwater, 13 miles away; from station, take bus.

ASHMOUR HOUSE HOSTEL

1 Hillsborough Terrace, Ilfracombe, Devon EX34 9NR

Phone Number: 01271–865337

Fax: 01271–862652
Rates: £5.95–£8.80 (about $9.00–$13.00 US) per HI member; doubles £21 (about $32 US)
Beds: 50
Affiliation: HI-YHA
Extras: TV, dinner ($), bike storage

Hostellers feel this Georgian home overlooking a tiny harbor is okay by them. Most of the dorm rooms are small enough, size-wise, and the stunning views out over Bristol Channel help, too. You can walk to a good set of beaches and glimpse the coast of Wales.

Gestalt: Walkin' shoes

Hospitality: 

Party index:

The added bonus here is that the hostel is situated close to a great walking track, the Southwest Coastal Footpath—a peninsular walk stretching more than 600 miles from Minehead to Poole Harbor, if you've got the time. One more thing to tuck in your rucksack: There's a ferry over to Wales in summertime from Ilfracombe, making it a good jump-off if you're only going to get a quick taste of things Welsh.

How to get there:

By bus: From Barnstaple take 3, 30, 300, 301, 302, or 303 bus to hostel.

By car: From Combe Martin, Ilfracombe, or Barnstaple, take A399 or A361 to harbor; hostel is across from Cliffe Hydro Hotel.

By train: Nearest station is at Barnstaple, 13 miles away; from station, take 3, 30, 300, 301, 302, or 303 bus to hostel.

WORLINGTON HOUSE HOTEL

New Road, Instow, Bideford, Devon EX39 4LW

Phone Number: 01271–860394

Fax: 01271–860055
Rates: £5.95–£8.80 per HI member (about $9.00–$13.00 US)
Beds: 58
Season: Call ahead for open days
Affiliation: HI-YHA
Extras: TV, laundry, dinner ($)

This hostel makes no bones about what it is—a Victorian house with views across water and a location in cute Instow village. Nice town, and the surroundings ain't bad, either, very green.

Party index: 

Two of the dorm rooms are huge, fourteen beds apiece, while the rest are more acceptable-sized. There are a TV and lounge you can use all day, so we'd consider this adequate as a base.

For fun, hit the Tarka Trail if you like. Who's Tarka? An otter. A very famous otter. You'll find out all about it when you get there, trust us. We did.

How to get there:

By bus: From Barnstaple take 1, 2, or 301 bus to Instow Quay; from stop walk 1 mile uphill on New Road to hostel.

By car: From Barnstaple drive B3233 or A39 to Instow; turn uphill onto New Road at signpost. Continue 1 mile to hostel.

By train: From Barnstaple Station take 1, 2, or 301 bus to Instow Quay; from stop walk 1 mile uphill on New Road to hostel.

LITTON CHENEY HOSTEL

Litton Cheney, Dorchester, Dorset DT2 9AT

Phone Number: 01308–482340

Fax: 01308–482636
Rates: £4.95–£7.20 per HI member (about $7.00–$11.00 US)
Beds: 24
Season: April 4 to September 6
Affiliation: HI-YHA
Extras: Bike storage

This Dutch-style barn set way-y-y outside central Dorchester used to be part of a cheese factory—maybe this is where they stored the cows, who knows? At any rate, it's an incredibly cheap joint that offers simplicity itself. Sling your pack in one of six dorm rooms of varying (but never very big) size.

Insiders' tip:
Hit the White Horse Pub

Gestalt:
Dutch treat

Party index:

The problem? You're nowhere near Dorchester, home to Thomas Hardy sights and castles galore. If you're going to use this hostel as a base, you'd best be prepared to make that 10-mile bus ride twice a day. So what else is there to do here during the day? Hike 3 miles to Chesil Beach, we'd say, or else head inland a few miles on the walking track.

How to get there:

By bus: From Dorchester take 31 or X31 bus 10 miles west to Whiteway. Walk 1½ miles to Litton Cheney; follow signs.

By car: Take A35 to Litton Cheney; follow signs to hostel.

By train: Dorchester Station, 10 miles away, is nearest; from station take 31 or X31 bus 10 miles west to Whiteway. Walk 1½ miles to Litton Cheney; follow signs.

LYNTON HOSTEL 

Lynbridge, Lynton, Devon EX35 6AZ

Phone Number: 01598–75237

Fax: 01598–753305
Rates: £5.95–£8.80 per HI member (about $9.00–$13.00 US); doubles £21 (about $32 US)
Beds: 34
Private/family rooms: Sometimes
Season: Call ahead for open days
Affiliation: HI-YHA

Extras: Laundry, bike storage, dinner ($), game room

Great place in a quiet setting, tucked in the West Lyn River gorge. That means double fun: woods and ocean.

The hostel dorms occupy six rooms of a Victorian home, and it's clean and friendly as can be here. Thank goodness for great management! Wonderful scenery surrounds you, too.

Hospitality:

Party index:

How to get there:

By bus: Take 311 bus to village.

By car: Take A39 to B3234, continue south on Lynmouth Road to Ye Olde Cottage Inn, make a left to hostel.

By train: Nearest station is at Barnstaple, 20 miles away; call hostel for transit route.

OKEHAMPTON HOSTEL

The Goods Yard, Okehampton, Devon EX20 1EJ

Phone Number: 01837–53916

Fax: 01837–53965
Rates: £6.55–£9.75 per HI member (about $10–$15 US)
Beds: 64
Private/family rooms: Sometimes
Season: January 29 to November 30
Affiliation: HI-YHA
Extras: Laundry, dinner ($)

Attention, attention. This new hostel has no lockout.

Yes, you read that right. Why? Who knows?? But we're glad to hear it; it's almost singular among English hostels for this reason. Not that it's great for hanging out, but still it's a nice touch.

Okay, let's get down to brass tacks. Formerly a railway shed, the place has good quad and six-bed rooms. There are also several five-bed family rooms for just £42 (about $63 US), quite a bargain for a couple with kids.

Gestalt: Okey

Party index:

We couldn't scratch up much to do around here, other than tooling around Dartmoor Park, maybe, or scoping out the local castle. Not bad, not thrilling.

Hmmm. Maybe that's why there's no lockout. Another mystery solved! (How come we feel like Robert Stack all of a sudden?)

How to get there:

By bus: Call hostel for transit route.

By car: Call hostel for directions.
By train: Call hostel for transit route.

CASTLE HORNECK 

Alverton, Penzance, Cornwall TR20 8TF

Phone Number: 01736–62666

Fax: 01736–62663 or 01736–362663
Rates: £6.55–£9.75 per HI member (about $10–$15 US)
Credit cards: Yes
Beds: 84
Season: February 3 to December 22
Affiliation: HI-YHA
Extras: Laundry, meals ($), garden
Lockout: 11:00 A.M. – 5:00 P.M.

This eighteenth-century mansion serves some of the best hostel chow in England, reason enough (we say) to come all the way west to Penzance at the tippy-toe of England. Views of the peninsula are spectacular.

Beds are no big thrill, however—just the usual stark bunks housed in rooms that sometimes seemed too big.

But those great meals are served after 5:30 P.M. and might include fresh-baked pizzas and (yes!) clotted-cream ice cream, among other offerings for around £4 to £5 ($6.00 to $7.00 US). So we can handle it. And there's tons to do in the area, everything from galleries to quaint seaside towns to tourist tack.

To paraphrase Ah-nold: We'll be back.

Best bet for a bite:
In-house chow

Insiders' tip:
See St. Ives or the Isles of Scilly

Gestalt:
Pirate of Penzance

Party index:

How to get there:

By bus: From downtown take 5B, 6B, or 10B bus to Pirate Inn; follow signs to hostel.

By car: Take A30 around Penzance, avoiding downtown, to Castle Horneck signs; turn north on Castle Horneck Road.

By train: From Penzance Station, 1½ miles away, walk to hostel, or take 5B, 6B, or 10B bus to Pirate Inn; follow signs to hostel.

PERRANPORTH HOSTEL

Droskyn Point, Perranporth, Cornwall TR6 0DS

Phone Number: 01872–573812

Fax: 01872–573319
Rates: £5.40–£8.00 per HI member (about $8.00–$12.00 US)

Beds: 26
Season: Call ahead for open days
Affiliation: HI-YHA
Extras: Garden

This hostel, on top of a seaside cliff, is super simple but has knockout views. A former Coast Guard station, its view of Ligger Point is major; there's also a really good stretch of beach—three miles' worth—down below.

Gestalt: Great surfing

Party index:

How to get there:

By bus: Take 87A, 87B, or 87C bus to Perranporth.

By car: Take B3284 or B3285 to Perranporth; turn onto Tywarnhale Road, then left at hostel sign. Pass through gate (locked until 5:00 P.M).

By train: Truro Station, 9 miles away, is nearest stop; take 87A, 87B, or 87C bus to Perranporth.

BELMONT HOUSE HOSTEL

Devonport Road, Stoke, Plymouth PL3 4DW

Phone Number: 01752–562189

Fax: 01752–605360
Rates: £6.55–£9.75 per HI member (about $10–$14 US); doubles £21.50 (about $32 US)
Beds: 68
Affiliation: HI-YHA
Extras: TV, game room, dinner ($), bike storage

Sorry to tell you that this place was not highly recommended by our hostel snoops despite its wonderful architecture and grounds—something about attitude. Geez, we might as well go to California instead.

Hospitality:

Party index:

Ah, well. If you're still going, it's got a variety of big (ten to twelve beds) and smaller (two to five bunks) accommodations. Once the home of a town banker, the building features a splendid eating area and nice rooms.

History buffs will go nuts over the fact that the Pilgrims set out from here on their way to, yes, Plymouth Rock, Massachusetts. Otherwise this town isn't worth the time of day, really; sorry.

How to get there:

By bus: From city center take 15A, 15B, 81A bus or local 3, 4,

16, 33, or 34 bus to hostel.

By car: Take A38 to A386; at sign to hostel, make a left

By train: Devonport Station, walk ¼ mile to hostel; from Plymouth Station take bus or walk 1½ miles.

BELLEVER HOSTEL

Postbridge, Yelverton, Devon PL20 6TU

Phone Number: 01822–88227

Fax: 01822–880302
Rates: £5.95–£8.80 per HI member (about $9.00–$14.00 US)
Beds: 36
Season: March 24 to October 31
Affiliation: HI-YHA
Extras: Dinner ($), bike storage
Lockout: 10:00 A.M.–5:00 P.M.

Not much to say about this place, except that it's located in the dead center of Dartmoor National Park and occupies a barnyard. This is for those who really crave that English countryside feel in a hostel.

Most hostellers go hiking in the granite hills and moors; horseback riding and mountain biking are also popular around here. You're locked out all day, so you'd best find something to do.

Party index:

How to get there:

By bus: Call hostel for transit route.

By car: Take B3212 to Postbridge, then turn onto road marked Bellever; hostel is 1 mile farther, on right.

By train: Call hostel for transit route.

SALCOMBE OVERBECKS HOSTEL

Sharpitor, Salcombe, Devon TQ8 8LW

Phone Number: 0154884–2856

Fax: 01548–842856
Rates: £5.95–£8.80 per HI member (about $9.00–$13.00 US); doubles £21 (about $32 US)
Beds: 51
Private/family rooms: Yes
Affiliation: HI-YHA
Extras: TV, bike storage, garden, dinner ($)

This is a place for those who love the ocean; it's simple as can be,

Salcombe Overbecks Hostel

Salcombe, England

(photo courtesy of HI-YHA)

but blessed with location on the water. A good coastal footpath, views from Bolt Head, two beaches, several acres of gardens—they're all here. Palm trees, too! Rub your eyes all you want, buster, they'll still be there. You can thank the Gulf Stream (or global warming) for that.

Inside this historic Edwardian house, which is protected by The National Trust, the dorms contain anywhere from two to fifteen beds; quad rooms are your most likely bet for maximum privacy. There are also private rooms for couples.

Party index:

How to get there:

By bus: From Kingsbridge catch Tally Ho! bus to Salcombe, walk 2 miles to hostel following signs to Overbecks.

By car: Take A381 to Salcombe, then follow signs to National Trust-Overbecks. Hostel is inside house.

By train: Closest station is at Totnes, 20 miles away; from station, catch Tally Ho! bus to Salcombe, walk 2 miles to hostel following signs to Overbecks.

MILFORD HILL HOUSE HOSTEL

Milford Hill, Salisbury, Wilthshire SP1 2QW

Phone Number: 01722–327572

Fax: 01722–330446

Rates: £6.55–£9.75 per HI member (about $10–$14 US)

Credit cards: Yes

Beds: 74

Affiliation: HI-YHA

Extras: Bar, garden, laundry, camping, TV, bike storage, volleyball

There are lots of beds here, in an eighteenth-century (and thus historic) house near the famous Salisbury Cathedral—one of England's most famous, and indisputably the one with the tallest spire, don'cha know.

Most of the dorms are big, but you might luck into the quads or the one and only single room. They're very gracious with the lockout here—it lasts only until 1:00 P.M.—and even then they let you use the TV room while you're waiting. Hanging out on nice big grounds that include an old cedar tree is an option, too. Or rap with fellow travelers in the hostel bar. All in all, it's quite a fun place considering it's in England.

Insiders' tip:
Public market Tuesdays and Saturdays

Party index:

We'd just as soon get out and see Salisbury, though, a great town for soaking up history. Besides that huge cathedral—which you always feel like you're right underneath, and which contains a super-rare copy of the *Magna Carta*—the Old Sarum medieval site is just 2 miles away. If you're really feeling ambitious, get stoned: Catch a bus in town for either Stonehenge or Avebury, and commune with those mysterious standing rocks.

How to get there:

By bus: Station and local buses in town. Call hostel for transit route.

By car: Take A36 around city center to Churchill Way East; turn south, go ¾ mile, then make left at Milford Hill.

By train: Salisbury Station, 1 mile away.

LAND'S END HOSTEL

Letcha Vean, St. Just-in-Penwith, Penzance, Cornwall

TR19 7NT

Phone Number: 01736–788437

Fax: 01736–787337
Rates: £5.95–£8.80 per HI member (about $9.00–$13.00 US)
Credit cards: Yes
Beds: 44
Season: Call ahead for open days
Affiliation: HI-YHA
Extras: Camping, bike storage

This is extremely simple living, but the location is terrific. Set in the Cot Valley, it's nothing if not scenic: Seals, sand beaches, and walking tracks compete for your attention. Most people here are either stuffing their sacks with postcards of this overtouristed area or else finishing/beginning a walk along the short, incredibly scenic Cornwall Coast Path.

Gestalt:
End Zone

Party index:

You can pick, if they're not too full, from either one enormous annex dorm (twenty beds there) or three other rooms with eight beds apiece. The hostel dinners are reported to be a decent value, but otherwise this is not a first choice. Use it if you must.

How to get there:

By bus: From Penzance take 10A, 10B, or 11A bus to St. Just. From station walk south past library, turn left, follow lane past chapel; turn right and walk down path ½ mile to hostel.

By car: Take B3306 to Kelynack Farm, north of Land's End, and turn east toward ocean; continue through barnyard and follow signs down lane.

By train: Nearest station at Penzance; from station, take 10A, 10B, or 11A bus to St. Just. From station walk south past library, turn left, follow lane past chapel; turn right and walk down path ½ mile to hostel.

STEPS BRIDGE HOSTEL

Steps Bridge, Dunsford, Exeter, Devon EX6 7EQ

Phone Number: 01647–252435

Fax: 01647–252948
Rates: £4.95–£7.20 per HI member (about $7.00–$11.00 US)
Beds: 24
Season: April 1 to September 27
Affiliation: HI-YHA
Extras: Bike storage

Super cheap for a reason, this small chalet-style building a mile from Dunsford is for nature-lovers and folks who don't mind hills. It's not really a great base for Exeter, being 10 miles away, but it is superbly positioned in moorlands.

The hostel is located right above the gorge of the Teign Valley, and you will find some serious walking challenges close at hand. (The hostel doesn't recommend bringing very young children here, in fact, because of those steep, slippery slopes.) Lots of flowers and birds here, too.

Party index:

Dorms have two to eight beds, all small, and some of the bathrooms are outdoors. It's pretty much self-service around here, and hostellers tend to head for the Dartmoor Tors.

How to get there:

By bus: From Exeter take 359 bus to hostel.

By car: Take B3212 to Morehampton Road, turn left 200 yards after bridge, and go up very steep driveway.

By train: Exeter Central Station is nearest, 9 miles away; take 359 bus to hostel.

KEY TO ICONS

- Attractive natural setting
- Ecologically aware hostel
- Superior kitchen facilities or cafe
- Offbeat or eccentric place
- Superior bathroom facilities
- Romantic private rooms
- Comfortable beds
- Editors' choice: among our very favorite hostels
- A particularly good value
- Wheelchair accessible
- Good for business travelers
- Especially well suited for families
- Good for active travelers
- Visual arts at hostel or nearby
- Music at hostel or nearby
- Great hostel for skiers
- Bar or pub at hostel or nearby

THE CHALET HOSTEL

Ivythorn Hill, Street, Somerset BA16 0TZ

Phone Number: 01458–442–961

Fax: 01458–442738
Rates: £5.40–£8.00 per HI member (about $8.00–$12.00 US)
Beds: 28
Season: Call ahead for open days
Affiliation: HI-YHA
Extras: Camping, bike storage

This hostel, which really isn't in Street's village center, has one great amenity: It's only 3 miles from New Agey Glastonbury, a chalet with wonderful views of famous Glastonbury Tor.

Gestalt: Grand Tor

Party index:

Once a holiday home for workers at a shoe factory, today it's a hilltop hostel. The chalet includes seven dorm rooms of varying configurations, plus a lounge and kitchen. You can also camp on the grounds for less dough.

How to get there:

By bus: From Bristol or Glastonbury take 376, 676, or 29A bus to Marshalls Elm; walk ⅓ mile to hostel.

By car: Take A39 to Street, then B3151 (Somerton Road) south 2 miles. Turn right at Marshalls Elm crossroads; hostel is ⅓ mile farther, on right.

By train: From Bristol Temple Meads Station, take 29A bus to Marshalls Elm. Walk ⅓ mile to hostel.

CLUNY HOSTEL

Cluny Crescent, Swanage, Dorset BH19 2BS

Phone Number: 01929–422113

Fax: 01929–426327
Rates: £6.55–£9.75 per HI member (about $10–$15 US); doubles £22 (about $33 US)
Beds: 105
Private/family rooms: Yes
Season: February 14 to October 31
Affiliation: HI-YHA
Extras: Laundry, TV, game room, bike storage, dinner ($)

A little too popular with school kids in summer, the Cluny Hostel is still one fine spot on the road. Located on the Isle of Purbeck, it's got small, medium, and large dormitories as well as family rooms. Lots to do on the island if you like sun, surf, and sand. Plus there's a steam railway for train buffs.

Insiders' tip: White Swan Pub

Party index:

How to get there:

By bus: From Bournemouth take 150 bus to Swanage, then walk ¼ mile to hostel.

By car: Take A357 to Swanage, turn onto Stafford Hill Road; hostel is on top of hill, on right.

By train: Closest station is Wareham, 10 miles away; take 142-4 bus to Swanage, then walk ¼ mile to hostel.

TINTAGEL HOSTEL 

Dunderhole Point, Tintagel, Cornwall PL34 0DW

Phone Number: 01840–770334

Fax: 01908–770733
Rates: £5.95–£8.80 per HI member (about $9.00–$13.00 US)
Beds: 26
Private/family rooms: Sometimes
Season: March 27 to October 3
Affiliation: HI-YHA
Extras: Bike storage

This tiny cottage, right on top of the huge seaside cliffs, was once the offices of a mining company in the area; now, after recent work to upgrade it, it's looking better. But we were so wowed by the views over Dunderhole Point that, frankly, we would have been happy sleeping here in a paper bag.

There's one double room and two big dorm rooms at this place—and that, as they say, is the rest of the story. It's only a half-mile hike back to Tintagel, which stands tall in Arthurian legend but is in fact just a pinprick on the map of time (and England). Nice castle here, but we might pass on King Arthur's Hall our next time through. Hang out at the hostel and check out the almost 1,000-year-old church nearby instead.

Gestalt: Excalibur

Hospitality: 

Party index:

How to get there:

By bus: From Bude take X4 bus to Tintagel, then walk to church and then up to clifftop, following signs to hostel.

By car: Call hostel for directions, parking limited.

By foot: On South West Coastal Path. Follow signs.

By train: Nearest station is in Bodmin Parkway, 20 miles away; take 44, 122, or 125 bus to Tintagel, walk to church and then up to clifftop, following signs for hostel.

TREYARNON BAY HOSTEL 

Tregonnan, Treyarnon, Padstow, Cornwall PL28 8JR

Phone Number: 01841–520322

Fax: 01841–520322
Rates: £5.95–£8.80 per HI member (about $9.00–$13.00 US)
Beds: 42
Season: March 29 to October 31
Affiliation: HI-YHA
Extras: Garden, bike storage, dinner ($)

Okay, we're giving this hostel our vote for top views in England. It's amazing, dude, and practically on the beach, as well. Don't fail to hike along the pathways around here—you might run into some Arthurian character.

There's a house and an annex; both are adequate, though you won't be spending much time indoors in this spot unless it's pouring madly. Surfing classes are sometimes conducted in the area by YHA instructors, and cycling is also popular. Hey, did we mention the sunsets over the Atlantic? Wolf down that hostel chow and don't miss 'em; they're great.

Insiders' tip:
Cycle the Camel Trail

Gestalt:
Bay watch

Party index:

How to get there:

By bus: From Bodmin take 55 bus to Padstow; from Newquay take 56 bus.

By car: Take A39 to A389 or B3276 to Padstow; change to B3276 and head to St. Merron, then take third right to Treyarnon.

By train: Newquay Station, 10 miles away, is nearest; take 56 bus to area. From Bodmin Parkway Station take 55 bus to Padstow.

LULWORTH COVE HOSTEL

School Lane, West Lulworth, Wareham, Dorset BH20 5SA

Phone Number: 01929–400564

Fax: 01929–400640
Rates: £5.95–£8.80 per HI member (about $9.00–$13.00 US)
Beds: 34
Season: Call ahead for open days
Affiliation: HI-YHA
Extras: Dinner ($)

Close to the South West Coastal Path, this chalet has built a reputation for its food; you can even get meals during the day. The rest of the setup includes seven dorm rooms of roughly equal size and not a whole lot more.

Party index:

But the walking's the thing here, and if you catch a view of Durdle Door—a natural stone formation letting in the blue, blue ocean—you won't believe your eyes. No, Dorothy, this isn't Greece; it's just England.

How to get there:

By bus: Call hostel for transit route.

By car: Take B3070 to West Lulworth, go 100 yards east, and turn opposite the Castle Inn into School Lane.

By train: Nearest station is Wool, 5 miles away; call hostel for transit route.

CENTRAL ENGLAND & EAST ANGLIA

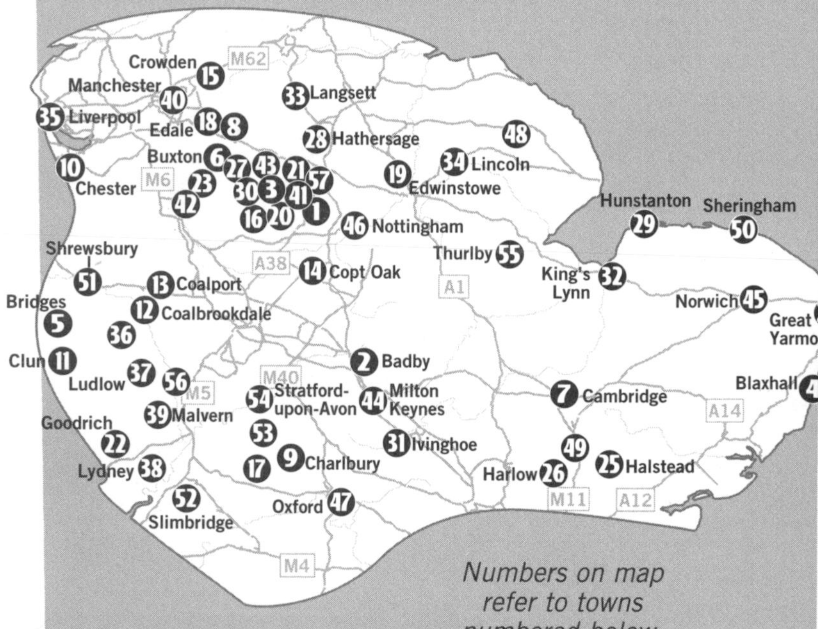

Numbers on map refer to towns numbered below.

1. Ambergate
2. Badby
3. Bakewell
4. Blaxhall
5. Bridges
6. Buxton
7. Cambridge
8. Castleton
9. Charlbury
10. Chester
11. Clun
12. Coalbrookdale
13. Coalport
14. Copt Oak
15. Crowden
16. Dimmingsdale
17. Duntisbourne Abbots
18. Edale
19. Edwinstowe
20. Elton
21. Eyam
22. Goodrich
23. Gradbach (Flash)
24. Great Yarmouth
25. Halstead
26. Harlow
27. Hartington
28. Hathersage
29. Hunstanton
30. Ilam
31. Ivinghoe
32. King's Lynn
33. Langsett
34. Lincoln
35. Liverpool
36. Longville in the Dale
37. Ludlow
38. Lydney
39. Malvern
40. Manchester
41. Matlock
42. Meerbrook
43. Millers Dale
44. Milton Keynes (Bradwell)
45. Norwich
46. Nottingham
47. Oxford
48. Ruckland
49. Saffron Waldon
50. Sheringham
51. Shrewsbury
52. Slimbridge
53. Stow-on-the-Wold
54. Stratford-upon-Avon (Alveston)
55. Thurlby
56. Wheathill
57. Youlgreave

CENTRAL ENGLAND & EAST ANGLIA

Parts of central England contain the highest density of hostels in the land. However, despite the gorgeous surroundings, most hostels here tend to be large and/or just plain boring.

At least the sights are nice. Cities like Oxford, Cambridge, and Stratford-upon-Avon cry out to be quaintly discovered (and, believe us, they have been), and the pretty Peaks District really isn't as touristed as you'd think it should be. Liverpool's a possible detour, though unremarkable except for its association with you-know-who, and Manchester thrums with a wild rave and gay scene between its smokestacks.

East Anglia is actually really nice in places, too, though much flatter and less pastoral than other parts of England. Ely is cute, Thetford a bit rough, and the coastal towns are nice: Great Yarmouth is a popular resort with locals, kinda tacky, while Cromer and Sheringham aren't as crowded except with campers and caravans. Ipswich has little coastal towns like Southwold.

SHINING CLIFF (AMBERGATE) HOSTEL

c/o Matlock Hostel, Bank Road, Matlock, Derbyshire DE4 3NF

Phone Number: 01629–760827

Rates: £4.00–£5.85 per HI member (about $6.00–$9.00 US)
Beds: 26
Season: Call ahead for open days
Affiliation: HI-YHA
Extras: Bike storage

You'll need a flashlight—maybe a microscope—to find this one-story hostel, tucked in the woods beneath a cliff outside already small Ambergate. Even if you come during the day, you'll need that light (the English call it a "torch," by the way), as the toilets are an outdoors walk from the bunks. And there are no showers. Remember this. We're telling you now so that you won't have to ask us later.

Five exceedingly basic rooms house the dorms, and there are a kitchen and a common room. To book, call the bigger Matlock hostel.

Gestalt:
Cliff note

Party index:

How to get there:

By bus: From Derby take 123, 124, or R1 bus to Ambergate.

By car: Take A6 to Ambergate, cross river at church. Turn uphill to Netherpark Farm; park on right side of road. Walk 10 minutes in to hostel.

By train: From Ambergate Station walk uphill 2 miles to hostel.

BADBY HOSTEL

Church Green, Badby, Daventry, Northamptonshire NN11 6AR

Phone Number: 01327–703883

Fax: 01327–703883
Rates: £4.95–£7.20 per HI member (about $7.00–$11.00 US)
Beds: 30
Season: March 31 to October 24
Affiliation: HI-YHA
Extras: Garden, bike storage, store

This is it! The only thatched hostel in England and, maybe, Europe. (We think. Our experts are still checking on it; do the croft houses of Scotland count?)

Set right on Badby's church green, this isn't sights-ville but, instead, a respite. The area's rich with tree-lined walking lanes, quaint villages, and everything you came to this island for. And the hostel, built in the 1600s, has all those stone floors and exposed beams you dreamt of seeing in England.

Not a complicated hostel, not supercomfortable, but as atmospheric as they get.

Gestalt: Thatch 'er

Party index:

How to get there:

By bus: From Northampton take 41 bus to Daventry; walk 3 miles to Badby.

By car: Take M1 to Junction 16 or 18, exiting toward Daventry. Get off A361 (Daventry-Banbury Road) at Badby, follow Main Street past pubs, turn left up Vicarage Hill, and ascend to Church Green. Turn left.

By train: Long Buckley Station, 6 miles away, is nearest station. From Northampton Station, take 41 or X64 bus to Daventry; walk 3 miles to Badby.

BAKEWELL HOSTEL

Fly Hill, Bakewell, Derbyshire DE45 1DN

Phone Number: 01629–812313

Fax: 01629–812313
Rates: £4.95–£7.20 per HI member (about $7.00–$10.00 US)
Beds: 36
Season: Call ahead for open days

Affiliation: HI-YHA
Extras: Dinner ($), store
Lockout: 10:00 A.M.–5:00 P.M.
Curfew: 11:00 P.M.

Uphill from the village, this hostel is plain but friendly. Dorms come in six-bed or twelve-bed rooms. There's a small hostel store, but grab your grub at the farmers' market on Mondays if you can. You can also get a dinner here.

During the daytime, when you're locked out anyway, you're close enough to walk among either limestone or gritstone peaks. The stone town is semi-interesting, with a really interesting church steeple and a weekly market that's been happening for the past 700 years. Lotsa buses fan out to the surrounding area's hostels so you'll probably come through anyway. What the heck.

Best bet for a bite: Local pudding

Insiders' tip: Monday is market day

Party index:

Better yet, hoof a couple miles outside town to historic Haddon Hall.

How to get there:

By bus: Lots of options; call hostel for transit route.

By car: From Buxton take A6 to North Church Street; turn right, then second right.

By train: From Matlock Station walk 8 miles to hostel.

BLAXHALL HOSTEL

Heath Walk, Blaxhall, Woodbridge, Suffolk IP12 2EA

Phone Number: 01728–688206

Fax: 01728–689292
Rates: £5.40–£8.00 per HI member (about $9.00–$12.00 US)
Beds: 40
Private/family rooms: Sometimes
Season: April 1 to October 31
Affiliation: HI-YHA
Extras: Lockers, bike storage, dinner ($)

Formerly a schoolhouse, this hostel doesn't exactly roll out the carpet of luxury: Bathrooms and showers are across a covered courtyard, making for some interesting late-night histrionics. Still, it's not too bad a place, especially considering the abundance of nature and sports opportunities at hand.

Raining? Then poke around Blaxhall instead, a speck of a village that's below the tourist radar.

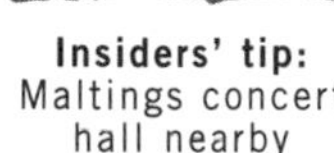

Insiders' tip:
Maltings concert hall nearby

Gestalt:
All Blaxhall

Party index:

How to get there:

By bus: From Ipswich take 80, 99, 124, or 166 bus to Stratford St. Andrew, then walk 2 miles to hostel.

By car: Take A12 to Wickham Market, turn off toward Capmsea Ashe, and follow signs to Tunstall. Then take B1078 to hostel, following signs.

By train: Wickham Market Station, 3 miles away. From Saxmundham Station take 166 bus to Stratford St. Andrew; walk 2 miles to hostel.

BRIDGES LONG MYND HOSTEL

Bridges, Ratlinghope, Shrewsbury SY5 0SP

Phone Number: 01588–650656

Fax: 01588–65056
Rates: £4.95–£7.20 per HI member (about $7.00–$11.00 US)
Beds: 35
Season: Call ahead in winter for open days
Affiliation: HI-YHA
Extras: Camping, bike storage, dinner ($)

Party index:

Positioned between the Long Mynd ridge and plenty of heather, this former school-turned-hostel makes a rather plain base in the Shropshire Hills. Four dorm rooms range from manageable (five beds) to bigger (a dozen). The scenery is nice, but you won't find anything resembling a party out here—and it's nigh on impossible to get here using public transport.

KEY TO ICONS

- Attractive natural setting
- Ecologically aware hostel
- Superior kitchen facilities or cafe
- Offbeat or eccentric place
- Superior bathroom facilities
- Romantic private rooms
- Comfortable beds
- Editors' choice: among our very favorite hostels
- A particularly good value
- Wheelchair accessible
- Good for business travelers
- Especially well suited for families
- Good for active travelers
- Visual arts at hostel or nearby
- Music at hostel or nearby
- Great hostel for skiers
- Bar or pub at hostel or nearby

How to get there:

By bus: Tuesdays only, from Shrewsbury, take 551 bus to village.

By car: Call hostel for directions.

By train: Church Stretton Station is closest, 5 miles away.

SHERBROOK LODGE HOSTEL

Harpur Hill Road, Buxton, Derbyshire SK17 9NB

Phone Number: 01298–22287

Fax: 01298–22287
Rates: £4.95–£7.20 per HI member (about $7.00–$11.00 US)
Beds: 56
Season: Call ahead for open days
Affiliation: HI-YHA
Extras: Bike storage, dinner ($)

A mile or so outside the good Peaks-area base town of Buxton, this fine-looking modern home has four- to twelve-bedded dorm rooms and a lounge and kitchen. Dinner is also served.

Pleasant and green Buxton makes a nice jump-off point for the park for two solid reasons: First, it's got more culture (an opera house, for example, and record and book fairs in the summer), food options, and nightlife than any of those other hamlets in the hills. Second, it's the end of the train line from Manchester. So if you don't have two to four wheels on your side, you're probably passing through here anyway.

Insiders' tip: Caverns nearby

Gestalt: Big Buxton

Party index:

For fun, traipse around one of several pedestrian walkways in town; check out the gardens; taste the local mineral water from a free-flowing spring across the street from the tourist information office. It's all great fun, almost like pretending you've inherited an English manor. The hostel ain't half bad, either.

How to get there:

By bus: From bus station walk 1½ miles up Harpur Hill to hostel.

By car: Take A6 to Buxton, turn into village, drive up Harpur Hill; hostel is at junction of Ashbourne Road.

By train: From Manchester take train to Buxton Station (one hour, about $12 US), walk 1½ miles up Harpur Hill to hostel, or take taxi.

CAMBRIDGE HOSTEL 

97 Tenison Road, Cambridge CB1 2DN

Phone Number: 01223–354601

Fax: 01223–312780
Rates: £7.30–£10.70 per HI member (about $11–$16 US)
Credit cards: Yes
Beds: 100
Affiliation: HI-YHA
Extras: Laundry, game room, garden, bike shed, dinner ($)
Lockout: 10:00 A.M.–2:00 P.M.

Despite the tight quarters, the hip and friendly staff manages to keeps things movin' pretty well here. A Victorian townhouse, it's usually full in summer—and we mean ful-l-l-l. Dorms range in size from two to eight beds, and they pack 'em in as best they can; not your greatest bet if you like tall-ceilinged, wide-open rooms. Bathrooms can get crowded and a bit grungy as a result. At least in a private room you'll have your own sink.

Best bet for a bite: Grocery store on main road

Insiders' tip: Cool Internet place nearby

Hospitality: 👍

Party index:

The kitchen here's pretty well stocked, although lighting the gas burners takes a little practice. (Chances are you'll quit and use the microwave instead.) A game room, laundry, in-hostel cafeteria with tons of seating, and nice courtyard garden all provide additional opportunities for goofing off or whiling away the four-hour lockout—which some folks spend philosophizing about the deeper meaning of navel lint, while others practice Shakespeare or boil ramen noodles. Different strokes for different folks, ya know?

Seriously, though, Cambridge is a pretty happenin' and attractive town, with lots of student-oriented pubs and clubs, quiet side streets, and a great open-air market where we found everything from organic soy milk to winter gloves at good prices.

The university has some amazing buildings, too, although much of it's off-limits to non-students like you and me. To see the best of it, the back lawns of the colleges, known simply as the "Backs," punt the Cam. What's that? If you've never punted the Cam—no, we don't mean kicked part of a car, you dolt—try it! It's good, clean fun, unless you embarrass yourself by losing that pole.

What do we mean by all that? Find out for yourself, man—we don't wanna talk about it. We're going for a beer.

Do note that the hostel is a bit of a walk from downtown, but on the other hand it's extremely close to the city train station (like a few minutes' walk). So you can do what we did—jump off the train, drop off your gear in your room, then hike into town to hit the pub scene running.

How to get there:

By bus: From downtown Cambridge take any local bus heading to train station; ask for dropoff at Tenison Road and walk short distance to hostel on right.

By car: From downtown follow A604 to rail station; make last left before station onto Tenison Road. Hostel is on right.

By train: From Cambridge Station walk less than ¼ mile down Station Road and turn right onto Tenison Road; hostel is on right.

CARPENTER'S ARMS BACKPACKERS' HOSTEL

182-186 Victoria Road, Cambridge CB1 2DN

Phone Number: 01223–351–814

Rates: £10–£11 per person (about $15–$17 US)
Beds: 14
Affiliation: None
Extras: Pickups (sometimes)

If you're looking for more fun while in Cambridge, grab that phone and try this joint—but hurry. See, it's awfully small and usually books up faster than you can say "hullo??"

Situated above a pub—and that gives you some idea of the clientele here, dudes who wanna party—this is the superhip alternative to the HI joint in town, with two to six beds per room and a shiny happy feeling most of the time. We'll definitely recommend it here, for those who are in it for the good times.

Gestalt: More fun, less filling.

Hospitality: 

Cleanliness: 

Party index: 

How to get there:

By bus: Call hostel for transit route.
By car: Call hostel for directions.
By train: Call hostel for transit route.

CASTLETON HALL

Castleton, Sheffield S30 2WG

Phone Number: 01433–620235

Fax: 01433–621767
Rates: £6.55–£11.65 per HI member (about $10–$18 US); doubles £22–£24 (about $33–$36 US)
Beds: 150
Private/family rooms: Yes
Season: February 6 to December 23
Affiliation: HI-YHA
Extras: TV, dinner ($)

On the road between Sheffield and Manchester, this big and popular place is pretty interesting. It's one of the oldest in this already-old town; the barn was used as a tithing area where peasants would bring their harvest for purchase by the landlord who, in turn, would sell it back to them at a higher price. Nice guy.

Best bet for a bite: The Castle (pub)

Gestalt: Peak perfomance

Hospitality: 

Cleanliness: 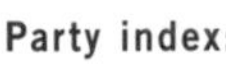

Party index: 

Anyhow, it's a good history lesson and provides decent rooms (some with en-suite bathrooms). But call ahead in summer, 'cause everyone in England knows about it, too. However, because it's used so heavily—mostly by school groups who come on the weekends for school parties and orienteering programs—it has a real worn look to it and smells a little bad upon entrance.

You will also encounter many folks who are walking through the park going hostel to hostel; they tend toward the retired set. Facilities have been upgraded to cater to all ages though; decent meals are served, bathrooms are serviceable if prison-like, and bunk beds are high enough so that your noggin doesn't get bumped in the night.

Dorms run from four to sixteen beds, and lots of renovations have been done in recent years; plus there are double rooms for couples. The adjacent vicarage house has been nicely decked out in nicer doubles and family rooms that cost an extra pound or two.

Your next-door neighbor (actually it's staring down on you from on high), Peveril Castle, was orignally built in 1066 (sound familiar?). Castleton itelf is a tourist town with narrow sidewalks and a few too many gift shops, although the local caves add a second interesting diversion. The hills (especially Mam Tor) and cliffs, of course, are the main draw. Also check out the local

Castleton Hall

Castleton, England

(photo by Martha Coombs)

Blue John quartz—which you can't miss, 'cause all those gift shops hawk the heck out of it.

How to get there:

By bus: From Sheffield take 272 or 274 bus to Castleton. Hostel is at base of castle.

By car: Take A625 to Castleton. Hostel is at Market Place, across from castle.

By train: From Hope Station walk 3 miles to hostel, or take 272 or 274 bus to Castleton. Hostel is at base of castle.

THE LAURELS HOSTEL

The Slade, Charlbury, Oxfordshire OX7 3SJ

Phone Number: 01608–810202

Fax: 01608–810202
Rates: £5.40–£8.00 per HI member (about $8.00–$12.00 US); doubles £19 (about $30 US)
Beds: 50
Season: Call ahead for open days
Affiliation: HI-YHA
Extras: Dinner ($), bike storage, laundry, garden
$

Better equipped than most of England's rural hostels, this former glove factory fits the bill neatly as a potential Cotswolds base. Private rooms are an especial bargain, but even if you're bunking up in one of the dorms—they range from two to eight beds apiece—you get the use of a laundry and can hang out in the gardens all day if you want.

Gestalt:
Laurel and Hardy

Party index:

How to get there:

By bus: From Oxford or Chipping Norton, take Worths bus to village.

By car: Take A44 to Enstone, turn onto B4022 and continue south to Charlbury. Make left at first crossroads; hostel is on left, 100 yards along.

By train: From Charlbury Station walk 1 mile into town on B4437.

HOUGH GREEN HOSTEL 

40 Hough Green, Chester CH4 8JD

Phone Number: 01244–680056

Fax: 01244–681204
Rates: £6.55–£9.75 per HI member (about $10–$15 US); doubles £20.50 (about $31 US)
Credit cards: Yes
Beds: 130
Private/family rooms: Yes
Season: January 9 to December 20
Affiliation: HI-YHA
Extras: TV, lockers, laundry, store, bike storage, pool table, garden
Lockout: 10:00 A.M.–3:00 P.M.
Curfew: 1:00 A.M.

This hostel fills a Victorian house a mile outside historic Chester, one of England's four walled cities. Some hostellers opt to walk the entire wall, but no matter where you head in this cutesy-dootsy town you'll run smack into a phalanx of tourists. Ah, well, enjoy the stroll into town anyway.

Dorms come in sizes of two to ten beds, and, yes, Virginia, that does mean there are couples' rooms here. Facilities are reasonable modern, including a television and laundry. Hostellers and families especially liked the rooms in the ground floor annex next to the hostel garden. We applaud YHA for actually locating one of its hostels in a real house, for once; though it's aging, it sure beats the heck out of those dungeon-like buildings we usually see.

Local sights include The Rows, a double-decker–style shopping area, and the famous cathedral. Not to mention a broadcasting museum and a zoo. But what everybody's really here to see are those half-timbered buildings in shades of brown, blue, white, and black. You'll feel like you're transported back to the Middle Ages for sure.

Insiders' tip: Grosvenor Park gardens

Gestalt: Chester grin

Hospitality:

Cleanliness:

Party index:

How to get there:

By bus: Walk downtown, and take 7 or 16 bus to hostel.

By car: From city take A55 to A483, turn right, exit next roundabout at A5104 going toward Saltney. Hostel is ¼ mile from traffic lights, on right.

By train: From Chester Station walk or take cab 1½ miles to hostel.

THE MILL HOSTEL

Clun, Shropshire SY7 8NY

Phone Number: 01588–640582

Fax: 01588–640582
Rates: £4.95–£7.20 per HI member (about $7.00–$11.00 US)
Beds: 24
Season: March 23 to September 1
Affiliation: HI-YHA
Extras: Camping, bike storage

A former mill, this hostel offers three dorm rooms plus standard common room and kitchen facilities. Nothing to write home about. Best advantage to staying here would appear to be the castles nearby and the farm museum a little farther afield. (Heh, heh.) And the place is well placed for walkers in the bunch, who might be trekking the Shropshire Way as it passes through the village of Clun.

Gestalt: Field Notes

Party index:

How to get there:

By car: Take A488 to Clun; turn onto B4368, then turn north onto Ford Street. Make a right and an immediate left; hostel is on right, 250 yards along.

By train: Craven Arms Station, 10 miles away, and Broome Station, 7 miles away, are nearest; no public transport.

IRONBRIDGE GORGE HOSTEL

Paradise, Coalbrookdale, Telford, Shropshire TF8 7NR

Phone Number: 01952–433281

Fax: 01952–433166
Rates: £6.55–£9.75 per HI member (about $10–$15 US)
Beds: 97
Season: February 1 to November 30
Affiliation: HI-YHA
Extras: TV, laundry, store, bike storage, dinner ($)

This hostel is a former Literary and Scientific Institute, built for local ironworkers in the 1800s. A sizable building, the structure sits in Severn Gorge, near the world's first iron bridge—a must-see for Industrial Revolution fans, possibly missable for the rest of us. A better bet is the nearby Museum of Iron.

Insiders' tip: Chocolate factory nearby

Gestalt: Ironclad

Party index:

As for the hostel, dorm rooms are small, but the hostel cafeteria has won awards for its meals. School kids swamp the place in summer, though, possibly marring the experience.

How to get there:

By bus: From Telford take bus to Ironbridge, hostel.

By car: Call hostel for directions.

By train: Wellington Telford West and Telford Central Stations, 5 miles away; from either, take bus to Ironbridge, walk to hostel.

COALPORT HOSTEL

John Road Building, High Street, Coalport, Telford, Shropshire TF8 7HT

Phone Number: 01952–58875

Fax: 01952–588722

Rates: £6.55–£9.75 per HI member (about $10–$15 US); doubles £22 (about $33 US)
Beds: 85
Season: February 1 to November 30
Affiliation: HI-YHA
Extras: TV, game room, meals ($), store, meeting rooms

Located just 3 miles from the more well-known Ironbridge Gorge hostel, this one's a bit easier to reach via public transportation: Buses run from Telford to the area until 5:20 P.M.

Gestalt:
Coal porter

Party index:

As with its sister hostel up the road, the real deal here is good in-house grub. There's also a pretty tiny kitchen if you want to cook your own meal and save those pounds for sight-seeing instead. This place is pretty well outfitted for school groups (shudder), so expect to get trampled by tiny feet; if you can secure the meeting rooms, TV, or hostel store ahead of them, good luck.

Several museums are the star attractions around these parts, including the popular Blist Hill Open Air Museum, a folk museum re-creating life as it appears to have been during the 1890s.

Whew. Thank goodness they didn't re-create life in the 1980s by mistake . . . don't know how much more Flock of Seagulls reunions we could take.

How to get there:

By bus: From Telford take 895 or 899 bus to China Museum.

By car: Call hostel for directions.

By train: Telford Central Station, take 895 or 899 bus to China Museum.

KEY TO ICONS

Attractive natural setting
Ecologically aware hostel
Superior kitchen facilities or cafe
Offbeat or eccentric place
Superior bathroom facilities
Romantic private rooms
Comfortable beds
Editors' choice: among our very favorite hostels
A particularly good value
Wheelchair accessible
Good for business travelers
Especially well suited for families
Good for active travelers
Visual arts at hostel or nearby
Music at hostel or nearby
Great hostel for skiers
Bar or pub at hostel or nearby

COPT OAK HOSTEL

Whitwick Road, Copt Oak, Markfield, Leicester LE67 9QB

Phone Number: 01530–242661

Rates: £4.45–£6.50 per HI member (about $7.00–$10.00 US)
Beds: 18
Season: March 23 to October 27
Affiliation: HI-YHA
Extras: Lockers, bike storage

Another schoolhouse hostel—England's chock-full of them—and again it's basic city. Just two dorm rooms, a lounge, a kitchen. But if you've just been walking and cycling about, or got shut out of the accommodations in Leicester or Nottingham, you'll be glad it's here.

How to get there:

By bus: From Leicester take 117, 119, 217, or 218 bus to Flying Horse roundabout, then walk 1 mile to hostel.

By car: Take M1 to Junction 22, taking A50 toward Leicester. Make first left, following signs to Copt Oak; hostel is on right, just before traffic lights.

By train: Leicester Station, 10 miles away, is nearest; from Leicester, take 117, 119, 217, or 218 bus to Flying Horse roundabout, then walk 1 mile to hostel.

PEAK NATIONAL PARK HOSTEL

Crowden, Hadfield, Hyde, Cheshire SK14 7HZ

Phone Number: 01457–852135

Fax: 01457–852135
Rates: £4.95–£7.20 per HI member (about $7.00–$11.00 US)
Beds: 50
Private/family rooms: Sometimes
Season: Call ahead for open days
Affiliation: HI-YHA
Extras: Dinner ($), bike storage

Gestalt:
Peakaboo

Party index:

Simple, of course, is the word here: 50 beds wedged into a row of former railwaymen's cottages on the Pennine Way outside Manchester. A meal is served at night, and there's also a kitchen.

How to get there:

By bus: From Sheffield or Manchester take National Express 350 bus.

By car: From Manchester take A628 (Barnsley Road) north to Crowden. Hostel is on left, at Pennine Way trailhead.

By foot: From Edale hostel walk 15 miles on Pennine Way.

By train: From Sheffield Station take National Express 350 bus.

LITTLE RANGER HOSTEL

Dimmingsdale, Oakamoor, Stoke-on-Trent, Staffordshire ST10 3AS

Phone Number: 01538–702304

Rates: £4.45–£6.50 per HI member (about $8.00–$12.00 US)
Beds: 20
Season: March 27 to October 31
Affiliation: HI-YHA
Extras: Bike storage, store

On the southern edge of the Peaks District, this place is plain and stuck in the woods near some quiet walking and biking areas. Dorms come in six- to eight-bed rooms, there's a tiny shop for essentials, and the kitchen works. Stoke-on-Trent isn't too far away as a destination.

Gestalt:
Peak-easy

Party index:

How to get there:

By bus: From Uttoxeter take 238 bus to Oakamoor, walk ¾ mile up hill to hostel, bearing right at fork and left at farm lane.

By car: Take B5417 to Oakamoor, turn off main road at Admiral Jervis pub, take next right and go to top of hill; turn left up farm lane and follow to hostel.

By train: Blythe Bridge Station, 6 miles away. From Uttoxeter Station take 238 bus to Oakamoor; walk ¾ mile up hill to hostel, bearing right at fork and left at farm lane.

DUNTISBOURNE ABBOTS HOSTEL

Duntisbourne Abbots, Cirencester, Gloucestershire GL7 7JN

Phone Number: 01285–821682

Fax: 01285–821697
Rates: £5.40–£8.00 per HI member (about $8.00–$12.00 US)
Beds: 53
Season: April 1 to November 1
Affiliation: HI-YHA
Extras: Laundry, meals ($)

Warning: At press time, this hostel was in danger of closing—we're not sure why, and we hope it doesn't, 'cause it's a good bet for your buck.

Party index:

Occupying an old rectory on two acres of hallowed grounds, this hostel makes up with its kitchen for the simplicity of the bunking. Meals, served at 7:00 P.M. sharp, are delicious; local gardens help supply the cooks' pots, we were told. This is hard to reach by public transportation, though, making it unlikely you'll get here without two or four wheels.

How to get there:

By car: Take A417 from Cirencester, turning left at sign just before Little Chef; hostel is 1 mile farther, on right.

By train: Kemble Station, 10 miles away, and Gloucester station, 14½ miles away, are closest; no public transport.

EDALE HOSTEL AND ACTIVITY CENTRE

Rowland Cote, Nether Booth, Edale, Derbyshire S30 2ZH

Phone Number: 01433–670302

Fax: 01433–670243
Rates: £6.55–£9.75 per HI member (about $10–$15 US)
Beds: 141
Season: January 1 to December 23
Affiliation: HI-YHA
Extras: Laundry, TV, dinner ($), bar, outings
Curfew: 11:00 P.M.

This is a real outdoorsperson's treat: A house on a hill, it's got super views of Mam Tor. The Pennine Way starts here. The hardbody staff runs regular hiking, biking, snowshoeing, bog-walking, orienteering, and rafting trips for groups just about any time of year; weather isn't a factor. (Book them in advance or get shut out. You have been warned.)

Gestalt: Hans and Franz

Party index:

That's only the beginning, though. They serve dinner—and a beer, if you want it. They make free pickups from the train station 2 miles away on Friday nights. Plus, get this, there's no lockout! You can lounge here all day and crash, enjoying the views (or the tube, or—bleck—the laundry) without the sweat if you're bushed.

But there's one big downside, and this is it: In summer, school kids are going to fill the place. You can't escape those little fingers and high-pitched squeals. Ah, well. Chances are you won't find a bed anyway if you're trying for a weekend.

How to get there:

By car: From Edale drive 1 mile toward Hope; hostel is on left, marked Rowland Cote.

By foot: From Crowden hostel walk 15 miles on Pennine Way.

By train: From Edale Station walk 2 miles.

SHERWOOD FOREST HOSTEL 

Forest Corner, Edwinstowe, Nottinghamshire NG21 9RN

Phone Number: 01623–825794

Rates: £6.55–£9.75 per HI member (about $10–$15 US); doubles £21.50 (about $32 US)
Beds: 46
Affiliation: HI-YHA
Extras: Bike storage, dinner ($)

This new joint was just built near Robin Hood's former stomping grounds. We don't know if they robbed from the rich to build bunks for the poor, but it sounds pretty good to us.

The hostel offers bunkrooms, double rooms, plus family accommodations in quads (£35.50, about $54 US). Those family rooms are located on the ground floor, with doors onto a patio; some have en-suite bathrooms, and all have sinks at least. The lounge is good and big, the views splendid. Management is really friendly, and even the building is smart—a sophisticated computer system controls the heating to conserve energy.

The Sherwood Forest visitor center is just a ¼ mile up the road (that's like a five-minute walk) and other sights aren't far off either. One more reason to go: This place is quickly building a rep for some of the best meals in the YHA system; a little heavy, sure, but tasty as heck.

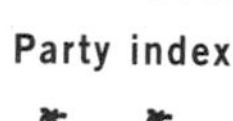

Gestalt:
Robin Good

Party index:

How to get there:

By bus: From Nottingham take 33 or 36 bus.

By car: Take B6034 to Edwinstowe; turn west just south of Sherwood Forest visitor center. Hostel is on left.

By train: Mansfield Woodhouse Station, 5 miles, is closest.

ELTON OLD HALL HOSTEL

Main Street, Elton, Matlock, Derbyshire DE4 2BW

Phone Number: 01629–650394

Rates: £4.45–£6.50 per HI member (about $7.00–$10.00 US)

Beds: 32
Season: February 13 to October 31
Affiliation: HI-YHA
Extras: Lunch ($), breakfast, snacks, bike storage

A seventeenth-century building right in Elton village, this hostel has everything from quad rooms to ten-bedded dorms. Snacks and box lunches are available for those day hikes; the village is mildly interesting for its little lanes.

Gestalt: Elton Jaunt

Party index:

How to get there:

By bus: From Matlock or Bakewell take 170 bus to Elton. Hostel is on main street, at east end.

By car: Take A6 to B5056 or B5057; continue to Elton turnoff. Hostel is on main street, at east end.

By foot: Walk 2½ miles from Youlgreave hostel; 7 miles from Bakewell hostel; 6 miles from Matlock hostel.

By train: From Matlock Station take 170 bus to Elton. Hostel is on main street, at east end.

BRETTON (EYAM) HOSTEL

c/o Whittington, 7 New Bailey, Crane Moore, Sheffield S35 7AT

Phone Number: 0114–2884541

Rates: £4.45–£6.50 per HI member (about $7.00–$10.00 US)
Beds: 18
Season: Call ahead for open days
Affiliation: HI-YHA
Extras: Bike storage

This is kind of a neat idea: a little home in the hills that's open during all of August, and Fridays and Saturdays most of the rest of the year, to run the hostel. Make sure the place is open before you come, and remember that you're calling a private home of John and Elaine Whittington in Sheffield, not the hostel, to book it. So don't phone at 3:00 in the morning, okay?

Party index:

The place itself has three dorm rooms plus a kitchen and common area; views are great, access by public transport occasional. Everything is fine and dandy.

This is miles from nowhere, but the nearby village of Eyam has a very important and dear place in English history—it's the village that walled itself off to keep from spreading the Great Plague throughout England. After a load of cloth from London brought the disease, villagers carted bodies daily to the graveyards, but they refused to seek help; today they are revered as heroes.

How to get there:

By bus: Call hostel for transit route.

By car: From Eyam go 1½ miles toward Hucklow. Hostel is on right, behind Barrel Inn.

By train: From Grindleford Station walk 4 miles to hostel. Or take bus from Sheffield or Buxton station.

EYAM HOSTEL

Hawkhill Road, Eyam, Sheffield S30 1QR

Phone Number: 01433–630335

Fax: 01433–630335
Rates: £5.40–£8.80 per HI member (about $8.00–$13.00 US)
Beds: 60
Season: Call ahead for open days
Office hours: 7:30 to 10:00 A.M.; 5:00 to 11:00 P.M.
Affiliation: HI-YHA
Extras: Bike storage, game room, dinner ($)
Lockout: 10:00 A.M.–5:00 P.M.
Curfew: 11:00 P.M.

Yet another big Victorian home on a hill is the scene of this hostel, built in 1887 for a judge. It's a bit of a hike uphill from Eyam proper, the village whose claim to fame—as mentioned above—was the unfortunate fate of most of the local population during the Great Plague. Among the unusual features here are a nice tower and a "crazy golf course." Hmmm. We'll let you see that one for yourself.

Party index:

The primary action around here is physical fitness: Burly he-men give classes year-round in stuff like ice climbing, extreme skiing, and bear wrasslin'. These classes are an integral part of the hostel's identity; it's gearheads all the way.

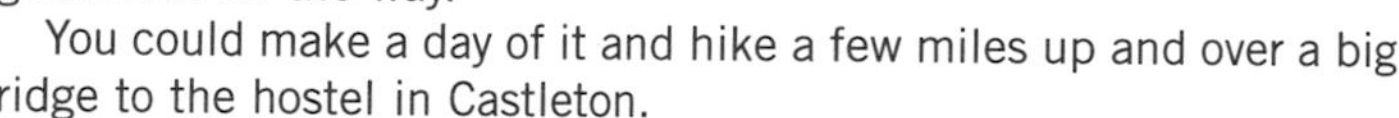

You could make a day of it and hike a few miles up and over a big ridge to the hostel in Castleton.

How to get there:

By bus: Call hostel for transit route.

By car: Take A623 to Eyam, turn off to village and continue up hill ⅓ mile to hostel.

By train: Grindelford Station, 3½ miles, is closest.

THE RECTORY HOSTEL

Welsh Bicknor, Goodrich, Ross-on-Wye, Herefordshire HR9 6JJ

Phone Number: 01594–860300

Fax: 01594–861276
Rates: £5.95–£8.80 per HI member (about $9.00–$13.00 US); doubles £20 (about $30 US)
Beds: 80
Season: Call ahead for open days
Affiliation: HI-YHA
Extras: TV, laundry, game room, camping, bike storage, dinner ($)

This former Victorian rectory on the Wye River includes twenty-five acres of grounds, with views of both the river below and the nicely wooded hills. This is perfect walking territory, though the area's a little remote by public transportation.

Dorm rooms come in two- to ten-bed configurations, lots of them suitable for families: You can get a double, a triple (£25, about $38 US) or even a quad (£31.50, about $48 US). The hostel is pretty well outfitted otherwise with several lounges, a television, dinner service, kitchen, a campground, and a laundry. Good spot, and a good hostel for a getaway en route to Wales; you won't fine nicer strolling territory than the Wye Valley.

How to get there:

Party index:

By bus: From Gloucester or Ross-on-Wye take 34 bus to Goodrich, then walk 1½ miles along sign-posted lane to hostel.

By car: From Ross-on-Wye or Monmouth turn off A40 at signs Goodrich/Goodrich Castle. From Goodrich, follow signs along lane for 1½ miles; after crossing cattle grid, make second right. Drive carefully along single lane to hostel.

By train: Gloucester Station, 19 miles away, is closest; from Gloucester, take 34 bus to Goodrich, then walk 1½ miles along sign-posted lane to hostel.

GRADBACH MILL HOSTEL

Gradbach (Flash), Quarnford, Buxton, Derbyshire SK17 0SU

Phone Number: 01260–227625

Fax: 01260–227334
Rates: £5.95–£8.80 per HI member (about $9.00–$13.00 US); doubles £20 (about $30 US)
Beds: 97
Season: February 6 to December 5

Affiliation: HI-YHA
Extras: Laundry, dinner ($), bike storage
Lockout: 10:00 A.M.–1:00 P.M.

This former mill on the River Dane has been retrofitted with thoughtful double rooms, triples (£25, about $38 US), quads (£32.50, about $50 US), and bigger dormitories; those on the first floor are wheelchair accessible. All in all, it's a nice place and quaint, if a bit lifeless. There's a laundry, which makes this a good choice as a base, plus dinner service and a very short lockout.

Party index:

How to get there:

By bus: From Sheffield or Hanley take X23 bus to Flash, then walk 2½ miles to hostel.

By car: Take A53 to Flash, follow signs.

By train: From Buxton Station walk 7 miles to hostel. From Sheffield Station, take X23 bus to Flash, walk 2½ miles to hostel.

GREAT YARMOUTH HOSTEL

2 Sandown Road, Great Yarmouth, Norfolk NR30 1EY

Phone Number: 01493–843991

Fax: 01493–843991
Rates: £5.95–£8.80 per HI member (about $9.00–$13.00 US)
Credit Cards: Yes
Beds: 40
Private/family rooms: Sometimes
Season: April 6 to September 1
Affiliation: HI-YHA
Extras: Dinner ($), bike storage
Lockout: 10:00 A.M.–5:00 P.M.
Curfew: 11:00 P.M.

This Victorian home sits close to the beach in the popular resort town of Great Yarmouth. Lots of typical English seaside fun and fluff here; good cycling, as well. The hostel itself consists of two- to ten-bedded rooms.

Gestalt: Beach bunk

Party index:

How to get there:

By bus: From bus station walk 1 mile north along sea, turn left at Sandown Road; hostel is on right.

By car: From downtown head toward ocean and turn left; Sandown Road is a left.

By train: From Great Yarmouth Station walk ¾ mile toward sea to hostel.

CASTLE HEDINGHAM HOSTEL

7 Falcon Square, Castle Hedingham, Halstead, Essex CO9 3BU

Phone Number: 01787–460799

Fax: 01787–461302
Rates: £5.95–£8.80 per HI member (about $9.00–$13.00 US)
Beds: 50
Private/family rooms: Sometimes
Affiliation: HI-YHA
Extras: Garden, grill, dinner ($), bike storage

A sixteenth-century structure plus an annex provide this hostel's bunking quarters. There's a big garden with a grill, a lounge, and they serve dinner each night at 7:00 P.M. sharp. Castle Hedingham's a quaint village of half-timbered homes.

Party index:

How to get there:

By bus: From Braintree take 89A bus to Hedingham. Hostel is in castle.

By car: Take A604 or B1058 to Castle Hedingham, then follow signs to castle; turn into Castle Lane. Hostel is on left, at bottom of hill.

By train: From Braintree Station take 89A bus to Hedingham. Hostel is in castle.

CORNER HOUSE HOSTEL

Netteswell Cross, Harlow, Essex CM20 2QD

Phone Number: 01279–421702

Fax: 01279–421702
Rates: £4.95–£7.20 per HI member (about $7.00–$11.00 US)
Beds: 21
Season: January 1 to December 23
Affiliation: HI-YHA
Extras: Game room, lockers

$

Insiders' tip: Pedal over to the cycle museum

Party index:

Note: At press time, this hostel was considering closing down. Call before making the journey.

A former village shop, the Corner House Hostel gives you a taste of quaint small-town life in East Anglia. Yet this little village offers more than just pubs and history; it's got a water sports center, museum, and swimming baths.

The hostel is plain, with four dorm rooms and nothing lavish at all. At least there's a kitchen, lounge, game room, and some grounds. All in all, just fine.

Hartington Hall Hostel
Hartington, England

(photo courtesy of HI-YHA)

How to get there:

By bus: Call hostel for transit route.

By car: Take A414 to Harlow, turn south onto Fifth Avenue, then left on First/Mandela Avenue. Continue to School Lane, and make a left; hostel is on left, across from pub.

By train: Harlow Town Station is ⅓ mile from hostel.

HARTINGTON HALL HOSTEL 

Hartington, Buxton, Derbyshire SK17 0AT

Phone Number: 01298–84223

Fax: 01298–84415
Rates: £5.95–£11.65 per HI member (about $9.00–$18.00 US)
Beds: 138
Season: February 13 to December 23
Office hours: 8:00 A.M. to 11:00 P.M.
Affiliation: HI-YHA
Extras: TV, laundry, bicycle storage, game room, store, dinner, bar, fireplaces, meeting rooms, bike rentals

One of YHA's stars, Hartington Hall is great. Recent new work has made it one of the best in the Peaks District—almost a hotel, really.

The main building is a Jacobean stone manor house, and an attached barn has recently been fixed up to add more family rooms; the area is also reportedly handicapped accessible, a big plus. There are some large dorms of eight to ten beds each, thirteen quad rooms, and a double. Some rooms have oak paneling, some common areas have a log fireplace. Nice! The restaurant here, which has a license to serve English hard cider and other liquor, even won awards for its food. And there's no lockout; you can come and go all day long.

Most visitors are here to explore the countryside, which is gentler than the rugged heart of the Peaks; the hostel's right on a walking path that runs along former railroad beds. You can hike down the Dovedale Valley and back up the Manifold Valley, for example, to get a great round-trip look at small-town England.

Gestalt:
Brave Hartington

Party index:

How to get there:

By bus: From Buxton take 442 bus to Hartington. Hostel is up lane beside school, 200 yards on left.

By car: Take B5054 to Hartington; from village center, turn onto lane by school, continue 200 yards to hostel on left.

By train: From Buxton Station, 12 miles away, take 442 bus to Hartington. Hostel is up lane beside school, 200 yards on left.

HATHERSAGE HOSTEL 

Castleton Road, Hathersage, Sheffield S30 1AH

Phone Number: 01433–650493

Fax: 01433–650493
Rates: £5.40–£8.00 per HI member (about $8.00–$12.00 US)
Beds: 42
Season: Call ahead for open days
Office hours: 8:00 to 10:00 A.M.; 5:00 to 11:30 P.M.
Affiliation: HI-YHA
Extras: Bike storage, dinner ($)
Lockout: 10:00 A.M.–5:00 P.M.
Curfew: 11:30 P.M.

This cute small town in nice hill country is Jane Eyre territory, and the hostel here's a Victorian house with adequate enough furnishings. Eight dorms contain either four or six bed apiece; dinner is offered at night in the attached kitchen/dining room/reception area. There's a nice area outside to sit and write postcards; if you arrive during the day when nobody's here, check in using the honor-system registration they've devised (it involves an envelope and a mail slot) and come back later.

The kitchen's pretty good for a hostel, by the way, including a toaster oven, aprons, microwave, and more in addition to the usual stuff. We also liked the giant hiking map of the area painted right onto an interior wall. But watch out for the usual English school groups who sometimes take over without warning.

You can walk to the White Peak Way from the village, and also check out the local swimming pool during summer. If you're walking through the Peaks, you'll find an interesting church here as well as the reputed grave of Robin Hood's buddy Little John.

Best bet for a bite: Sangam's Balti

Insiders' tip: Walking path to church at edge of town

Gestalt: Plain Jane

Cleanliness: 

Party index:

How to get there:

By bus: From Sheffield or Castleton take 272 or 274 bus to Hathersage.

By car: Take A625 to Hathersage; hostel is 100 yards west of George Hotel.

By train: From Hathersage Station, walk ½ mile down B6001 into village, then go left on main road to hostel on right.

HUNSTANTON HOSTEL

15 Avenue Road, Hunstanton, Norfolk PE36 5BW

Phone Number: 01485–532061

Fax: 01485–532632
Rates: £5.95–£8.80 per HI member (about $9.00–$13.00 US)
Beds: 46
Private/family rooms: Yes
Season: April 1 to November 7
Affiliation: HI-YHA
Extras: TV, dinner ($), bike storage

Two Victorian town houses sit in the middle of Hunstanton, and that's the hostel. Nine dorm rooms offer everything from an eight-bed dorm to triple bedrooms perfect for families—and, at just £26 (about $39 US) a super bargain for your buckaroo.

Lounging facilities are key here, and they include telly and chill-in' room, plus a cycle shop, dining room, and kitchen. Meals are served at 7:00 P.M. You're also in primo beach and cliff country, so ramble around a little or a lot.

Insiders' tip: Blue Flag beaches

Party index:

How to get there:

By bus: From King's Lynn take 410 or 411 bus to Hunstanton; walk ¼ mile to hostel.

By car: Take A149 to Hunstanton; turn off at B1161 (Southend Road) toward South Beach, then turn onto Park Road and make immediate left onto Avenue Road. Hostel is on left.

By train: Nearest station is King's Lynn, 16 miles away; take 411 bus to Hunstanton; walk ¼ mile to hostel.

ILAM HALL

Ilam, Ashbourne, Derbyshire DE6 2AZ

Phone Number: 01335–350212

Fax: 01335–350350
Rates: £6.55–£9.75 per HI member (about $10–$15 US)
Beds: 148
Private/family rooms: Sometimes
Season: February 1 to October 31
Affiliation: HI-YHA
Extras: TV, laundry, dinner ($), bike storage

A stately nineteenth-century mansion on nice grounds, Ilam Hall supplies two types of digs. In the main house you can stay in dorms with from three to sixteen beds. In the adjacent Brew House nicer four-bed (£40, about $60 US) and bigger rooms good for families are also available. (Ale is served, but not in the brewhouse; the kitchen has a license to sell liquor with meals.) Just don't get shut out by the conference and school groups that periodically take over the place.

Party index:

Derbyshire (say Darby-sure and you've about got it right) is one of the prettiest counties in all England, so don't pass up the opportunity to walk round the area.

How to get there:

By bus: Call hostel for transit route.
By car: Call hostel for directions.
By train: Call hostel for transit route.

THE OLD BREWERY HOUSE HOSTEL

Ivinghoe, Leighton Buzzard, Bedfordshire LU7 9EP

Phone Number: 01296–668251

Fax: 01296–662903
Rates: £5.40–£8.00 per HI member (about $8.00–$12.00 US)
Beds: 50
Season: Call ahead for open days
Affiliation: HI-YHA
Extras: TV, bike storage, dinner ($)

Once home to a local brewer—oh, unhappy day when he left—this Georgian mansion in the center of inviting little Ivinghoe is plain. Six dorm rooms handle the visitors, and a regular evening meal brings everyone together at night. A zoo, an abbey, and Iron Age ruins are in the countryside nearby.

Gestalt:
Brew crew

Party index:

How to get there:

By bus: From Aylesbury or Luton take 61 bus.

By car: Take B488 or B489 to Ivinghoe; hostel is in center of village, beside church and across from village green.

By train: Cheddington Station, 1½ miles away, is closest.

KING'S LYNN HOSTEL

Thoresby College, College Lane, King's Lynn, Norfolk PE30 1JB

Phone Number: 01553–772461

Fax: 01553–764312
Rates: £5.40–£8.00 per HI member (about $8.00–$12.00 US)
Beds: 35
Season: April 2 to October 31
Office hours: 7:00 to 10:00 A.M.; 5:00 to 9:00 P.M.
Affiliation: HI-YHA
Extras: Bike storage, catered meals for groups
Lockout: 10:00 A.M.–5:00 P.M.
Curfew: 11:00 P.M.

$

A somewhat smallish—but venerable—former college building in the oldest part of the village, this hostel's quarters are 500 years old, they tell us. (Hopefully the original plumbing isn't still here.)

Placed nicely alongside the Great River Ouse and directly across from town hall and a tourist information office, it packs 'em into six rooms of varying size. Scramble like heck for the lone single room if you get there early in the morning: It offers the ultimate in privacy, a rarity in English hostels. The tourist info booth is right at hand, as are lots of buildings that might be three times older than the country you just flew in from. Or maybe not. Depends.

Keep in mind that this joint sometimes closes up tight as a drum on certain days during shoulder season (in other words, spring and fall); don't find out the hard way.

Insiders' tip:
Tuesday Market Place

Party index:

How to get there:

By bus: Call hostel for transit route.

By car: From downtown take St. James Street to river; turn into College Lane.

By train: King's Lynn Station is ¾ mile from hostel; walk toward river.

LANGSETT HOSTEL

c/o Whittington, 7 New Bailey, Crane Moor, Sheffield S35 7AT

Phone Number: 0114–2884541

Rates: £4.45–£6.50 per HI member (about $7.00–$10.00 US)
Beds: 34
Season: Call ahead for open days
Affiliation: HI-YHA
Extras: Garden, bike storage

Another plain-Jane place, just six bunkrooms in two buildings on the edge of the Peak District, but it's surrounded by moors. Two kitchens and a common room help you meet new friends, while a garden is a good place to hang if you're waiting to check in. Remember that you're calling a private home, not the hostel, to book here—so be respectful of hours.

Party index:

How to get there:

By bus: From Barnsley or Penistone take 381 bus to hostel.
By car: From A616 go 1 mile south of Flouch Inn roundabout.
By train: From Penistone Station walk 3 miles, or take 381 bus to hostel.

LINCOLN HOSTEL

77 South Park, Lincoln LN5 8ES

Phone Number: 01522–522076

Fax: 01522–567424
Rates: £5.95–£8.80 per HI member (about $9.00–$13.00 US)
Beds: 47
Private/family rooms: Sometimes
Season: February 1 to December 21
Affiliation: HI-YHA
Extras: TV, laundry, bike storage, lockers, dinner ($)

This big, oh-so-English mansion gets so-so reviews for its blah location. Otherwise, it's pleasant enough—and Lincoln is a blast. The food they serve here's really good, too.

Let's start with the basics. Dorms come in sizes of two to eight beds, and they're generous with the lockout: You can get access to your locker. Later, returning, they've actually got a telly where you can catch up on the football (er, soccer) scores.

Lincoln, as we said, is well worth a side trip from the main London-Edinburgh train line. How about this, for starters: a hilltop castle that dates from 1068! Plus long cobblestoned sidestreets to explore, a connection to Tennyson, and one of the best cathedrals in all England. Interested yet? If you got wheels, don't forget to check out Robin Hood country nearby during the daytime.

Gestalt: Lincoln logs

Party index:

How to get there:

By bus: From station walk along Canwick Road past traffic lights. At cemetery turn left on South Park. Hostel is on right.

By car: Call hostel for directions.

By train: From Lincoln Station, 1 mile walk. Turn right onto St. Mary's Street and continue to Oxford Street. Walk under underpass and up steps to right, along Canwick Road, and over traffic lights. At cemetery turn left on South Park. Hostel is on right.

EMBASSIE HOSTEL

1 Falmber Square, Liverpool L8 7NU

Phone Number: 0151–707–1089

Rates: £9.50 per person (about $14 US)
Beds: 32
Office hours: Call hostel for hours
Affiliation: None
Extras: Breakfast, meals, game room, laundry, coffee

A house in a residential neighborhood, this nineteenth-century building was a Venezuelan consulate until the late 1980s—and it appeared in the film *In the Name of the Father.* They provide free continental breakfast and sometimes free dinners, apparently; a game room and laundry. No rules here, that's the rule.

Party index:

How to get there:

By bus: Call hostel for transit route.

By car: Call hostel for directions.

By train: From Lime Street Station take 80 bus to hostel.

Liverpool Hostel
Liverpool, England
(photo courtesy of HI-YHA)

LIVERPOOL HOSTEL 

Wapping, Liverpool, Merseyside L1 8EE

Phone Number: 0151–709–8888

Rates: £11.75–£15.75 per HI member (about $18–$24 US)
Beds: 100
Affiliation: HI-YHA
Extras: TV, laundry, lockers, bike storage, dinner ($), bar, free breakfast

It's a hostel, yeah, yeah, yeah.

Insiders' tip: Paul is not dead

What hostellers say: "Yesterday . . ."

Gestalt: Fab floor

Hospitality: 

Cleanliness: 

Party index:  

Sorry. But hostelling types are just so darned excited about this place we couldn't help it. It's brand-new and good, affording plenty of opportunities to check out the city's former docks . . . okay, okay, we'll quit it. You're here for one reason only—because a couple of chaps rose from these gritty, uninspiring streets to everlasting superstardom.

The hostel is mostly made up of two- to six-bedded rooms. Quad rooms with breakfast cost around £56 (about $84 US) for four and include breakfast, a heckuva good deal. Every room has its own en-suite bathroom facilities, a great addition. A diner serves burgers and other suspiciously North American fare. There's also a television room with new TV.

While here, you're gonna hit the Beatles sights: the real Penny Lane, the real Strawberry Fields building, the McCartney home. And you're gonna empty your pockets.

This place isn't cheap, you're thinking, so it better be good. And it is.

How to get there:

By bus: Call hostel for transit route.

By car: Call hostel for directions.

By train: From Liverpool Station call hostel for directions.

THE JOHN CADBURY MEMORIAL HOSTEL

Wilderhope Manor, Longville in the Dale, Much Wenlock, Shropshire TF13 6EG

Phone Number: 01694–771363

Fax: 01694–771520
Rates: £5.95–£8.80 per HI member (about $9.00–$13.00 US)
Beds: 70
Season: February 1 to October 30
Affiliation: HI-YHA
Extras: Camping, porch, dinner ($)

The manager here likes to tout this big building's spiral staircases and banquet room, and, indeed, it is a National Trust property. Okay, so it's historic. No argument there.

Still, it's overly simple and not too too comfortable. There's not much privacy, either: four quad rooms, a sixer, and two bigger ones with ten to fourteen bunks.

At least it's beautifully set on the lower slopes of Wenlock Edge, nice hills for walking.

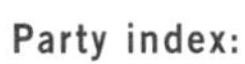

Party index:

How to get there:

By bus: From Ludlow take 712 bus (Mondays and Fridays only). Or take bus to Shipton, and walk 2 miles along footpath to hostel.

By car: From B4371 turn south at Longville in the Dale; turn left in ½ mile to hostel. From B4368 turn north toward Longville in the Dale at Seven Stars pub; in ½ mile, turn right to hostel.

By train: Church Stretton Station, 8 miles away, is closest stop.

LUDFORD LODGE HOSTEL

Ludford, Ludlow, Shropshire SY8 1PJ

Phone Number: 01584–872472

Fax: 01584–872095
Rates: £4.95–£7.20 per HI member (about $7.00–$11.00 US)

Beds: 50
Season: Call ahead for open days
Affiliation: HI-YHA
Extras: TV, bike storage, dinner ($)

This hostel sits on a river bank, facing Ludlow from across a bridge. Eight dorm rooms range from quad to eight-bedded situations, and there is not one but two lounges plus a television for lazing around. Ludlow, said to be one of the realm's most attractive towns, is packed with sights: castle ruins, town houses, and lots more.

Party index:

How to get there:

By bus: From Birmingham or Hereford take 192 or 292 bus to Ludlow. Walk into town and cross river.

By car: From Ludlow drive down Broad Street and cross Ludford Bridge; hostel is immediately to left, on river bank.

By train: Ludlow Station, walk ¾ mile into town; cross Ludford Bridge. Hostel is immediately to left, on river bank.

ST. BRIAVELS CASTLE HOSTEL

St. Briavels, Lydney, Gloucestershire GL15 6RG

Phone Number: 01594–530272

Fax: 01594–530849
Rates: £6.55–£9.75 per HI member (about $10–$15 US)
Beds: 70
Season: February 13 to October 31
Affiliation: HI-YHA
Extras: Bike storage, store, dinner ($), bar, banquets

Now this is why we came to England!

Not far from Wordworth's famous Tintern Abbey, set in a nice valley, this hostel actually is a castle—it was used by King John as a hunting lodge when he wasn't working on the *Magna Carta*. There's a decent Welsh folk museum nearby, too, just across the border.

Gestalt:
King for a day

Party index:

Dorm rooms, occupying dungeons and a guard room, are pretty big (what'd you expect, the lap of luxury?) but otherwise okay.

If you're into it, you can take a tour that includes the prisoners' cells, chapel, 30-foot dungeon (shudder—they dropped prisoners in there) and (double shudder) a hanging room. On second thought, we'll skip all that and come on a Wednesday or Saturday during August, when the management hosts a series of delicious banquets in the feasting hall. Even if you can't come then, dinners are served whenever the place is open, which is almost always. And get this: They've got a license to sell you a drink with your meal.

Make the trip; you'll love it, we think, both the ambience and the local hills. Just think twice about the creepy tour; personally, dinner didn't quite sit so well afterward!

How to get there:

By bus: From Chepstow, take 69 bus to Bigsweir Bridge, then walk 2 miles to hostel.

By car: From M4 take M48 toward Chepstow. Exit onto A466 and follow signs to St. Briavels. Hostel is located in center of village, in castle.

By train: Lydney or Chepstow Station, both 7 miles away; from Chepstow Station, take 69 bus to Bigsweir Bridge, then walk 2 miles to hostel.

MALVERN HILLS HOSTEL 

18 Peachfield Road, Malvern Wells, Malvern, Worcestershire WR14 4AP

Phone Number: 01684–569131

Fax: 01684–565205
Rates: £5.40–£8.00 per HI member (about $8.00–$12.00 US)
Beds: 57
Private/family rooms: Sometimes
Season: February 16 to October 31
Affiliation: HI-YHA
Extras: TV, garden, bike storage, dinner ($)

Not the prettiest face, this building, but it makes up for it with good food and a good rural location tucked into the hills. It's also more accessible by public transport than many other British hostels.

Five dorms contain four to six beds each, and two coveted doubles contain twin beds. A television, lounge, garden, and game room make this a good place to hang.

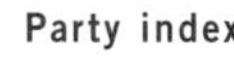

Party index:

How to get there:

By bus: From Worcester take 44 bus to Barnards Green; walk 1 mile to hostel.

By car: Take A449 to Malvern Hills; at Railway Inn near train crossing, turn east onto Peachfield Road. Hostel is on right.

By train: From Great Malvern Station walk 1 mile south on Court Road, turn right on Peachfield Road. Hostel is on left.

MANCHESTER HOSTEL 

Potato Wharf, Castlefield, Greater Manchester M3 4NB

Phone Number: 0161–839–9960

Fax: 0161–835–2054
Rates: £9.00–£13.00 per HI member (about $13–$20 US)
Beds: 152
Private/family rooms: Yes
Office hours: Twenty-four hours
Affiliation: HI-YHA
Extras: TV, game, laundry, meals ($), lockers, conference rooms

Attention: Some call this best hostel in the world. And we've got to agree that it certainly deserves all the thumbs up we can muster.

Lots of thought seems to have gone into the joint, which is almost like a sleek modern hotel. There are plenty of private rooms, for starters, and even the dorms never have more than six beds; every room has its own en-suite bathroom, a rarity in the world of Eurohostelling. Some of the rooms are wheelchair accessible, too, and some have televisions. Staff is incredibly friendly, the place is spotless, good meals are served—and you can actually have fun here in the common rooms talking with people! It's so unlike a YHA hostel we almost fell over in surprise.

Best bet for a bite: Rusholme neighborhood (Indian)

Insiders' tip: Hacienda dance club nearby

Gestalt: Manchester United

Hospitality: 

Cleanliness: 

Party index:

As a bonus, it's right across the road from the good Museum of Science and Industry, which charts the Industrial Revolution and central England's crucial role in it.

As a city, Manchester's definitely on the comeback trail after years of industrial gray. Despite the smog and bricks, you can find tons of veggie eats, pubs, gay culture, bars, and a pumpin' music scene. Raves that the likes of Madonna might drop in for (at the Hacienda dance club), beers at any of a hundred pubs (the Ox Noble and the White Lion next door are great), gardens, universities, a Roman fort . . . the list goes on and on.

Tack on Europe's best Indian food—a mile-long strip of curry houses—and you'll be sticking around at least a night or two. This place is getting' fun.

How to get there:

By bus: From Piccadilly Gardens take 33 bus to hostel. From main bus station walk 1 mile to hostel, behind Castlefield Hotel, or take Metro to G-Mex Centre and walk along Liverpool Road to Potato Wharf on left; turn left and walk to hostel on left. Take cab at night.

By car: Call hostel for directions.

By train: From Deansgate Station walk to Chester Road, then turn left at Liverpool Road; take next left. Hostel is on left, behind Castlefield Hotel. From Piccadilly Station walk 1 mile through city center, following signs to Castlefield/Museum of Science and Industry, or take Metrolink to G-Mex station and walk 2 blocks up Bridgewater and Liverpool to hostel. Hostel is behind Castlefield Hotel. Take cab at night.

PEPPERS HOSTEL

17 Great Stone Road, Stretford, Manchester M32 0ZP

Phone Number: 010370–303009

Rates: £8.00 per person (about $12 US)
Beds: 14
Affiliation: None
Extras: TV, breakfast ($), laundry, coffee

Another Manchester hostel, this one's much smaller than the hip and modern YHA joint, and it's way out in the suburbs. Only worth checking if the other one's full, though it's surely more laid back. And it's located—surely on purpose—very near the soccer stadium (only they call it "football") where Manchester's home team plays before raucous crowds.

Party index:

How to get there:

By bus: Call hostel for transit route.
By car: Call hostel for directions.
By train: Call hostel for transit route.

MATLOCK HOSTEL 

40 Bank Road, Matlock, Derbyshire DE4 3NF

Phone Number: 01629–582983

Fax: 01629–583484
Rates: £6.55–£9.75 per HI member (about $10–$15 US); doubles £21.50 (about $32 US)
Beds: 49
Season: January 1 to December 23
Affiliation: HI-YHA
Extras: TV, laundry, bike storage, meeting room, game room, dinner ($)
Lockout: 10:00 A.M.–1:00 P.M.

You'd better book ahead if you're rolling into the Peaks District on a summer weekend, because this place is internationally famous among hostellers-in-the-know.

Matlock Hostel

Matlock, England

(photo by Paul Karr)

It's a decent place, blessed with good staff and a good mix of English and non-English hostellers. Dorm rooms with international themes in the Victorian house hold up to nine beds, and there are four couples' rooms for sweethearts who just can't get enough of each other. Families are especially well taken care of here: There are triples (£29.50, about $45 US), quads (£35.50, about $54 US), and bigger rooms suited for them, and the village has stuff like a swimming pool and cinema. Take care with the bunk beds though, they are quite low and not suitable for tall people.

Best bet for a bite: Natural foods market

Insiders' tip: Norwegian room has great view

Gestalt: Peak experience

Hospitality:

Cleanliness:

Party index:

Dinnertime means one of the hostel's renowned meals, scrumptious and affordable. There's a TV room that's always tuned to some news station; the lockout is mercifully brief; and public transportation comes really close. That's about all you could ask for in a hostel (except maybe a hot tub).

Matlock's not the greatest place to land for the night, though; a nice little park on a river was about the only living thing that interested us here. There's also a really scenic hike up to a wildlife preserve inside a castle! And you can see the castle from your bedroom if you've got the right one. Lots of bus connections and a train station also converge here.

How to get there:

By bus: From bus station walk ¼ mile to roundabout, left on Bank Road, to hostel on right.

By car: Take A6 to Matlock. From Crown Square go 200 yards up Bank Road to hostel on right.

By train: From Matlock Station walk ¼ mile across river to hostel.

OLD SCHOOL HOSTEL

Old School, Meerbrook, Leek, Staffordshire ST13 8SJ

Phone Number: 01538–300148

Rates: £4.45–£6.50 per HI member (about $8.00–$12.00 US)
Beds: 22
Family/private rooms: Sometimes
Season: Call ahead for open days
Affiliation: HI-YHA
Extras: Bike storage

Two big and two small dorm rooms make up this smallish hostel, once the schoolhouse for Meerbrook village. Consider yourself lucky to have a kitchen and bathroom. Most people are here on their way to climb the Roaches or ramble around looking into Staffordshire's various museums and pottery kilns.

Note that you're calling Mrs. Nettel in Upperhulme to book, though, instead of the hostel itself; so pleeeeease don't ring her at 3:00 A.M. or she might throw this book at us. Ouch! Hey, we were only kidding!

Gestalt: School days

Party index:

How to get there:

By bus: From Sheffield take X23 bus to Blackshaw Moor and walk 2 miles to hostel.

By car: From A53 turn off main road at Three Horseshoes pub toward Meerbrook. Pass reservoir and enter village; hostel is on right, just past pub.

By train: From Stoke-on-Trent Station take X23 bus to Blackshaw Moor and walk 2 miles to hostel.

RAVENSTOR HOSTEL

Millers Dale, Buxton, Derbyshire SK17 8SS

Phone Number: 01298–871826

Fax: 01298–871275
Rates: £6.55–£9.75 per HI member (about $10–$15 US)
Beds: 82
Private/family rooms: Sometimes

Season: January 1 to October 31
Affiliation: HI-YHA
Extras: TV, bike storage, dinner ($), fireplace, store

Lovely setting is the appeal here. This National Trust historic home—once the home of a local mill owner—stands above the River Wye in plenty of woods. Dorms come in many sizes, from two (yes) to twenty beds (yikes); the place is fairly remote, so it's either empty or full with schoolkids. Staff was right friendly, and the showers were super: strong and hot after a hard day of hiking. They also offer dinner in addition to the option of using the kitchen and even sell beer with meals.

Best bet for a bite: In-hostel grub

Insiders' tip: Great wildflowers in spring

Gestalt: Raven haven

Hospitality:

Cleanliness:

Party index:

Best thing to do in the area, we'd say from a look-see, is to check out the White Peak Way. After all, the hostel overlooks great scenery—and a hiking trail built over old railroad tracks passes right by. You can walk from here to Eyam (the Plague village), Castleton, and Buxton.

How to get there:

By bus: Call hostel for transit route.

By car: Take A6 to B6049, exit, continue to Millers Dale; hostel is 1 mile east.

By train: Buxton Station, 8 miles away, is nearest. Bus available; call hostel for transit route.

MILTON KEYNES HOSTEL

Manor Farm, Vicarage Road, Bradwell (Milton Keynes)

MK13 9AJ

Phone Number: 01908–310944

Fax: 01908–310944
Rates: £5.40–£8.00 per HI member (about $8.00–$12.00 US)
Beds: 38
Season: March 31 to September 5
Affiliation: HI-YHA
Extras: Locker, bike storage, catering for groups

This seventeenth-century farmhouse overlooks earthworks for a former Norman Castle. It's actually a little ways outside Milton Keynes proper, in the suburbs; popular local attractions include cycling the local paths or following the Grand Union Canal into the countryside.

For sleeping, there's one single room (catch it if you can) plus six other rooms ranging from four to ten bunks apiece. This is also the office for group-booking lots of the smaller English hostels during wintertime, so jot down that number if you're bringing a horde.

How to get there:

By bus: Call hostel for transit route.

By car: Take A55 to A422, then turn into Bradwell. From M1, take Junction 14 exit; follow A509 to central Milton Keynes, then take V6 north, following signs to Bradwell.

By train: Milton Keynes Station is ¾ mile from hostel.

Party index:

NORWICH HOSTEL

112 Turner Road, Norwich NR2 4HB

Phone Number: 01603–627647

Fax: 01603–629075
Rates: £5.95–£8.80 per HI member (about $9.00–$13.00 US); doubles £19.50 (about $30 US)
Credit cards: Yes
Beds: 66
Season: January 5 to December 21
Affiliation: HI-YHA
Extras: TV, bike storage, dinner ($)
Lockout: 10:00 A.M. to 5:00 P.M.

$

Thumbs up to this hostel, placed a mile or two outside Norwich center in a pleasant enough area. Couples' rooms are an outstanding bargain, and the rest of the place is just as nice. Dorm rooms are kept small and intimate without being shoeboxes. There's even a reading room in addition to the usual TV-lounge combo.

Don't forget to see one of an unbelievable thirty-three medieval churches within city limits, including an absolutely amazing cathedral. Norwich has really improved in recent years as a nightspot; social aspects apart, it has always been a nice place to explore: lots of hidden buildings and little suprise streets. There's a canal as well, so if you fancy a trip to the area this good hostel is a good place to start from.

Party index:

How to get there:

By bus: Bus station downtown, 1 mile from hostel; call hostel for transit route.

By car: From A47 or Outer Ring Road exit onto A1074 going toward center of city. Make immediate left onto Waterworks Road; hostel is short distance farther, on right, at corner of Turner Road.

By train: Norwich Station is 2 miles from hostel.

IGLOO HOSTEL

110 Mansfield Road, Nottingham NG1 3HL

Phone Number: 0115–947–5250

Rates: £8.50 per person (about $13 US)
Beds: 34
Office hours: Call hostel for hours
Affiliation: None
Extras: TV

This place's obvious attraction is its closeness to Sherwood Forest and all that, plus an abbey. Otherwise, Nottingham's so-so as a destination—though suprisingly hip and hippie.

The hostel occupies a Victorian home divided into bunkrooms, and its chief selling point is the pub right across the street. Management is relaxed.

Gestalt: North pole

Party index:

How to get there:

By bus: Call hostel for transit route.
By car: Call hostel for directions.
By train: Call hostel for transit route.

OXFORD YOUTH HOSTEL

32 Jack Straw's Lane, Oxford, Oxfordshire OX3 0DW

Phone Number: 01865–62997

Fax: 01865–69402
Rates: £6.55–£9.75 per HI member (about $10–$15 US)
Credit cards: Yes
Beds: 112
Affiliation: HI-YHA
Extras: TV, laundry, camping, dinner ($), pool tables

Two words: Book early. Real early.

Okay, wise guy, that's four words. But you'd better listen, because this big Victorian building is wildly popular; show up last-minute and you don't have a chance. First thing in the morning might land you a bunk, but be ready with backup plans.

What's amazing, though, is that this perpetually packed joint's staff manages to keep things moving. Dorms are mostly six- to eight-bed affairs, tightly packed of course, with a few closely watched doubles. There's a lounge, campground, that good hostel food—and great kitchen facilities, too.

Really nice surroundings, too. Oxford is a little overtouristed for our tastes, but years of hype will do that to you. The colleges are amazing, of course, if you can get a look at 'em, as is the Bodleian Library—which has sought to archive every book printed in the British Empire since, well, the printing press. A refreshing antidote to some of that crap on the Internet, we say: a place that worships the written word.

Insiders' tip:
Botanic gardens are great

Hospitality:

Cleanliness:

Party index:

How to get there:

By bus: From downtown take 13 or 14 bus to Jack Straw's Lane.

By car: Take A40 ring road to Headington roundabout; exit onto London Road, turn right at White Horse Pub. Hostel is on left, ¼ mile along.

By train: Oxford Station is 2½ miles away.

WOODY'S TOP HOSTEL

Woody's Top, Ruckland, Louth Lincolnshire LN11 7RF

Phone Number: 01507–533323

Rates: £4.45–£6.50 (about $7.00–$10.00 US) per HI member
Beds: 22
Season: March 23 to September19
Affiliation: HI-YHA
Extras: Bike storage, woodstove

These converted farm buildings make up a simple-as-pie hostel, a rather quiet and sedate retreat from which to base explorations of East Anglia towns. Dorms come in five rooms.

Gestalt:
Woody

Party index:

How to get there:

By bus: Call hostel for transit route.

By car: From A16 take road toward Ruckland, then turn left at crossroads; hostel is 100 yards farther, on right.

By train: Grimbsy Town Station is 22 miles away; take 25, 51, or Z21 bus to area, then walk 6 miles to hostel.

SAFFRON WALDEN HOSTEL

1 Myddylton Place, Saffron Waldon, Essex CB10 1BB

Phone Number: 01799–523117

Fax: 01799–520840
Rates: £5.40–£8.00 per HI member (about $8.00–$12.00 US)
Beds: 40
Season: Call ahead for open days
Affiliation: HI-YHA
Extras: Dinner ($), bike storage, garden

Formerly a brewery maltings, this hostel is just off downtown of a little village. Its courtyard garden is popular, though the two big dorm rooms aren't. A good place to get a cheap bed in the area if Cambridge, 15 miles distant, is booked solid.

Insiders' tip: Get lost—in the local maze

Party index:

How to get there:

By bus: Call hostel for transit route.

By car: Call hostel for directions.

By train: Audley End Station is 2½ miles away; from station take 59 bus to Saffron Walden. Hostel is ½ mile north of bus stop, just off B184 on Myddylton Place.

SHERINGHAM HOSTEL

1 Cremer's Drift, Sheringham, Norfolk NR26 8HX

Phone Number: 01263–823215

Fax: 01263–824679
Rates: £6.55–£9.75 per HI member (about $10–$15 US); doubles £21 (about $32 US)
Credit cards: Yes
Beds: 109
Private/family rooms: Yes
Season: Call ahead for open days
Office hours: 7:00 A.M. to noon; 1:00 to 10:30 P.M.
Affiliation: HI-YHA
Extras: TV, bike storage, meals ($), restaurant, game room, meeting rooms

This place, built for tree-huggers and leaf-peepers and little ones, satisfies even the crustiest, baddest hosteller. Don't expect a party, but if you want Mother Nature and some snazzy digs, this is your joint. Designed as a center for Field Study and set on a quiet street, it's really nice.

Party index:

Accommodation at the YHA Centre is in the usual single-sex bunkrooms, but an unusual number of couples' and family rooms are also available—some, even, with en-suite bathrooms. Hallelujah! Bed-and-breakfast packages are available, too.

The sharp staff here hosts special events on Christmas and New Year's; there's a licensed restaurant serving breakfast and dinner. And—we love this—there are six special rooms outfitted for wheelchair. Bravo!

School groups often swamp the place, however, since it's so nice and located in this great little not-too-touristy town. That's probably because of the seminar and meeting rooms they've got; not that you care, but you can hire 'em out. There's a nature study room, too.

A local steam railway and theatre company are other cultural options, should you tire of throngs of schoolkids.

How to get there:

By bus: From bus station walk less than ¼ mile to hostel.

By car: Take A149 to to St. Joseph's Church; hostel is behind church.

By train: From Sheringham Station walk less than ¼ mile to hostel.

THE WOODLANDS HOSTEL

Abbey Foregate, Shrewsbury, Shropshire SY2 6LZ

Phone Number: 01743–357423

Fax: 01743–357423
Rates: £5.40–£8.00 per HI member (about $8.00–$12.00 US)
Beds: 60
Season: February 1 to October 31
Affiliation: HI-YHA
Extras: TV, porch, laundry, bike storage, lockers, dinner ($)
Lockout: 10:00 A.M.–5:00 P.M.
Curfew: 11:00 P.M.

We've reserved a special place in our heart for Shrewsbury—a great town that's visited, as it should be, but not swamped. And the sights here are among our favorite in all of England. The city's closeness to some of Wales' finest scenery is key, too.

But what about the hostel? Well, this former ironmasters' house built of red stone is pretty well stocked with a laundry, lounge, television, even a porch to while away those daytime lockout blues. Nine dorm rooms split up bunk duty, some as big as ten beds and others just quads, which are quite manageable.

Party index:

How to get there:

By bus: Call hostel for transit route.

By car: Take A49 to Shrewsbury, then follow signs to Abbey. Hostel is just off A49 on Abbey Foregate, sign-posted from Abbey.

By train: From Shrewsbury Station walk 1 mile to hostel.

SLIMBRIDGE HOSTEL

Shepherd's Patch, Slimbridge, Gloucestershire GL2 7BP

Phone Number: 01453–890275

Fax: 01453–890625
Rates: £6.55–£9.75 per HI member (about $10–$15 US); doubles £22 (about $33 US)
Beds: 56
Private/family rooms: Yes
Season: February 1 to December 31
Affiliation: HI-YHA
Extras: Store, laundry, bike storage, game room

Fairly well equipped, including a laundry, this joint maintains a pond; big windows give you views of waterfowl, and that gives you some idea of what this place is like.

Dorms contain four to ten beds, plus there are five double rooms that sometimes go fast to couples. Otherwise, it's off to the kitchen, hostel store, lounge, or game room. For something to do during the daytime, the popular and fun Cotswold Way walking trail is nearby.

Party index:

How to get there:

By bus: From Bristol take 308 bus or from Gloucester, take 91 or 308 bus to Slimbridge roundabout. Walk 1½ miles through town to Tudor Arms pub, turn right to hostel.

By car: Take A38 to Slimbridge roundabout, exit, drive through village; turn right at Tudor Arms pub. Hostel is on right.

By train: Cam & Dursley Station, 3 miles, is closest. From Gloucester Station, take 91 bus to Slimbridge roundabout; walk 1½ miles through town to Tudor Arms pub, turn right to hostel.

STOW-ON-THE-WOLD HOSTEL

The Square, Stow-on-the-Wold, Cheltenham, Gloucestershire GL54 1AF

Phone Number: 01451–830497

Fax: 01451–870102
Rates: £5.40–£8.00 per HI member (about $8.00–$12.00 US)
Beds: 56
Season: February 13 to October 31
Affiliation: HI-YHA
Extras: TV, dinner ($), laundry, bike storage
Lockout: 10:00 A.M.–5:00 P.M.

Located right on the main drag of cute little Stow, this nice place is the ideal base for hitting the Cotswolds.

Best bet for a bite: The Organic Shop

Insiders' tip: Walk to Oddington pub

Gestalt: Wold party

Party index:

The hostel is stuck next to a pub—appropriate, since it used to be a brewhouse itself.

It's a sixteenth-century building, with dorm rooms of all sizes. Amenities like a laundry, television, and meal service give it the nudge over simpler joints around this part of England, especially if you've been walking from Bourton or the Slaughters.

As a destination, Stow is great—one of the cutest of the Cotswold villages, but not completely crazed with tourists. It's also quite centrally positioned for exploring less-touristed villages: Walk any direction from town and you'll hit one within a couple miles. Two or three good pubs, two natural foods stores, a top-notch tourist office . . . well, it's just fine.

We can't overemphasize the number of things to do in the Cotswold Hills, either, a truly quaint area. We love walking the field pathways here, which are public domain by English law, and checking out pubs and shops in places like Broadwell, Oddington, Chipping Camden, and Lower Slaughter. However, be aware that the English themselves also love this area—so meal prices get a little steep.

How to get there:

By bus: From Cheltenham Spa or Moreton-in-Marsh, take Pulhams bus to Stow.

By car: Take A429 or A424 to Stow-on-the-Wold. Hostel is in center of village, across from green, between White Hart and Old Stocks Hotel.

By train: Moreton-in-Marsh, 4 miles away. Walk or take Pulhams bus to Stow.

HEMMINGFORD HOUSE HOSTEL 

Alveston (Stratford-upon-Avon), Warwickshire CV37 7RG

Phone Number: 01789–297093

Fax: 01789–205513
Rates: £10.05–£13.45 per HI member (about $15–$20 US)
Beds: 130
Private/family rooms: Yes
Season: January 5 to December 15
Affiliation: HI-YHA
Extras: Breakfast, TV, game room, laundry, bike storage, bureau de change, meals ($)

This hostel is a lovely stroll from overly schlocky Stratford-upon-Avon, but a long one—not something you'd want to try navigating late at night, especially since you'd miss the wonderful architecture along the way. And certainly not with lots of stuff. Fortunately, buses make the run once an hour.

Insiders' tip:
Dirty Duck pub

Gestalt:
Milk Shakespeare

Party index:

It's a good enough place, though very expensive as hostels go. And there's a definite sense that they're out to milk you of your every last dime: Towel rentals cost 50 pence (almost a dollar US), and you must pay for breakfast with room—even if you don't want it! They also sell the tackiest imaginable souvenirs at the front desk.

Room setups vary, as usual: There are eight doubles—some with en-suite bathrooms—seven quads, and ten even larger rooms. In high season, of course, you'll struggle to find anything at all unless you call way-y-y-y ahead. The in-house cafeteria serves up breakfast and dinners, which cost even more than the breakfasts. At least you can mix and match the food to your heart's content. Other amenities include a much-needed laundry, game room, and lounge with a telly. That's a television, Yank.

What to do in Stratford? Don't get us started. See the Shakespeare stuff if you must; everyone and his or her brother come here to madly shove their way around some fairly lukewarm attractions, so you'll have plenty of company. The town itself is only so-so, much too commercial and not great at all. Only the Royal Shakespeare Theatre, the river, and a few obscure sights are really worth seeing. We're outta here at dawn, heading for the pretty Cotswolds nearby.

How to get there:

By bus: From Stratford-upon-Avon or Leamington Spa, take 18 bus to Alveston.

By car: From M40 take Junction 15 to A429 south. Follow signs to Charlecote Park, turn right onto B4086 and go 2 miles; hostel is on right. From downtown Stratford's Clopton Bridge, take B4086 (Wellesbourne Road) 1½ miles to hostel on left.

By train: Stratford-upon-Avon Station, 2½ miles; walk or take 18 bus to Alveston.

THURLBY HOSTEL

16 High Street, Thurlby, Bourne, Lincolnshire PE10 0EE

Phone Number: 01778–425588

Fax: 01778–425588
Rates: £5.40–£8.00 per HI member (about $8.00–$12.00 US)
Beds: 34
Season: March 30 to October 31
Affiliation: HI-YHA
Extras: Camping, shop, bike storage, gardens

Once a forge, this fifteenth-century building is now—with its annex—a small hostel. Five dorm rooms split up the bunks; nice lawns and gardens, as well as a good campsite, are also here. We'd recommend that you hit the Viking Way if you're hankering to hike some; you're sure to find stone villages and woods galore.

Best bet for a bite: Horseshoe Pub

Insiders' tip: Find some Wool Churches

Party index:

How to get there:

By bus: From Peterborough take Delaine's bus to Thurlby, get off at pub, walk ¼ mile up High Street to hostel.

By car: From Peterborough or Bourne take A15 to Thurlby; turn off main road into High Street at sign.

By train: Peterborough Station, 13 miles away, is closest; take Delaine's bus to Thurlby, get off at pub, walk ¼ mile up High Street to hostel.

MALTHOUSE FARM HOSTEL

Wheathill, Bridgnorth, Shropshire WV16 6QT

Phone Number: 0174633–236

Rates: £4.00–£5.85 per HI member (about $6.00–$9.00 US)
Beds: 28
Affiliation: HI-YHA
Extras: Laundry, bike storage, snack shop, store, camping

$

This is a good bargain if you don't mind the absence of showers —the cheapest hostel in south England is actually pretty nice, that flaw notwithstanding. Management goes the extra mile with

Party index:

touches like a hot snack shop, campground, lounge, store, and laundry.

This was once part of a seventeenth-century farm; now it's within a short distance of several good walking trails and an old church that dates even further back, back to the swingin' 1100s. Really. Honest. They swung.

How to get there:

By bus: From Hereford or Birmingham take 192 or 292 bus to Hopton Bank, 5 miles away. No public transport.

By car: From Bridgnorth or Ludlow take B4364 to Wheatmill. At Three Horse Shoes pub, turn east. Go 1 mile; hostel is on right.

By train: Ludlow Station, 9 miles away, is nearest.

YOULGREAVE HOSTEL 

Fountain Square, Youlgreave, Bakewell, Derbyshire DE4 1UR

Phone Number: 01629–636518

Fax: 01629–636518
Rates: £5.40–£8.00 per HI member (about $8.00–$12.00 US)
Beds: 46
Private/family rooms: Yes
Season: Call ahead for open days
Affiliation: HI-YHA
Extras: Dinner ($), bike storage

Newly renovated, this three-story hostel has added family rooms to a previously basic setup. The new manager has also proudly decked the place out in early 1900s-era fittings, and the meals served here are rapidly gaining notice on the hostel circuit. Dorm rooms contain four to eight beds, and the kitchen and common area are just as you'd expect them to be. Quad rooms for £30.50 (about $45 US) are an especially good deal.

Gestalt: Youl love it

Party index:

Lots of walking in the limestone dales here; in fact, two other hostels—Bakewell and Elton—are just 3 miles away, and the great Matlock joint rewards a 10-mile jaunt. Also check the history of this place—it used to be a cooperative store where workers owned the place, and it harkens back to a simpler, more useful ideal that's very much in tune with hostelling.

How to get there:

By bus: From Bakewell or Matlock take 170 or 171 bus to Youlgreave.

By car: Take A6 to B5056. Turn off for Youlgreave; hostel is in center of village, across from Fountain Well.

By train: From Matlock Station take 170 or 171 bus to Youlgreave.

ORTHERN ENGLA D

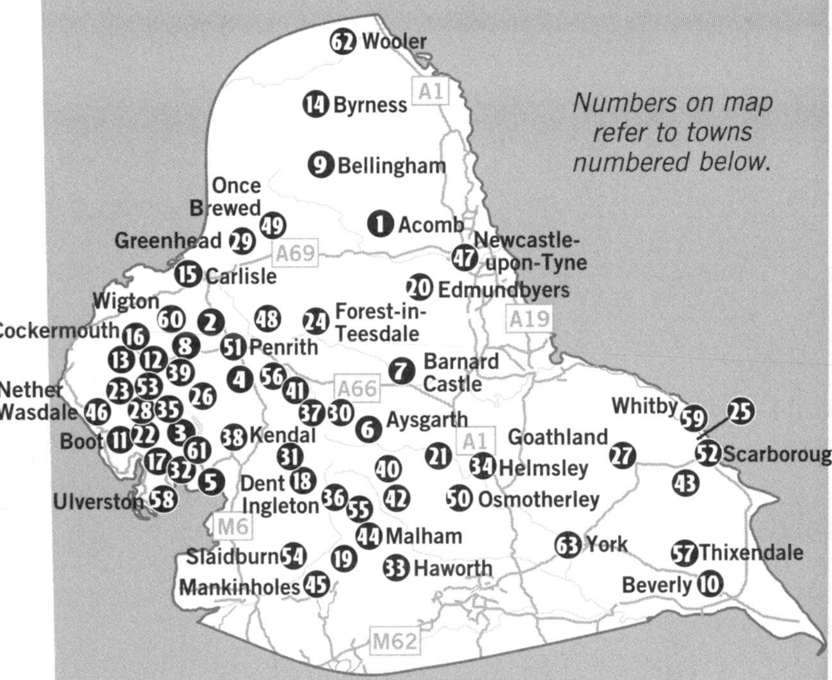

1. Acomb
2. Alston
3. Ambleside
4. Appleby
5. Arnside
6. Aysgarth
7. Barnard Castle
8. Bassenthwaite
9. Bellingham
10. Beverley
11. Boot
12. Borrowdale
13. Buttermere
14. Byrness
15. Carlisle
16. Cockermouth
17. Coniston
18. Dent
19. Earby
20. Edmundbyers
21. Ellingstring
22. Elterwater
23. Ennerdale
24. Forest-in-Teesdale
25. Fylingthorpe
26. Glenridding
27. Goathland
28. Grasmere
29. Greenhead
30. Grinton
31. Hawes
32. Hawkshead
33. Haworth
34. Helmsley
35. High Close
36. Ingleton
37. Keld
38. Kendal
39. Keswick
40. Kettlewell
41. Kirkby Stephen
42. Linton-in-Crave
43. Lockton
44. Malham
45. Mankinholes
46. Nether Wasdale
47. Newcastle-upon-Tyne
48. Ninebanks
49. Once Brewed
50. Osmotherley
51. Penrith
52. Scarborough
53. Seatoller
54. Slaidburn
55. Stainforth
56. Tebay
57. Thixendale
58. Ulverston
59. Whitby
60. Wigton
61. Windermere
62. Wooler
63. York

NORTHERN ENGLAND

Northern England comprises a big area, and there are a lot of hostels here—especially in the Lake District, a lovely area of big bodies of water. Just remember before you come that most of the Lake District hostels are closed some day or days of the week; it varies wildly, but you can be sure—if you come in spring and fall, especially—that some of the hostels listed in this book will not be open on the day when you're there. Make sure to check ahead!

A nice touch here is that YHA runs a shuttle bus from hostel-to-hostel (and to parts in between) around the Lakes. You get picked up at at the Windermere train station; call 015394–32304 for more information.

There's also a system of camping barns in the area, an extremely rural experience if you're into roughing it: You throw your tent on the floor of a barn, and a farmer sometimes sells you eggs. Water and toilets are all you get, but it can be fun.

ACOMB HOSTEL

Main Street, Acomb, Hexham, Northumberland NE46 4PL

Phone Number: 01434–602864

Rates: £4.00–£5.85 per HI member (about $6.00–$9.00 US)
Beds: 36
Season: Call ahead for open days
Affiliation: HI-YHA
Extras: bike storage
Lockout: 10:00 A.M.–5:00 P.M.
Curfew: 11:30 P.M.

This hostel, a couple miles from Hadrian's Wall, might be a better choice than the Once Brewed hostel, perpetually overrun with school groups. Former stables have been fashioned into two big bunkrooms and a third, smaller quad room. Kitchen and common area are standard-issue; bathrooms are outside in a separate building.

Party index:

How to get there:

By bus: From Hexham take 880 or 882 bus to Acomb; from Carlisle or Newcastle take 685 bus to Hexham, then walk 2½ miles or switch to 880 or 882 bus to Acomb.

By car: From Newcastle take A69 1 mile past Bridge End roundabout, turn right at A6079, then make right at Acomb Village sign, then take Main Street uphill to hostel.

By train: From Hexham Station walk 2 miles or switch to 880 or 882 bus to Acomb.

ALSTON HOSTEL

The Firs, Alston, Cumbria, CA9 3RW

Phone Number: 01434–381509

Fax: 01434–381509
Rates: £5.40–£8.00 per HI member (about $8.00–$12.00 US)
Beds: 30
Season: March 27 to October 31
Affiliation: HI-YHA
Extras: Dinner ($), bike storage

This hostel's located in prime strategic position on both the Pennine Way walking trail and the Sea-to-Sea cycle trail. Four dorm rooms contain four to eight beds apiece; dinner is served in the dining room each night. Real adventurers head for Cross Fell, the tallest peak around here at almost 3,000 feet high.

Party index:

How to get there:

By bus: From Halwhistle take 681 bus; from Penrith take 888 bus.

By car: Take A689 or A686 to Alston; at south end of village, turn into The Firs, then make first right at top of bank.

By train: From Halwhistle Station take 681 bus; from Penrith Station take 888 bus.

AMBLESIDE HOSTEL

Waterhead, Ambleside, Cumbria LA22 0EU

Phone Number: 015394–32304

Fax: 015394–34408
Rates: £7.30–£10.70 per HI member (about $11–$16 US); doubles £26 (about $39 US)
Beds: 245
Private/family rooms: Yes
Office hours: 7:15 A.M. to midnight
Affiliation: HI-YHA
Extras: Dinner ($), coffeeshop, bar, bike rentals, laundry, TV, game room, travel agency, bureau de change
Lockout: 11:30 P.M.

If you're looking for a quaint and quirky hostel owned by an eccentric, Wellie-wearing Englishman, where the breakfast milk comes

Ambleside Hostel

Ambleside, England

(photo courtesy of HI-YHA)

straight from the cow and the evenings are filled with cozy campfire entertainment, you won't find it here. With 226 beds, Ambleside's hostel is as big as . . . well, a big youth hostel, but it's also as efficient as the manager's well-organized Filofax.

This bastion of smooth operation began life as an Edwardian hotel. Informal gardens slope down to the waterfront and private jetty; it's only a ten-second walk to the pleasures of duck feeding and dabbling toes in the cold gray waters of Lake Windermere.

Best bet for a bite: In town

Insiders' tip: Shower at night

Gestalt: Ambler

Hospitality:

Cleanliness: 

Party index: 

Having been recently refurbished, the interior is now modern, if a little too functional. Three floors of rooms vary in size from two to eight beds and family rooms are available. Bunkrooms consist of forty-three rooms with two to five beds each, and sixteen rooms with six to eight beds each; the private rooms are especially nice, some of them with sweeping views of the lake. Industrial showers and toilets are well within streaking distance.

The kitchen's especially good at handling the load of hostellers, and they also serve decent dinners—with liquor if you like—from 5:30 to 7:30 each night. Nice. Further conveniences include a good laundry, rented bikes for tooling around the area, game rooms, lounges, and a quiet room.

This hostel is so big it even has its own restaurant, the Lakeside, which serves breakfast, lunch, and dinner and will provide packed meals if you're going out for the day. The place also has a full wine and beer list, but the pub has a fuller one and better atmosphere to boot. If the restaurant feels too school cafeteria-like, well, there's an excellent self-catering kitchen, too.

Management seem really helpful and offer many services: tourist information, a bureau de change, ticket agency, bike rental, reservations for other hostels, and so on and on and on.

Location? The town center is a short walk away, the steamer boat pier is right next the hostel, and there's a bus stop close by. It's an ideal base for exploring the South Lakes, with lots of water sports and outdoor activities all accessible from here. Just be warned that this place is very popular with school groups and families—if you don't feel up to being surrounded by fourteen year olds, it may be best to avoid the end of June or beginning of July.

This is still more hotel than hostel, but the trade-off of character for efficiency and comfort is sometimes worth it. Besides, any place that advertises "duck food" has to have some potential.

Ignore the hugeness—it's big because it has to be, since everyone wants to be here in this lakeside location. This could be the best hostel in the Lake District.

How to get there:

By bus: Take Cumberland bus to Windermere. From Windermere Station, take YHA shuttle bus or walk 1 mile to hostel.

By car: Drive A591 to Ambleside, continue 1 mile south of village; hostel is at Waterhead, next to Steamer Pier on lake.

By train: From Windermere Station, 4 miles away, take YHA shuttle bus or walk 1 mile to hostel.

REDSTONES HOSTEL

Dufton, Appleby, Cumbria CA16 6DB

Phone Number: 017863–51236

Fax: 017683–51236
Rates: £5.40–£8.00 per HI member (about $8.00–$12.00 US)
Beds: 36
Season: Call ahead for open days.
Affiliation: HI-YHA
Extras: Garden, dinner ($), bike storage, ski rentals, outings

Another hikers' and bikers' hostel, this one is a stone house on the green in Dufton—yet another quaint village. (No, this is not a replay.) One plus here is the additional focus on skiing: You can rent cross-country skis and take a class in winter. As for the building, five dorms do the job adequately. Dinner service and a small garden are bonus perks.

Party index:

How to get there:

By car: Take A66 to Appleby, follow signs to Long Marton and Dufton for 3½ miles. Hostel is in village center.

By train: From Appleby Station walk 3½ miles to hostel.

OAKFIELD LODGE

Redhills Road, Arnside, Carnforth, Lancashire LA5 0AT

Phone Number: 01524–761781

Fax: 01524–762589

Rates: £5.95–£8.80 per HI member (about $9.00–$13.00 US); doubles £20.50 (about $32 US)

Beds: 72

Private/family rooms: Yes

Season: Call ahead for open days

Affiliation: HI-YHA

Extras: TV, garden, game room, dinner ($), bike storage, bike rentals

This prettily located hostel sits on the Kent estuary, a mixing of salty and fresh waters. Rooms range in size from two to nine beds, and they serve dinner each night at 7:00 P.M. for a charge. Lots of common space here, too—a game room, a sitting room, a television room, a map room . . . lots of room. They rent bicycles at the front desk, too.

Party index:

How to get there:

By bus: From Kendal take 552 bus to Arnside.

By car: Take M6 to junction 35 or 36, then take A6 to Milnthorpe. Take B5282 to Arnside, turning right at T-stop. Continue through village; hostel is on right.

By train: From Arnside Station walk 1 mile to hostel.

KEY TO ICONS

Attractive natural setting	Comfortable beds	Especially well suited for families
Ecologically aware hostel	Editors' choice: among our very favorite hostels	Good for active travelers
Superior kitchen facilities or cafe	A particularly good value	Visual arts at hostel or nearby
Offbeat or eccentric place	Wheelchair accessible	Music at hostel or nearby
Superior bathroom facilities	Good for business travelers	Great hostel for skiers
Romantic private rooms		Bar or pub at hostel or nearby

AYSGARTH FALLS HOSTEL

Aysgarth, Leyburn, North Yorkshire DL8 3SR

Phone Number: 01969–663260

Fax: 01969–663110
Rates: £5.40–£8.80 per HI member (about $8.00–$13.00 US); doubles £20 (about $30 US)
Beds: 67
Season: Call ahead for open days
Affiliation: HI-YHA
Extras: TV, game room, bike storage

This place is big enough to handle the hordes of schoolkids or hikers who might descend on it, putting them in twelve rooms of just three to eight beds apiece. Dinner is served, and there's a television room for the perpetually bored.

Gestalt: True falls

Party index:

Most hostellers here want to walk the Heriot Way. Still others hit Bolton Castle, which (as every Brit history major knows) is the place Mary Queen of Scots was imprisoned for a time.

How to get there:

By bus: Call hostel for transit route.

By car: Take A684 to Aysgarth Village. Hostel is ½ mile east of village center.

By train: Garsdale Station, 16 miles away, is closest.

BALDERSDALE HOSTEL

Blackton, Baldersdale, Barnard Castle, Co. Durham DL12 9UP

Phone Number: 01833–50629

Fax: 01833–650629
Rates: £4.95–£7.20 per HI member (about $7.00–$11.00 US)
Beds: 40
Season: Call ahead for open days
Affiliation: HI-YHA
Extras: TV, dinner ($), bike storage, store, game room

Gestalt: Balderdash

Party index:

Pretty simple, this stone farmhouse. Seven dorm rooms, a TV, a small store for basic foodstuffs, a kitchen. You know the drill. Dinner is thrown in as a possible option, too. It's right on the Pennine Way and not far from the bigger village of Barnard Castle.

But it's pretty hard to get here by public transit, making it unlikely you'll get here unless you're either walking the Way or driving four wheels.

How to get there:

By bus: From Darlington take 75A bus to Cotherstone; walk 6 miles to hostel.

By car: Call hostel for directions.

By train: From Darlington Station take 75A bus to Cotherstone; walk 6 miles to hostel.

SKIDDAW HOUSE HOSTEL

Skiddaw Forest, Bassenthwaite, Keswick, Cumbria CA12 4QX

No phone (Call 016974–78325 for information)

Rates: £4.00–£5.85 per HI member (about $6.00–$9.00 US)
Beds: 20
Season: March 27 to October 31
Private/family rooms: Sometimes
Affiliation: HI-YHA
Extras: Bike storage, store

Gestalt: Peak preview

Hospitality: 

Party index:

This former hunting lodge, way up near the top of Skiddaw peak, boasts terrific location but no showers and limited lighting. This is a good place to rough it, as you'll need to hike up to 1,500 feet of elevation to sleep here. Bunkrooms contain four to six beds each, and there's a kitchen and very limited supply shop.

Still wanna stay? Okay, here's the drill. Write or call at least two weeks in advance. Bring a flashlight and the warmest clothes you've got. Don't think you can leave your car nearby. And be prepared for some great long views out over the woods and mountains.

How to get there:

By bus: From Penrith take X5 or 888 bus to Threlkeld and walk 4½ miles to hostel.

By car: Call hostel for directions.

By train: From Penrith Station take X5 or 888 bus to Threlkeld and walk 4½ miles to hostel.

BELLINGHAM HOSTEL

Woodburn Road, Bellingham, Hexham, Northumberland NE48 2ED

Phone Number: 01434–220313

Rates: £4.45–£6.50 per HI member (about $7.00–$10.00 US)
Beds: 34
Season: March 27 to October 31

Affiliation: HI-YHA
Extras: Bike storage
Lockout: 10:00 A.M.–5:00 P.M.
Curfew: 11:00 P.M.

Gestalt: Parking place

Party index:

This teeny-tiny hostel, a cedar building on the Pennine Way, sits above Bellingham. Totally simple, but fairly close at least to Hadrian's Wall and Northumberland Park. Two massive dorms and one smaller one house the bodies; a little kitchen and common area make up the rest of the place.

How to get there:

By bus: From Hexham take 880 bus.

By car: Take B6320 to West Woodburn turnoff, continue on road ¼ mile to hostel on left.

By train: From Hexham Station take 880 bus.

THE FRIARY HOSTEL

Friar's Lane, Beverley, North Humberside HU17 0DF

Phone Number: 01482–881751

Fax: 01482–880118
Rates: £4.95–£7.20 per HI member (about $7.00–$11.00 US)
Beds: 34
Season: March 26 to November 1
Affiliation: HI-YHA
Extras: Dinner ($), bike storage

Gestalt: Deep friary

Party index:

Located in a renovated old friary (read all about the original in the *Canterbury Tales*), this hostel features just three bunkrooms: a triple plus two biggies. There's a pleasant walled garden, and the village minster (church, that is; you know, like Westminster Abbey) is close at hand, as well.

Dinner is served every night, and there's a pub next door for knocking one back. Also of note: This hostel is just 12 miles from the overnight ferry from Hull to Rotterdam, the Netherlands.

How to get there:

By bus: Call hostel for transit route.

By car: Take A164 to Beverley; hostel is ¼ mile southeast of town center.

By train: From Beverley Station walk ½ mile south to hostel.

ESKDALE HOSTEL

Boot, Holmrook, Cumbria CA19 1TH

Phone Number: 019467–23219

Fax: 019467–23163
Rates: £5.95–£8.80 per HI member (about $9.00–$13.00 US); doubles £20 (about $30 US)
Beds: 54
Season: Call ahead for open days
Private/family rooms: Yes
Affiliation: HI-YHA
Extras: Dinner ($), games, classroom, bike storage

Nine dorm rooms make up this hostel, set in the woods and equipped with a classroom and games for kids. Six of the rooms contain two to six beds, so families like the place; three more dormitories have eight to ten beds apiece.

Some hostellers hike into this place via another of the local hostels; it's a rough day's walk, though, and don't try it if you're not fit. Another interesting way to get here is to take the local Ravenglass & Eskdale Railway, a scenic ride of about 10 miles through peaks and passes.

And, yes, the town is named Boot. We didn't get a chance to ask why, but you can.

Gestalt: Boot camp

Party index:

How to get there:

By train: Call hostel for transit route.

By foot: From Wastwater, Coniston Coppermines, or Elterwater hostels, walk 7 to 10 miles by pathway to hostel.

By car: Call hostel for directions.

BORROWDALE HOSTEL

Longthwaite, Borrowdale, Keswick, Cumbria CA12 5UR

Phone Number: 017687–77257

Fax: 017687–77393
Rates: £6.55–£9.75 per HI member (about $10–$15 US)
Beds: 88
Private/family rooms: Yes
Season: February 13 to December 31
Affiliation: HI-YHA
Extras: Dinner ($), bike storage
Lockout: 10:00 A.M –1:00 P.M.

A cedar building on the Coast to Coast and Cumbria Way walking paths, this hotel was recently fixed up some.

It's fairly simple, but they do maintain a kitchen and grounds and serve dinner nightly. And there are plenty of different-sized rooms good for different sizes of families or groups. Plenty of trails strike out from here, obviously, and paddling on the adjacent river is also an option if you've brought a watercraft.

Hospitality: 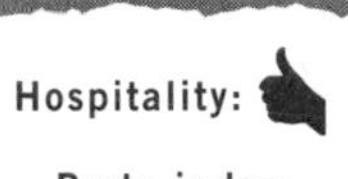

Party index:

How to get there:

By bus: From Keswick take 79 bus to Borrowdale.

By car: From Keswisk take B5289 to Borrowdale.

By train: Penrith Station, 26 miles away, and Windermere Station, 28 miles away, are closest stops; call hostel for transit routes.

DERWENTWATER HOSTEL 

Barrow House, Borrowdale, Keswick, Cumbria CA12 5UR

Phone Number: 01–7687–77246

Fax: 01–7687–77396
Rates: £6.55–£9.75 per HI member (about $10–$15 US)
Credit cards: Yes
Beds: 89
Private/family rooms: None
Season: January 1 to October 31
Office hours: 7:30 A.M. to 10:30 P.M.
Affiliation: HI-YHA
Extras: Dinner ($), bar, laundry, pool table, game room
Curfew: 11:00 P.M.

This old house perched above a lake practically drips atmosphere all over you. Amazing walking opportunities abound, and the facilities are good—some common space, a decent kitchen, and available laundry mean that famlies tend to find this place and use it as a base for holidays. Visiting the Lake District is all about enjoying the stunning countryside—and with that in mind, this is a perfect base.

The building itself is a 200-year-old mansion, designed by famous architect John Adam, so that's all very impressive. Even better are the fifteen acres of grounds that include (drumroll please) a 108-foot waterfall. The hostel is set on a steep slope overlooking the lake, and you couldn't ask for a better view, so that's a great big spit in the eye for those city joints.

The place is comfortable and clean, nicely decorated with a pool room, table tennis room, common rooms, and a dining area. They've managed to stuff eighty-nine beds in, mostly in rooms with five to eight beds apiece. There's one quad room, but beware the big dorm room: Come when they're pretty full and you'll get stuck in this twenty-two-bed monster.

Best bet for a bite: At the hostel

Gestalt: Derwentwater world

Hospitality: 

Cleanliness:

Party index: 

Like at most large English hostels, meals and packed lunches are available. There's a well-stocked kitchen and a small provisions shop at the front desk for those who prefer to cook.

Most rooms accommodate four to eight bodies in bunk-bedded dorms; family rooms are also available. The hostel definitely tries to be the exception to the Lake District's rule of big, boring hostels, and management is keen on explaining that it's a big place with the feel of a small one. (They still douse the lights at 11:00 P.M., though.)

In winter the hostel organizes courses for hiking, mountaineering, even survival . . . all handy for the intrepid backpacker. In summer and fall there are classes in drawing and painting and opportunities to do conservation work in the area with the Lake District National Park staff. So be prepared to get involved.

The highest "mountains" in England are also within reach: Scafell Pike, Skiddaw, and Great Gable among them—if you're up for the challenge. They're mostly just rocky walks or scrambles, but don't underestimate the landscape or climate. Inexperienced walkers who find it too rugged should hit the market town of Keswick nearby instead, which offers a dose of civilization such as it is around here.

How to get there:

By bus: From Keswick take 79 bus to Borrowdale.

By car: From Keswick take B5289 south 2 miles; hostel is on left, 100 yards past left-hand turnoff to Ashness Bridge/Watendlath.

By train: Call hostel for transit route.

KING GEORGE VI MEMORIAL HOSTEL

Buttermere, Cockermouth, Cumbria CA13 9XA

Phone Number: 017687–70245

Fax: 017687–70231
Rates: £5.95–£8.80 per HI member (about $9.00–$13.00 US)
Beds: 70
Private/family rooms: Sometimes
Season: Call ahead for open days
Affiliation: HI-YHA
Extras: Dinner ($)

This is another of the Lake District's quiet hostels, blessed with a waterfall nearby, which is nice. There's not much in town or at the hostel, although they do serve dinner nightly.

Gestalt: By George
Party index:

Accommodations here consist of mostly four- to six-bedded dorms, plus there's one double room for couples. A kitchen and two common rooms round out the operation. Curiously, during the daytime lockout women can take showers if they want—but men can't. Boo!

How to get there:

By bus: From Keswick take 77 bus to hostel (runs May through October only).

By car: Take B5289 to Buttermere village and continue ¼ mile south; hostel is on left.

By train: Penrith Station, 27 miles away, is nearest stop; call hostel for directions.

BYRNESS HOSTEL

7 Otterbrun Green, Byrness, Newcastle-upon-Tyne NE19 1TS

Phone Number: 01830–520519

Rates: £4.45–£6.50 per HI member (about $7.00–$10.00 US)
Beds: 26
Private/family rooms: Sometimes
Season: March 27 to October 5
Affiliation: HI-YHA
Extras: Store, bike storage, garden

This is a so-so place, if friendly—and sometimes crowded, 'cause it's on that popular Pennine Way where walkers galore congregate to, um, get away from it all. Five dorm rooms make up the bulk of this joint, which includes two doubles and a quad room just 5 miles from the invisible border with Scotland. It used to be a pair of Forest Commission houses.

Gestalt: Half biked

Hospitality: 

Party index:

How to get there:

By bus: From Edinburgh or Newcastle take National Express to Byrness.

By car: Take A68 to Byrness turnoff. Hostel is in village.

By train: From Edinburgh or Newcastle Station take National Express to Byrness.

CARLISLE HOSTEL

University of Northumbria, The Old Brewery Residences,

Bridge Lane, Caldewgate, Carlisle, Cumbia CA2 5SR

Phone Number: 01228–597352 or 01228–59486

Fax: 01228–597352
Rates: £10 per HI member (about $15 US)
Beds: 56
Private/family rooms: Yes
Season: July 1 to September 15
Office hours: 8:00 A.M. to 2:00 P.M.; 7:00 to 11:00 P.M.
Affiliation: HI-YHA
Extras: Laundry, bike storage

This new hostel occupies a former Theakston's Brewery that's been converted into university residence halls; in summertime it morphs into a pretty nice hostel, if plain. Bedrooms contain one to seven beds each, all with their own private bathrooms, and there's a kitchen. Unfortunately, there's no longer any beer running through the taps at this place. Sigh . . .

You couldn't be closer to the local castle, and Hadrian's Wall and cycling and walking paths are also close at hand.

Gestalt: Beer today, gone tomorrow

Party index:

How to get there:

By bus: Take 62 bus to hostel.

By car: From downtown Carlisle take A595 west to Old Brewery Residences, just past castle on right.

Cockermouth Hostel
Cockermouth, England
(photo courtesy of HI-YHA)

COCKERMOUTH HOSTEL

Double Mills, Cockermouth, Cumbria CA13 ODS

Phone Number: 01900–822561

Fax: 01900–822561
Rates: £4.95–£7.20 per HI member (about $7.00–$11.00 US)
Beds: 28
Private/family rooms: None
Season: Call ahead for open days
Affiliation: HI-YHA
Extras: Dinner ($), bike storage

A former mill built in the sixteenth century, this place supplies spare but adequare bunking for hostellers. Three rooms contain six, ten, and twelve bunks respectively; dinner is served at night.

The area's attractions are quaint. Poet William Wordsworth's birthplace isn't very far away, for instance, and several little towns can be walked or cycled to from here.

Insiders' tip: Jennings Brewery in town

Party index:

How to get there:

By bus: From Penrith or Workington take X5 bus to Cockermouth. From center of town walk footpath to hostel.

By car: Take A66 and then A5086 to Cockermouth; make second right on Fern Bank. Park and walk down trail to hostel.

By train: From Workington Station, 8 miles away, take X5 bus to Cockermouth. From center of town walk footpath to hostel.

CONISTON COPPERMINES HOSTEL

Coppermines House, Coniston, Cumbria LA21 8HP

Phone Number: 015394–41261

Fax: 015394–41261
Rates: £4.95–£7.20 per HI member (about $7.00–$11.00 US)
Beds: 28
Season: Call ahead for open days
Private/family rooms: None
Affiliation: HI-YHA

The quieter of Coniston's two hostels, this one's set in pretty and sedate scenery a mile outside of town on a bit of a rough road. It once served as the local copper mine boss's house, but now it's just a little twenty-eight-bed joint with three bunkrooms, a kitchen, common room, and bathroom.

No frills at all—but, boy, that scenery!

Party index:

How to get there:

By bus: From Ambleside or Windermere take 505 or 506 bus to Coniston and walk 1¼ miles to hostel.

By car: Take A593 to Coniston, then drive down road between Black Bull and Co-Op. Continue for 1¼ miles to hostel.

By train: From Windermere Station, 13 miles away, take 505 or 506 bus to Coniston and walk 1¼ miles to hostel.

CONISTON HOLLY HOW HOSTEL

Holly How, Far End, Coniston, Cumbria LA21 8DD

Phone Number: 015394–41323

Fax: 015394–41803

Rates: £5.40–£8.00 per HI member (about $8.00–$12.00 US)
Beds: 60
Private/family rooms: Yes
Season: Call ahead for open days
Affiliation: HI-YHA
Extras: Dinner ($), game room, TV, laundry

Just like the other hostel in Coniston, this place is set in beautiful hillside scenery. It's closer to town—only ¼ mile—and much better equipped if you're looking for comfort or toting young ones. The nightly dinners here, we'll add, are delicious. We recommend 'em. Other amenities we noted here included a game room, laundry, and television room.

Insiders' tip:
Sculpture trail in Grizedale Forest

Gestalt:
Holly hobby

Party index:

Among the cool stuff you can do around town are windsurfing and sailing on the lake here known as Coniston Water (how's that for tellin' it like it is?) or mountain biking the local hills.

How to get there:

By bus: From Ambleside or Windermere take 505 or 506 bus to Coniston and walk to hostel.

By car: Take A593 to Coniston. Hostel is on A593, ¼ north of village center.

By train: From Windermere Station, 13 miles away, take 505 or 506 bus to Coniston and walk to hostel.

DENTDALE HOSTEL

Cowgill, Dent, Sedbergh, Cumbria LA10 5RN

Phone Number: 015396–25251

Fax: 015396–25251
Rates: £5.40–£8.00 per HI member (about $8.00–$12.00 US)
Beds: 40
Season: Call ahead for open days
Affiliation: HI-YHA
Extras: Bike storage, fireplace, dinner ($)

Once a shooting lodge, this hostel is made up of four biggish dorm rooms, plus a kitchen and a dining room. They lock you out of your dorm and kitchen all day, like most every other hostel in England, but kindly allow use of the bathroom and common room anytime after noon. Dent village, a quaint stop, is 5 miles away.

Party index:

How to get there:

By bus: Call hostel for transit route.
By car: Call hostel for directions.
By train: From Dent station, walk 2 miles to hostel.

KATHARINE BRUCE GLASIER MEMORIAL HOSTEL

Glen Cottage, 9-11 Birch Hall Lane, Earby, Colne, Lancashire BB8 6JX

Phone Number: 01282–842349

Fax: 01282–842349
Rates: £4.95–£7.20 per HI member (about $7.00–$11.00 US)
Beds: 22
Season: March 27 to October 31
Affiliation: HI-YHA
Extras: Store, bike storage, garden

A small cottage, this hostel has a nice bonus: a garden and little nature conservatory on its grounds. Otherwise, the place has three six- to eight-bedded dorms and one double. Most come for walking on the Penine Way, but Skipton Castle's also a great quick trip.

Party index:

How to get there:

By bus: Take National Express from London to Skipton; walk 8 miles to hostel, or call hostel for bus route to hostel.

By car: Take A56 to Earby, turn off main road at Lead Mining Museum, turn left onto Water Street and continue across bridge to Birch Hall Lane. Hostel is ¼ mile past Red Lion pub, on left.

By foot: Walk about 15 miles on Pennine Way from hostels in Haworth or Malham.

By train: Colne Station, 5 miles away, and Skipton, 8 miles away, are closest. Call hostel for transit route.

LOW HOUSE HOSTEL

Edmundbyers, Consett, Durham DH8 9NL

Phone Number: 01207–5651

Fax: 01207–255345
Rates: £4.45–£6.50 per HI member (about $7.00–$10.00 US)

Beds: 36
Private/family rooms: Sometimes
Season: March 27 to October 31
Affiliation: HI-YHA
Extras: Bike storage

This used to be an inn, but now—just 400 short years later—it's, well, still an inn, only for budget travelers. Five dorms contain up to twelve beds apiece, and one is a double room with private room potential. It's on the Sea-to-Sea (also known as the C2C) bicycle route, too.

Party index:

How to get there:

By bus: Call hostel for transit route.
By car: Call hostel for directions.
By train: From Newcastle take 745, 770, or 771 bus to Consett; then walk 5 miles to hostel.

LILAC COTTAGE HOSTEL

Ellingstring, Masham, Ripon, North Yorkshire HG4 4PW

Phone Number: 01677–460216

Rates: £4.00–£5.85 per HI member (about $6.00–$9.00 US)
Beds: 20
Season: Call ahead for open days
Affiliation: HI-YHA
Extras: Garden, store, bike storage

Nothing fancy here, just three dorm rooms in a stone cottage plus the requisite kitchen and common room. At least there's a garden and a small hostel store for basic food supplies. The to-do list around here usually includes a stop at Middleham, a look around the local abbeys, or walking in the national park.

A beer, Black Sheep Ale, is now also brewed in these parts. Call the brewers in town and ask about a tour or a tasting. Couldn't hurt.

Party index:

How to get there:

By bus: Call hostel for transit route.
By car: Take A6108 to Ellingstring turnoff; hostel is in village center, in stone cottage.
By train: Thirsk Station, 16 miles away, is closest.

ELTERWATER HOSTEL

Elterwater, Ambleside, Cumbria LA22 9HX

Phone Number: 015394–37245

Fax: 015394–37120
Rates: £5.40–£8.00 per HI member (about $8.00–$12.00 US)
Beds: 46
Private/family rooms: Sometimes
Season: Call ahead for open days
Affiliation: HI-YHA
Extras: Bike storage, garden, dinner ($)

Once a farmhouse, now a hostel, this joint's well placed on the Cumbria Way and near the two Langdale valleys, famous (around England, anyway) for their walking.

The hostel itself puts you in rooms as small as a double or as big as ten beds. Evening dinner, a garden, kitchen, and common space are among the amenities when you stay here.

How to get there:

By bus: From Ambleside or Windermere, 9 miles away, take 516 bus to Elterwater.

By car: Take A593 to B5343; continue 2 miles, pass over cattle grid, and then take next left into Elterwater village. Continue through village to hostel on right. Limited parking in town.

By train: From Windermere Station, 9 miles away, take 516 bus to Elterwater.

Party index:

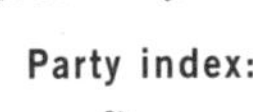

BLACK SAIL HUT HOSTEL

Ennerdale, Cleator, Cumbria CA23 3AY

Phone Number: 01411–108450

Rates: £4.45–£6.50 per HI member (about $7.00–$10.00 US)
Beds: 16
Private/family rooms: Sometimes
Season: May 21 to October 31
Affiliation: HI-YHA
Extras: Store, dinner ($)

You can't even drive here; that's how remote this little hostel is. Once a shepherd's bothy (simple house), it's got loads of atmosphere and hearty food—but no electricity or heat. So bring lots of warm clothes and a thick sleeping bag, and be prepared to hike in.

What an experience, though. Isolated on a rocky point, you won't hear anyone but the birds. Numerous climbs and walks are at hand, and they serve nightly dinner and sell a few plain staples at the hostel. Beds consist of two quad rooms and one with eight beds, and that's it. Extra points for being a no-smoking place, though.

Gestalt:
Yard sail

Party index:

How to get there:

By bus: From Keswick take 77, 77A, or 79 bus to Honister, and walk 3 miles to hostel.

By car: Drive B5389 to Honister, and hike 3 rugged miles to hostel.

By foot: From Honister hostel walk 3 miles by footpath to hostel.

By train: Whitehaven Station, 19 miles away, is nearest stop; call hostel for transit route.

ENNERDALE HOSTEL

Cat Crag, Ennerdale, Cleator, Cumbria CA23 3AX

Phone Number: 01946–861237

Rates: £4.45–£6.50 per HI member (about $7.00–$10.00 US)
Beds: 24
Private/family rooms: Sometimes
Season: Call ahead for open days
Affiliation: HI-YHA
Extras: Store, dinner ($)

This is quite a simple hostel, but it's ideal for walkers on the Coast to Coast Way. (Even the rest of us must walk between 2 and 5 miles into the woods to get here.)

Party index:

The two cottages that make up the place are lit by gas lamps—there is no electrical power—and surrounded by woods and hills. Yet somehow they still manage to supply hot showers, a kitchen, and evening dinners to hostellers. A good rustic hostel when you're tired of city grime, and no smoking's allowed.

How to get there:

By bus: From Keswick take bus to Buttermere (runs May through October only), then walk 3 miles along path to hostel. Rest of year, from Keswick take 79 bus to Seatoller and walk 7 miles to hostel on path.

By car: From Cockermouth take A5086 to Crossdale turnoff; turn off and go through Crossdale, continuing to Bowness Knott parking lot. Park and walk 2½ miles to hostel along Forest Road pathway.

By foot: From Buttermere hostel walk 3 miles on Coast to Coast Way to hostel.

By train: Call hostel for transit route.

LANGDON BECK HOSTEL

Langdon Beck, Forest-in-Teesdale, Barnard Castle, Co Durham DL1 0XN

Phone Number: 01833–22228

Fax: 01833–622228
Rates: £5.95–£8.80 per HI member (about $9.00–$13.00 US); doubles £20 (about $30 US)
Beds: 34
Season: Call ahead for open days
Affiliation: HI-YHA
Extras: Dinner ($), laundry, bike storage

Close to the High Force waterfall, this stone hostel was opened for walkers along the challenging Pennine Way. Six dorm rooms divide up the bunkage, including a double and a quad room among them.

Party index:

How to get there:

By bus: From Darlington take 75A bus High Force; walk to hostel.

By car: Take B6277 for 7 miles north of Middleton.

By foot: Walk on Pennine Way from Dufton (12 miles) or Baldersdale (15 miles) hostels.

By train: From Darlington Station take 75A bus High Force; walk to hostel.

KEY TO ICONS

- Attractive natural setting
- Ecologically aware hostel
- Superior kitchen facilities or cafe
- Offbeat or eccentric place
- Superior bathroom facilities
- Romantic private rooms
- Comfortable beds
- Editors' choice: among our very favorite hostels
- A particularly good value
- Wheelchair accessible
- Good for business travelers
- Especially well suited for families
- Good for active travelers
- Visual arts at hostel or nearby
- Music at hostel or nearby
- Great hostel for skiers
- Bar or pub at hostel or nearby

BOGGLE HOLE HOSTEL

Boggle Hole, Mill Beck, Fylingthorpe, Whitby, North Yorkshire YO22 4UQ

Phone Number: 01947–880352

Fax: 01947–880987
Rates: £5.95–£8.80 per HI member (about $9.00–$13.00 US); doubles £20.50 (about $32 US)
Beds: 80
Family/private rooms: Yes
Season: February 13 to November 30
Affiliation: HI-YHA
Extras: TV, lockers, bike storage, dinner ($)
Lockout: 10:00 A.M.–1:00 P.M.
Curfew: 11:30 P.M.

Man, this place is popular . . . very full when we dropped in. Must be because of that great beach, where schoolkids love to muck about: During low tide you can walk right to the water from this hostel. Just remember to get back before high tide.

Anyhow, it takes a little desire to get here: You walk the last ¼ mile even if you have a car, so bring a flashlight. (Cigars won't do the trick. Sorry.) A former corn mill right on Robin Hood's Bay, it features knockout views of cliffs, water, and headlands. Inside, dorms range from four to sixteen beds; there's a goodly number of doubles and quads for couples and families, especially in the adjacent annex building. Staff fixes dinners for a price, locks you out for only three hours, and lets you come in as late as 11:30 P.M.

Two walking trails pass through here, the Coast to Coast Way and the Cleveland Way, so they make two obvious day hikes from the hostel.

Gestalt:
Boggler

Party index:

How to get there:

By bus: From Whitby or Scarborough, take 93A bus to Robin Hood's Bay and walk 1 mile to hostel.

By car: Take A171 to Boggle Hole turnoff; continue 3½ miles to parking area. Park and walk ¼ mile down lane to hostel.

By train: From Whitby or Scarborough Stations, take 93A bus to Robin Hood's Bay and walk 1 mile to hostel.

HELVELLYN HOSTEL

Greenside, Glenridding, Penrith, Cumbria CA11 0QR

Phone Number: 017684–82269

Fax: 017684–82269
Rates: £5.40–£8.00 per HI member (about $8.00–$12.00 US)
Beds: 64

Season: Call ahead for open days
Private/family rooms: Yes
Affiliation: HI-YHA
Extras: Dinner ($), bike storage

This hostel enjoys a spectacular setting in Glenridding valley, with big mountains and hills around it. Beds here come two to six to a room, and they serve dinner each night.

Needless to say, the walking, biking, and photographing are superb around here. Or you could head down to the lake instead for walking or water sports.

How to get there:

Party index:

By bus: From Penrith, 14 miles away, take 108 bus to Glenridding (runs Monday through Saturday) and walk 1½ miles west to hostel.

By car: Take A593 to Glenridding, then turn west at sign and follow 1½ miles up rough road to hostel.

By train: From Penrith Station, 14 miles away, take 108 bus to Glenridding (runs Monday through Saturday) and walk 1½ miles west to hostel.

WHEELDALE LODGE HOSTEL

Wheeldale Lodge, Goathland, Whitby, North Yorkshire YO22 5AP

Phone Number: 01947–896350

Rates: £4.00–£5.85 per HI member (about $6.00–$9.00 US)
Beds: 30
Season: Call ahead for open days
Affiliation: HI-YHA
Extras: Garden, bike storage, fireplace, store

Another simple hostel, yeah: This former shooting lodge in the heather has great location but no showers or central heating. (So that explains the cheap rates.)

Four dorm rooms hold the beds, and the common room does have a fireplace, a good touch. Bring a flashlight, though. It's a quarter-mile hike in from the parking lot.

Party index:

How to get there:

By bus: Call hostel for transit route.

By car: From Goathland take Egton Bridge Road ½ mile to Hunt House Road; make a left, go past farm ¼ mile on dirt lane. Park and walk ¼ mile to hostel.

By train: From Grosmont Station walk 6 miles. From Grosmont change to North York Moors Railway and ride to Goathland station; walk 3 miles to hostel.

Butterlip How Hostel
Grasmere, England
(photo courtesy of HI-YHA)

BUTTERLIP HOW HOSTEL 

Butterlip How, Easedale Road, Grasmere, Ambleside, Cumbria LA22 9QG

Phone Number: 015394–35316

Fax: 015394–35798
Rates: £5.95–£9.75 per HI member (about $9.00–$15.00 US); doubles £20–£22 (about $30–$33 US)
Beds: 80
Private/family rooms: Yes
Office hours: 7:30 A.M. to 10:00 P.M.
Season: April 1 to October 31
Affiliation: HI-YHA
Extras: TV, laundry, dinner ($)

Smack in the middle of the Lake District, in yet another gorgeous setting, this place is a traditional Lakeland slate Victorian house in the center of the National Park overlooking extensive grounds and a village beyond. They've got exceptionally comfortable beds here, large bunkrooms, and generally excellent facilities. Other nice touches include the large yet homey lounge—big windows and an open fire here.

Facilities include rooms that contain no more than six beds each and often contain just two to four. The main building is for catered accommodation (meals must be reserved and paid for in advance). In the basement is a game room with pool tables, arcades, and drink and snack vending machines. The other, self-catering rooms (i.e., with kitchens) are in How Lodge, a separate annex with an excellent kitchen (open from 7:00–11:00 A.M. and 12:00–11:00 P.M.) and a functional lounge, showers, and a dining room. If good showers and toilets are a priority for you, this place is great . . . they're everywhere, private and clean.

Among the favorite activities here is the renting of a rowboat to test the waters of Grasmere Lake. Poet William Wordsworth's first home at Dove Cottage is a short bus trip away, and special events and exhibits are organized each year, so be prepared for poetry pilgrims.

Wordsworth aside, this area is also famous for some annual festivals. Among the attractions here: the Gingerbread shop, the Peace Oak, and walking routes. Nearby is Grizedale Forest Park, with a forest theater plus a whole lot of trees. This village is also very popular with artists, so the hostel's location and recent improvements make it a favorite target of families and groups.

All in all, this is a quiet, comfortable hostel where the guests all smell good—not exactly edge-of-the-seat stuff, but hey! Everyone needs to relax once in a while. This hostel is really popular in summertime; so book early, kiddos.

Best bet for a bite: Gingerbread shop

Insiders' tip: Art show in August

What hostellers say: "These showers are great!"

Gestalt: Butterlip balm

Hospitality: 

Cleanliness: 

Party index:

How to get there:

By bus: From Keswick, Lancaster, take 555 bus to Grasmere and walk ¼ mile up Easedale Road to hostel. From Windermere take 555 or 599 bus to Grasmere and walk ¼ mile up Easedale Road to hostel

By car: Take A591 to Grasmere, then take Easedale Road ¼ mile to hostel on right.

By train: From Windermere Station, 8½ miles away, take 555 or 599 bus to Grasmere and walk ¼ mile up Easedale Road to hostel.

THORNEY HOW HOSTEL 

Thorney How, Grasmere, Ambleside, Cumbria LA22 9QW

Phone Number: 015394–35591

Fax: 015394–35866
Rates: £5.95–£8.80 per HI member (about $9.00–$13.00 US)
Credit cards: Yes
Beds: 48
Private/family rooms: Sometimes
Season: Call ahead for open days

Affiliation: HI-YHA
Extras: Dinner ($), bike storage
Curfew: 11:00 P.M.

Of the two hostels in Grasmere, this one's our preference. It's practically next door to the Butterlip How hostel, and a cut above it for our money. Didja know? This farmhouse was the very first YHA hostel, and it was built way back in the 1660s.

Gestalt: How nice

Hospitality: 

Cleanliness: 

Party index:

It's a cozy, converted farmhouse filled with forty beds in rooms ranging from four to twelve beds in size. (Half the beds come four to six to a room, and the rest are housed in two larger bunkrooms.) Rooms 8 and 9 are actually situated in a (former) outhouse! The ceilings are low, the rooms are smallish, and the corridors are odd-shaped: a place with atmosphere galore, and one that's popular as heck with bearded walkers exploring central Lakeland rather than the usual family types. Priorities here are warmth, food, and comfortable beds.

There's no TV or pool table, which actually builds a strong sense of companionship. The lounge is small with an open fire; you're guaranteed to end up in conversation with someone and find yourself inventing strange games involving music, chairs, and, maybe, tent poles. As with most hostels in the Lakes District, meals are available—there's a small self-catering kitchen if you prefer—yet another gentle push toward social mixing among hostellers.

The only bad thing about this place is the showers: There's one for guys, one for gals, and that's it. Washrooms are single-sex but communal; then again, what's a little public tooth-cleaning among all those friends you've made in the lounge? People here don't shave and wear bright clothes. Call it a comfortable, up-market hippie commune of sorts.

Call us daft, but we liked this place.

How to get there:

By bus: From Keswick, Lancaster, take 555 bus to Grasmere and walk ½ mile up Easedale Road to hostel sign; turn right and walk ¼ mile down road to hostel on left. From Windermere take 555 or 599 bus to Grasmere and walk ½ mile up Easedale Road to hostel sign; turn right and walk ¼ mile down road to hostel on left.

By car: Take A591 to Grasmere, then take Easedale Road. Pass Butterlip How hostel, go ¼ mile farther to sign on right; turn and go ¼ mile down road. Hostel is on left.

By train: From Windermere Station, 8½ miles away, take 555 or 599 bus to Grasmere and walk ½ mile up Easedale Road to hostel sign; turn right and walk ¼ mile down road. Hostel is on left.

GREENHEAD HOSTEL

Greenhead, Carlisle, Cumbria CA6 7HG

Phone Number: 016977–47401

Fax: 016977–47401
Rates: £4.95–£7.20 per HI member (about $7.00–$11.00 US)
Beds: 40
Season: March 27 to December 20
Affiliation: HI-YHA
Extras: Dinner ($), bike storage
Lockout: 10:00 A.M.–5:00 P.M.
Curfew: 11:30 P.M.

Cool—a chapel converted into a hostel. Superpopular with walkers, this makes a fun stop on the Pennine Way. You're sure to meet more than just Brits, all of you tramping around the hills or checking out Hadrian's Wall. Dorms contain six to eight beds each; they open the common room at 1:00 P.M. so that you can rest your weary bod and dinner is served nightly.

Gestalt:
Green jeans

Party index:

How to get there:

By bus: From Carlisle or Newcastle take 685 bus to Greenhead.

By car: Take A69 to Greenhead, turn into village. Hostel is on left, across from hotel.

By train: From Haltwhistle Station walk 3 miles, or take 685 bus to Greenhead.

GRINTON LODGE HOSTEL

Grinton, Richmond, North Yorkshire DL11 6HS

Phone Number: 01748–884206

Fax: 01748–884876
Rates: £5.40–£8.00 per HI member (about $8.00–$12.00 US)
Beds: 66
Private/family rooms: Sometimes
Affiliation: HI-YHA
Extras: Bike rental, bike storage, game room, TV, laundry, courtyard, fireplace, dinner ($)

This former shooting lodge is now a good hostel, blessed with fireplace and good services. They'll rent you a bike, serve you dinner, let you watch the tube, or just leave you alone while you

Gestalt: Grinton and bear it

Party index:

watch the laundry go round and round, play in the games room, or sit watching the fire. Dorms range from four to eight beds apiece, and there's also one double room.

How to get there:

By bus: Call hostel for transit route.

By car: Take B6270 to Grinton, turn off, continue south on Reeth-Leyburn road ¾ mile. Hostel is on left.

HAWES HOSTEL 

Lancaster Terrace, Hawes, North Yorkshire DK8 3LQ

Phone Number: 01969–67368

Fax: 01969–667723
Rates: £5.95–£8.80 per HI member (about $9.00–$13.00 US)
Beds: 58
Family/private rooms: Yes
Season: Call ahead for open days
Affiliation: HI-YHA
Extras: TV, dinner ($), bike storage, laundry, porch

Right on the Pennine Way, this hostel has more thoughtful touches than it needs to. We like that.

Try a laundry, good family rooms, and a television room. Dorm rooms are never bigger than eight beds, often smaller; the dinners here have won awards, too. While in the area don't miss Hardraw Force, a tall waterfall. Or hit the cheese factory nearby for a, well, cheesy experience.

Hospitality:

Party index:

How to get there:

By bus: Call hostel for transit route.

By car: Take A684 to Hawes, turn onto B6255 (Ingleton Road). Hostel is on left.

By train: From Garsdale Station walk 6 miles to hostel or take bus; call hostel for transit route.

HAWSKEAD HOSTEL 

Esthwaite Lodge, Hawkshead, Ambleside, Cumbria LA22 0QD

Phone Number: 015394–36293

Fax: 015394–36720
Rates: £6.55–£9.75 per HI member (about $10–$15 US)
Beds: 115

Private/family rooms: Yes
Season: Call ahead for open days
Affiliation: HI-YHA
Extras: TV, game room, laundry, dinner ($), bar

This mansion in the woods by a river is quite comfortable, as hostels go. Dinner service, liquor, a television room, and games for the kiddies—all make for a pleasant stay. It's got lots of beds, too: twelve smaller rooms of three to four bunks each, five rooms of six to eight beds each, and two huge rooms with sixteen or more bunks each. The private rooms, located in an adjacent courtyard complex, are especially nice.

Hawkshead village isn't very big, but it does pack in some cobbled streets and a quaint-looking town square.

Gestalt: Hawkshead revisited

Party index:

How to get there:

By bus: From Ambleside or Windermere take 505 or 506 bus to Hawkhead, and walk 1 mile south along Newby Bridge Road to hostel.

By car: Take B5285 to Hawkshead turnoff; from village, go south 1 mile on Newby Bridge Road. Hostel is on right.

By train: From Windermere Station take 505 or 506 bus to Hawkhead, and walk 1 mile south along Newby Bridge Road to hostel.

LONGLANDS HALL

Longlands Drive, Lees Lane, Haworth, Keighley, West Yorkshire BD22 8RT

Phone Number: 01535–642234

Fax: 01535–643023
Rates: £5.95–£8.80 per HI member (about $9.00–$13.00 US)
Beds: 100
Season: February 13 to December 19
Affiliation: HI-YHA
Extras: Laundry, bike storage, dinner ($), game room
Curfew: 11:00 P.M.

Once home to a mill owner, this Victorian building hosts a surprisingly big hostel overlooking Haworth village. It caters to fans of the Brontë family (they lived here) as well as walkers and cyclists. Dorm rooms come mostly in big sizes, but there are a few smaller ones as well. The best part here is the place doesn't lock you out; reception is open all day.

Party index:

How to get there:

By bus: Call hostel for transit route.

By car: From Haworth center take B6142 toward Keighley. Go ¾ mile, turn up Longlands Drive. Hostel is on left.

By train: From Keighley Station walk 4 miles to hostel. On Worth Valley Railway, walk ½ mile from Haworth Station.

HELMSLEY HOSTEL

Carlton Lane, Helmsley, North Yorkshire YO6 5HB

Phone Number: 01439–770433

Fax: 01439–770433
Rates: £5.40–£8.00 per HI member (about $8.00–$12.00 US)
Beds: 40
Season: March 27 to October 31
Affiliation: HI-YHA
Extras: Porch, dinner ($), laundry, bike storage

Not much to report about this one, which consists of forty beds in six dorm rooms. Dinner and laundry are amenities offered. Three walking trails do pass by—the Cleveland, Link, and Ebor Ways—so that's something to do in the area, plus the town castle is only half a mile away.

Party index:

How to get there:

By bus: From York take Stevensons 57 or 58 bus; from Scarborough, take Scarborough & District 128 bus.

By car: Take A170 to Helmsley, turn onto Carlton Road at garage; hostel is at corner of Carlton Lane, on left.

By train: Call hostel for transit route.

HIGH CLOSE HOSTEL

High Close, Loughrigg, Ambleside, Cumbria LA22 9HJ

Phone Number: 015394–37313

Fax: 015394–37101
Rates: £5.95–£8.80 per HI member (about $9.00–$13.00 US)
Beds: 96
Private/family rooms: Sometimes
Season: Call ahead for open days
Affiliation: HI-YHA
Extras: TV, dinner ($), bike storage

This National Trust–protected mansion, high on a hill, isn't near anything except wooded ridges and valleys; that alone might be enough to draw you here. Plenty of common space, a television room, and dinner service are additional reasons to think about it as an option. The rooms lay out like this: Two of them contain three to four beds, eight contain five to eight beds, and four have eleven beds.

Party index:

How to get there:

By bus: Take bus to Grasmere, then walk 1½ miles to hostel.

By car: Take A593 to Langdale turnoff; turn north and go 1½ miles to smaller road, turn right and continue uphill 1¾ miles. At top of hill turn left and go ¼ mile to hostel.

By train: From Windermere Station take 516 bus to just before Elterwater, then walk ¾ mile.

INGLETON HOSTEL

Greta Tower, Sammy Lane, Ingleton, Carnforth, Lancashire LA6 3EG

Phone Number: 015242–41444

Fax: 015242–41854
Rates: £4.95–£7.20 per HI member (about $7.00–$11.00 US)
Beds: 58
Season: April 4 to December 22
Affiliation: HI-YHA
Extras: Bike storage, dinner ($)

Right off Ingleton's market square, this hostel benefitted from recent renovations. All rooms are quads (£30.50, about $46 US) or six-bedded dorms. They won't lock you out of your bedroom during the day, and they serve dinners. A village swimming pool nearby is popular in summer.

Party index:

How to get there:

By bus: From Lancaster take 80 bus.

By car: From High Street in Ingleton, go down lane between Barclays Bank and carpet shop to hostel.

By train: From Betham Station walk 3 miles to hostel; from Clapham Station walk 4 miles to hostel.

KELD LODGE

Upper Swaledale, Keld, Richmond, North Yorkshire DL11 6LL

Phone Number: 01748–86259

Fax: 01748–886013
Rates: £4.95–£7.20 per HI member (about $7.00–$11.00 US)
Beds: 40

Season: Call ahead for open days
Affiliation: HI-YHA
Extras: Dinner ($), TV, bike storage, porch

Gestalt:
Swell deal

Party index:

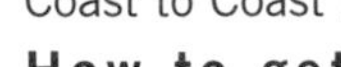

A former shooting lodge, this hostel is packed with dorms of four to ten beds each. Walking is popular in the Swaledele region, known for its flowery fields and unique barn architecture; try the Pennine Way or Coast to Coast route.

How to get there:

By bus: Call hostel for transit route.
By car: Take B6270 to Keld; hostel is west of village.
By train: Kirkby Stephen Station, 11 miles away, is closest.

KENDAL HOSTEL

118 Highgate, Kendal, Cumbria LA9 4HE

Phone Number: 01539–724066

Fax: 01539–724906
Rates: £5.95–£8.80 per HI member (about $9.00–$13.00 US)
Beds: 54
Private/family rooms: Yes
Season: Call ahead for open days
Affiliation: HI-YHA
Extras: Dinner ($), TV

Talk about a marriage made in heaven. That's what Kendal's cool little hostel, a town house located smack downtown, is: great.

See, the hostel is joined at the hip with the hoppin' and boppin' Brewery—not a brewery, for once, but rather an arts center with music, food, galleries, and so on. So your entertainment is already set: Just hang out here, catching the Festival of Mime (April), a folk festival (August), and a jazz and blues festival (in fall). Or check out the shops, which cluck busily during the day and on weekends.

Best bet for a bite:
Right here

Gestalt:
Brew haha

Hospitality:

Cleanliness:

Party index:

There's one big eleven-bedded dorm room in the hostel for lonely travelers; the rest are quite small, and you get a choice of two common rooms—one that's nuts and one that's pensive. Facilities are good, with a sink in every room plus a nice lounge and quiet room.

This place is popular with walkers and those stopping off en route to Scotland. You're also close to all those great cheap pubs. (Smell them first. Pipe smoke: dodgy old men and cloudy ale. Cigarettes, perfume, or cologne? Youth, good beer, and fun.) Plus there are tons of good family rooms and delicious dinners served each night. How can you go wrong?

Kendal, while not a prime example of cosmopolitan city life, is as close to a city as you'll find in Cumbria. Brochures call it "the gateway to the southern Lake District," but don't let that put you off. It really is worth visiting, a pretty market town with some great hidden and historic lanes and quirky shops. (Don't even think about driving here, though; in town, it's all one-ways. Once you're in, you're never gonna get back out.)

In a region that's made up of small towns and depends upon its traditional vernacular gray stone appearance for tourists, it's good to see the odd splash of kitsch and cool here.

One downside: The hostel doesn't open until 5:00 P.M., so unless you're booked in, you can't get in until then. So take off for those winding streets, check out the chip shops, and dare to try batter-fried haggis. It's "an experience" with a capital E. And brush your teeth after the mint cake, a local delicacy: It tastes like toothpaste, but it's actually very sugary.

How to get there:

By bus: From bus station walk ¼ mile to hostel in center of town.

By car: Hostel is in center of downtown Kendal. Park free in adjacent lot.

By train: From Kendal Station walk ¾ mile into town to hostel.

KESWICK HOSTEL

Station Road, Keswick, Cumbria CA12 5LH

Phone Number: 017687–72484

Fax: 017687–74129
Rates: £6.55–£9.75 per HI member (about $10–$15 US)
Credit cards: Yes
Beds: 91
Private/family rooms: Sometimes
Season: February 12 to December 28
Affiliation: HI-YHA
Extras: TV, laundry, bike storage, dinner ($), game room
Lockout: 10:00 A.M.–1:00 P.M.

A refurbished wool mill on the banks of the Greta River that once turned its mill wheel, this hostel is a five-minute walk from the center of Keswick, facing a park and lofty Skiddaw Pike. It's big and bustling here. Most rooms have three or four beds; some have five, ten, or twelve beds—for the late or unfortunate. Meals are available in a dining room on the ground floor next to reception: Book in and go straight over there for free tea and coffee.

Best of all is the balcony overlooking the river, perfect for evening beer drinking (er, relaxation). They ban alcohol here except when they sell it to you with meals; there are also plenty of pubs around. Other guests are a good mix of hostelling types—lots of individual backpackers plus some families and groups.

It gets busy here in summer, probably because they maintain a high level of service. The nightly dinners in the dining room, a television room, a laundry—all good enough.

If Kendal is gateway to the southern Lakes District, then Keswick is the northern hub. It's a busy market town and a good base for walkers. Several hills are within easy reach, and there are plenty of easier paths, too, for those with less-developed calf muscles. Action around here consists mostly of walking or shopping.

Best bet for a bite: Java coffeehouse

Hospitality: 

Cleanliness: 

Party index:

How to get there:

By bus: Many bus connections locally. Call hostel for transit route.

By car: From Penrith take A591 to Keswick. Park in town, walk up Station Road, and turn left at hostel walkway just before bridge.

By train: Many bus connections locally. Call hostel for transit route.

KETTLEWELL HOSTEL

Whernside House, Kettlewell, Skipton, North Yorkshire BD23 5QU

Phone Number: 0175676–232

Fax: 01756–760402
Rates: £5.95–£8.80 per HI member (about $9.00–$13.00 US); doubles £20.50 (about $32 US)
Beds: 58
Private/family rooms: Yes
Season: Call ahead for open days
Affiliation: HI-YHA
Extras: Lockers, bike storage, dinner ($)

Right on the Dalesday walking track, this stone house hostel is useful for its position on a number of riverside trails. It includes an interesting ten-bed annex where an entire large group could crash. There are also double and quad rooms and dorms with up to seven beds apiece. Dinner is served at 7:00 P.M. each evening.

One of the fun things to do around here—ask at the front desk—is to canoe the whitewater at Linton Falls. (Make sure you know what you're doing first, of course.)

Party index:

How to get there:

By bus: Call hostel for transit route.

By car: Take B6160 to Kettlewell; follow signs to hostel.

By train: From Skipton Station take 72 bus to Grassington, 6 miles away.

KIRKBY STEPHEN HOSTEL

Fletcher Hill, Market Street, Kirkby Stephen, Cumbria CA17 4QQ

Phone Number: 017683–71793

Fax: 017683–71793
Rates: £5.40–£8.00 per HI member (about $8.00–$12.00 US); doubles £20 (about $30 US)
Beds: 44
Private/family rooms: Yes
Season: March 27 to October 31
Affiliation: HI-YHA
Extras: Laundry, bike storage, dinner ($)

What a nice building! Once a chapel, this lovely hostel has retained the wooden pews, oak beams, and—of course—stained-glass windows of the country church it was.

Dorms come in four and eight bed configurations, plus there are two double rooms for couples. Plus there's the intangible thrill of sleeping and eating dinner on holy ground. A tourist information center is located across the street for ease in planning day trips.

Gestalt:
Peace be with you

Party index:

How to get there:

By bus: Call hostel for transit route.

By car: Take A66 or M6 to A685; follow to Kirkby Stephen. Hostel is on main street in center of village.

By train: Kirkby Stephen Station is 1½ miles from hostel.

OLD RECTORY HOSTEL

Linton-in-Crave, Skipton, North Yorkshire BD23 5HH

Phone Number: 01756–752400

Fax: 01756–752400
Rates: £5.95–£8.80 per HI member (about $9.00–$13.00 US)
Beds: 38
Season: Call ahead for open days

Affiliation: HI-YHA
Extras: Dinner ($), bike storage, porch, garden

Yep, it's a seventeenth-century rectory built of stone and just a mile from some touristic stuff (like actual restaurants) in Grassington. Dorms range from four to ten beds apiece, and there is indeed a kitchen and common area. They'll serve you dinner if you don't wanna cook.

Party index:

Linton isn't bad, either, with old-fashioned bridges, a waterfall and those oh-so-quaint cottages, all of which you'd just love to photograph. Or just hang out on the big lawn here with a Frisbee and watch friends appear as if by magic.

How to get there:

By bus: From Skipton take 72 bus to Linton.

By car: Take B6160 or B6265 to Linton village. Hostel is adjacent to village green, on east side of bridge.

By train: From Skipton Station, 8 miles away, walk to hostel or take 72 bus to Linton.

THE OLD SCHOOL HOSTEL

Lockton, Pickering, North Yorkshire YO18 7PY

Phone Number: 01751–60376

Rates: £4.00–£5.85 per HI member (about $6.00–$9.00 US)
Beds: 22
Season: March 27 to September 26
Affiliation: HI-YHA
Extras: Bike storage
Lockout: 10:30 A.M.–5:00 P.M.
Curfew: 10:30 P.M.

Once a schoolhouse, this hostel has just three dorms of varying size, plus a kitchen. Toilet and shower are outside. We're talking basic with a capital B—not the place to take Mom and Dad, maybe, but close to walking trails near the North York Moors.

Insiders' tip:
Steam train nearby

Gestalt:
School's out

Party index:

How to get there:

By bus: From Whitby or Malton take 840 bus.

By car: Take A169 to Lockton turnoff; hostel is in village.

By train: From Malton Station take 840 bus.

JOHN DOWER MEMORIAL HOSTEL

Malham, Skipton, North Yorkshire BD23 4DE

Phone Number: 01729–830321

Fax: 01729–830551
Rates: £6.55–£9.75 per HI member (about $10–$15 US); doubles £22 (about $33 US)
Beds: 82
Season: January 1 to December 19
Affiliation: HI-YHA
Extras: Lockers, laundry, dinner ($), TV, bike storage, garden

Recent work has improved this roomy place, which is notable for its wide variety of family-style rooms—everything from couples' rooms to triples, quads, and more. Between the main building and the annex there are fifteen dorm rooms, none bigger than eight beds and most a good deal smaller. The laundry and television room really help, too.

Most visitors were heading to outings at the local caves, or else walking the Pennine Way (it passes right by the hostel). A lesser known network of paths also connects Malham with other local villages, several of which have their own hostels. Connect the dots if you want.

Insiders' tip: Listers Arms pub

Party index:

How to get there:

By bus: From Skipton take 210 bus or Postbus to Malham.

By car: Take A65 to Malham turnoff, turn and go to village; hostel is in center.

By foot: Walk 7 miles from Linton hostel by path or 10 miles from Kettlewell hostel by path.

By train: From Skipton Station take 210 bus to Malham.

MANKINHOLES HOSTEL

Mankinholes, Todmorden, Lancashire OL14 6HR

Phone Number: 01706–812340

Fax: 01706–812340
Rates: £4.95–£7.20 per HI member (about $7.00–$10.00 US)
Beds: 40
Season: Call ahead for open days
Affiliation: HI-YHA
Extras: Laundry, dinner ($), bike storage

More basic digs from YHA here, five nearly identical dorm rooms housing forty beds total. They do serve dinner, though, and let you

Gestalt: Mankind

Party index:

enter part of the building after 1:00 P.M. The laundry on site is also handy.

How to get there:

By bus: From Todmorden take T6 or T8 bus to Mankinholes.

By car: Call hostel for directions.

By train: From Todmorden Station walk 2 miles to hostel, or take T6 or T8 bus to Mankinholes.

WASTWATER HOSTEL

Wasdale Hall, Nether Wasdale, Seascale, Cumbria CA20 1ET

Phone Number: 019467–26222

Fax: 019467–26056
Rates: £5.95–£8.80 per HI member (about $9.00–$13.00 US)
Beds: 50
Private/family rooms: Sometimes
Season: Call ahead for open days
Affiliation: HI-YHA
Extras: Game room, dinner ($), library

This place is close to some big-league climbing and hiking, such as Scafell Pike, and a cool lake called Wastwater. No, not Wastewater . . . Wastwater. It's England deepest lake.

Party index:

Anyway, the building's half-timbered (gosh, we love saying that) and was built in 1829; you'll feel a king, walking or riding up the gravel path beneath trees to the mansion. Inside it features a big library/reading room, game room, and dining room where they serve dinner each night for a charge. Beds come in quads, six-bedded rooms, eight-bedded rooms, and two fourteen-bedded rooms.

How to get there:

By bus: From Whitehaven or Seascale take 6 bus to Gosforth and walk 5 miles to hostel.

By car: Call hostel for directions.

By foot: From Black Sail, Eskdale, or Borrowdale hostels, walk 7-10 rugged miles to hostel.

By train: From Seascale Station take 6 bus to Gosforth and walk 5 miles to hostel.

NEWCASTLE-UPON-TYNE HOSTEL

107 Jesmond Road, Newcastle-upon-Tyne NE2 1NJ

Phone Number: 0191–2812570

Fax: 0191–281–8779
Rates: £5.95–£8.80 per HI member (about $9.00–$13.00 US)
Beds: 60
Private/family rooms: Sometimes
Season: February 1 to November 30
Affiliation: HI-YHA
Extras: TV, game room, bike storage, dinner ($)

This big town house isn't as lavish as you might expect; then again, Newcastle isn't exactly a huge destination, unless you're taking a ferry somewhere else. At any rate, thirteen dorms at this hostel range from two to eight beds, nicely sized. There's a telly and game room, too, plus dinner is served each night at 7:00 P.M. sharp.

Party index:

Like we said, Newcastle's pretty big and uninspiring, but there is the option of taking a ferryboat to Norway (it takes, like, twenty-four hours) if you're so inclined.

How to get there:

By bus: Call hostel for transit route.

By car: Call hostel for directions.

By train: From Jesmond Station walk ¼ mile to hostel; from Newcastle Station walk 1½ miles.

ORCHARD HOUSE HOSTEL

Mohope, Ninebanks, Hexham, Northumberland NE47 8DO

Phone Number: 01434–345288

Fax: 01434–345288
Rates: £4.00–£5.85 per HI member (about $6.00–$9.00 US)
Beds: 26
Affiliation: HI-YHA
Extras: Bike storage, fireplace

Just twenty-six beds at this plain bunkhouse, built 300 years ago as a lead miner's cottage. Not on your beaten track, certainly, though it is on the C2C (get it?) bike route. Cross-country skiing is also popular around this area.

Party index:

How to get there:

By bus: From Newcastle, Haxham, or Alston take Wright Bros. 888 bus to Ouston, then walk 1 mile to hostel.

By car: Take A686 to 2½ miles south of Whitefield, turn off main road at signs.

By train: Haydon Bridge Station (11 miles) and Hexham (15 miles) Station are nearest.

ONCE BREWED HOSTEL

Military Road, Once Brewed, Bardon Mill, Hexham, Northumberland NE47 7AN

Phone Number: 01434–344360

Fax: 01434–344045
E-mail: yhaoncebrewed@compuserve.com
Rates: £6.55–£9.75 per HI member (about $10–$15 US)
Beds: 87
Family/private rooms: Sometimes
Season: February 2 to November 28
Office hours: 7:00 to 10:00 A.M.; 1:00 to 11:00 P.M.
Affiliation: HI-YHA
Extras: Laundry, dinner ($), garden, bike shop, Minicom
Lockout: 10:00 A.M.–1:00 P.M.
Curfew: 11:00 P.M.

This place is slighly nuts, what with all the tourists and schoolchildren piling in for a look at Hadrian's Hall. The puny kitchen and longish walk from public transit stops is partly made up for by the quad bunkrooms, frequently rented out by entire families for £35.50 (about $53 US).

Next time around, we'd probably skip it and and head for, oh, the hostel in Acomb maybe 'cause it's loads quieter. We've gotta admit, though, that if you're Wall-bound this is the best hostel: It sits near a great section.

Insiders' tip:
Visitors' center next door

Gestalt:
Once Brewed, twice shy

Party index:

How to get there:

By bus: From Newcastle or Carlisle take Northumbria 685 bus to Henshaw and walk 2 miles to hostel. Buses also run from Hexham to hostel, summer only; call hostel for details.

By car: Take B6318 to Once Brewed; hostel is above Bardon Mill, on corner of crossroads next to park visitor center.

By train: From Bardon Mill Station walk 2½ miles to hostel.

OSMOTHERLEY HOSTEL

Cote Ghyll, Osmotherley, Northallerton, North Yorkshire DL6 3AH

Phone Number: 01609–883575

Fax: 01609–883715
Rates: £5.95–£8.80 per HI member (about $9.00–$13.00 US); £20 doubles (about $30 US)

Beds: 80
Season: February 1 to November 7
Affiliation: HI-YHA
Extras: TV, laundry, bike storage, game room, dinner ($)

This former mill was turned into an eighty-bed hostel that includes a television, dinner service, and even a laundry. They've got everything from doubles to triples to quad rooms, and the joint is located pretty close to a number of walking trails. A campground sits adjacent to the hostel.

Party index:

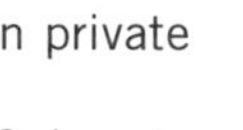

How to get there:

By bus: From Middlesbrough or Northallerton take 90 or 190 bus to Osmotherley. Walk ¾ mile to hostel.

By car: Take A19 to Osmotherley turnoff, go into village, turn left at stop, and bear right into hostel down private driveway.

By train: From Northallerton Station take 90 or 190 bus to Osmotherley. Walk ¾ mile to hostel.

PATTERDALE HOSTEL

Goldrill House, Patterdale, Penrith, Cumbria CA11 0NW

Phone Number: 017684–82394

Fax: 017684–82034
Rates: £6.55–£9.75 per HI member (about $10–$15 US)
Beds: 82
Private/family rooms: Yes
Season: Call ahead for open days
Affiliation: HI-YHA
Extras: Bicycle storage, dinner ($)

A wooden, so-called Scandinavian-style building, this place packs in eighty-two beds. Most come in big dorms, but there are three doubles available as well. They serve dinner nightly.

A local steamboat cruises the Ullswater lake, and there's climbing and walking in the area, too.

Party index:

How to get there:

By bus: From Penrith, 15 miles away, take 108 bus to Patterdale (runs Monday to Saturday).

By car: Take A592 just south of Patterdale.

By train: From Penrith Station, 15 miles away, take 108 bus to Patterdale (runs Monday to Saturday).

SCARBOROUGH HOSTEL

The White House, Burniston Road, Scarborough, North Yorkshire YO13 0DA

Phone Number: 01723–361176

Fax: 01723–500054
Rates: £4.95–£7.20 per HI member (about $7.00–$10.00 US)
Beds: 64
Season: March 27 to December 31
Affiliation: HI-YHA
Extras: Dinner ($), bike storage

This former mill building sits just inland from the sea, close to the Cleveland Way Path and other walking trails. Dorms contain six to fourteen beds each, and the coastline is the obvious draw.

Gestalt: Scarborough fare

Party index:

How to get there:

By bus: Call hostel for transit route.

By car: From Scarborough, take A165 north toward Whitby for 2 miles; make sharp left just after bridge.

By train: From Scarborough Station walk 2 miles to hostel, or call hostel for bus route.

HONISTER HAUSE HOSTEL

Seatoller, Keswick, Cumbria CA12 5XN

Phone Number: 017687–77267

Fax: 017687–77267
Rates: £4.45–£6.50 per HI member (about $7.00–$10.00 US)
Beds: 26
Private/family rooms: Yes
Season: Call ahead for open days
Affiliation: HI-YHA
Extras: Dinner ($)

Simplicity itself, but okay with us. This hostel's twenty-six beds all come just two, three, or four to a room. The usual kitchen and dinner service are available. Some of the most famous peaks in the Lake District are within a day's walk of the place, so expect a crowd of grinnin' gearheads.

Party index:

How to get there:

By bus: From Keswick take 77 or 77A bus (runs May to November) to hostel.

By car: From Keswick take B5289 9 miles to Seatoller. Hostel is on left, just west of village.

By train: Call hostel for transit route.

SLAIDBURN HOSTEL

King's House, Slaidburn, Clitheroe, Lancashire BB7 3ER

Phone Number: 01200–446656 or 015242–41567

Rates: £4.00–£5.85 per HI member (about $6.00–$9.00 US)
Beds: 22 (winter), 36 (summer)
Season: April 9 to September 26
Affiliation: HI-YHA
Extras: Store, bike storage, fireplace

This incredibly cheap hostel is a good bet if you're saving bucks, though you'd do well to remember that it's a little basic. Located in a seventeenth-century inn, it's made up of four dorm rooms plus an additional annex that opens doors in summertime only. As usual in these parts, there's good walking available in the area.

Party index:

How to get there:

By bus: From Clitheroe take 110 or 111 bus to Slaidburn.

By car: Take B6478 (Settle Road) to Slaidburn; hostel is in village center.

By train: From Clitheroe Station take 110 or 111 bus to Slaidburn.

TAITLANDS HOSTEL

Stainforth, Settle, North Yorkshire BD24 9PA

Phone Number: 01729–823577

Fax: 01729–825404
E-mail: dmcgui@netcomuk.co.uk
Rates: £5.40–£8.00 per HI member (about $8.00–$12.00 US)
Beds: 50
Season: April 1 to October 31
Affiliation: HI-YHA
Extras: Dinner ($), bike storage, gardens

Inside Yorkshire Dales National Park, this hostel's chief advantage is location near the Pennine Way. Dorms come in five to twelve bed sizes; dinner's available, as well as a kitchen and nice, gardeny

Party index:

grounds. Check out the neat bridge across the River Ribble, too.

How to get there:

By bus: Contact hostel for transit route.

By car: Take B6479 to Settle; continue 2 miles north.

By train: From Settle Station walk 2½ miles to hostel, or take taxi.

TEBAY HOSTEL

The Old School, Tebay, Penrith, Cumbria CA10 3TP

Phone Number: 015395–24286

Fax: 015395–24286
Rates: £5.40–£8.00 per HI member (about $8.00–$12.00 US)
Beds: 46
Private/family rooms: Yes
Season: Call ahead for open days
Affiliation: HI-YHA
Extras: TV, dinner ($)

Just a little stone schoolhouse, this hostel's best for walkers and cyclers who want to hit the Dales or North Pennines using it as a base. Most of the dorms contain five to eight beds, although you might luck into a double or quad—or get crammed into the eighteen-bedder. A television room and evening meals are about the only special touches they offer here.

Party index:

How to get there:

By bus: From Kendal, Penrith, or Kirkby Stephen, take bus to Tebay.

By car: Take M6 to Junction 38; continue 200 yards to hostel.

By train: From Kendal or Penrith Stations take bus to Tebay.

THIXENDALE HOSTEL

The Village Hall, Thixendale, Malton, North Yorkshire YO17 9TG

Phone Number: 01377–88238

Rates: £4.00–£5.85 per HI member (about $6.00–$9.00 US)
Beds: 18
Season: Call ahead for open days
Affiliation: HI-YHA

This is one of England's simplest hostels, a tiny schoolhouse with two dorms. There is a kitchen and a dining room, and that's it! Even the bathrooms are outside, in a separate building. But it still makes a fairly convenient, if austere, crash pad for walkers on the Wolds Way.

Gestalt: Chip 'n' Dale

Party index:

How to get there:

By bus: Call hostel for transit route.

By car: From Malton take Beverley Road to small roundabout; turn right toward Birdsall and Langton. Go through Birdsall, up hill, make a left at crossroads to village of Thixendale; hostel is in center.

By train: Call hostel for transit route.

WALKERS HOSTEL

Oubas Hill, Ulverston, Cumbria LA12 7LB

Phone Number: 01229–585588

Rates: £10–£15 per person (about $15–$18 US)
Beds: 30
Affiliation: None
Extras: Breakfast, dinner ($)

They sure get points for ecological consciousness at this out-of-the-way hostel: The place is geared to walkers, of course, and the owner also serves "fair trade" coffee and tea—products that have been obtained directly from growers rather than some unscrupulous landowner/middleman.

Beds come in spartan rooms of two to seven bunks each. Ulverston's a tiny village near the Cumbria Way and two more well-known walking paths; it's not easy to get here, but if you're driving you are fairly near the Lakes District, too.

Insiders' tip: Laurel and Hardy museum nearby

Gestalt: Earth Day

Party index:

How to get there:

By bus: Call hostel for transit route.

By car: From M6 turn onto A590 and drive 25 miles to Ulverston; hostel is on left.

By train: Call hostel for transit route.

WHITBY HOSTEL

East Cliff, Whitby, North Yorkshire YO22 4JT

Phone Number: 01947–602878

Fax: 01947–602878

Rates: £4.95–£7.20 per HI member (about $7.00–$10.00 US)
Beds: 66
Season: Call ahead for open days
Affiliation: HI-YHA
Extras: Dinner ($), garden, bike storage, lockers
Lockout: 10:00 A.M.–5:00 P.M.
Curfew: 11:00 P.M.

Formerly a stable, this hostel sits right atop the famous 199 steps that seem to lead from sea to sky. It claims a superb view of the ruined village abbey and Whitby's harbor. Most of the bunkrooms are pretty big, but they do have lockers and a decent garden on site. This is at the end of the train line, too, making it a quicker and easier destination than some other hostels.

Party index:

Whitby is a historical little find amid the Moors: Check out the cobblestone streets, and think about that abbey. (It was built in 1220, by the way—and part of the novel *Dracula* was set in this church's graveyard!)

How to get there:

By bus: From bus station walk ½ mile to hostel.

By car: Take A171 to Whitby, following signs to abbey and turn into Green Lane. Continue beyond Abbey to parking lot, walk to hostel. Small fee for parking.

By train: From Whitby Station walk ½ mile to hostel.

CARROCK FELL HOSTEL

Haltcliffe, Hesket Newmarket, Wigton, Cumbria CA7 8JT

Phone Number: 016974–78325

Fax: 016974–78325
Rates: £4.95–£7.20 per HI member (about $7.00–$11.00 US)
Beds: 20
Private/family rooms: None
Season: Call ahead for open days
Affiliation: HI-YHA
Extras: Dinner ($), fireplace

This old farmhouse is just what you'd expect: made of wood and stone, warmed by an open fire, simple as heck.

There are just three bunkrooms all told here, containing four, six, and ten beds respectively. Kitchen, bathrooms, and common room are all standard as could be. They also serve dinners here each night.

The arca has some nice trips, including a Bronze Age fort and craft shops. It's not very easy to get to by public transportation, though, even in bus-filled England; without a car, you might as well skip it.

Party index:

How to get there:

By bus: From Penrith, 15 miles away, take bus (runs Tuesdays only) to Hesket Newmarket and walk 2½ miles to hostel. Otherwise call hostel for transit route from Penrith.

By car: Take A66 to Mungrisdale turnoff, and from Mungrisdale go 3 miles north on unnumbered road toward Caldbeck; turn right at Caldbeck Road. Hostel is first house on left.

By train: From Penrith Station, 15 miles away, take bus (runs Tuesdays only) to Hesket Newmarket and walk 2½ miles to hostel. Otherwise call hostel for transit route from Penrith.

WINDERMERE HOSTEL

High Cross, Bridge Lane, Troutbeck, Windermere, Cumbria LA23 1LA

Phone Number: 015394–43543

Fax: 015394–47165
Rates: £5.95–£8.80 per HI member (about $9.00–$13.00 US)
Credit cards: Yes
Beds: 73
Private/family rooms: Yes
Season: January 1 to December 28
Affiliation: HI-YHA
Extras: TV, laundry, dinner ($), bike rentals
Lockout: 10:00 A.M.–1:00 P.M.
Curfew: 11:00 P.M.

You'll have to make tracks to get a spot at this place in summer—it's that well located and popular, though set in the middle of sheep-inhabited nowhere.

Initially intended as a private guest house, the original timber-framed building burnt down in 1915, and the slightly upset and singed owner swore that would never happen again. Rather than install a fire alarm or something similar, he rebuilt the whole thing in solid concrete. Gray concrete.

Turrets and a tower were added later so that he could call it a castle instead of a dam, but were later removed upon being declared structurally hazardous. So this place ain't pretty, but it's sure busy.

A big house, basically, the place has superb views of lake and mountain alike. To get here, however, you must make a little uphill climb away from the water that discourages some and invigorates others. Dorms are so big and airy we almost fell off the mountain, and they mostly contain just a couple beds.

Best bet for a bite: Villa Lostitano

Insiders' tip: Bowness is worth a visit

Hospitality:

Cleanliness:

Party index:

The joint is adequately clean and comfortable, though decked in drab shades of brown. We're not talking lap of luxury here, but the essentials are in place—well-stocked kitchen, shop, television. The TV is small and placed in the dining room, but you should be outside enjoying the air anyway. Grounds are large and include foundations of castles, fountains, trees, and ponds. Staff are helpful, but they won't sing you any lullabies, that's for sure.

The nightly curfew sounds bad, but you're not staying up late around here anyway unless you know some crazy sheep who know where the key to the warden's liquor cabinet is kept! Ambleside's the nearest town, and that's 3 long miles away. At least the YHA shuttle bus will whisk you and your rucksack away to any other hostel in the Lakes. So getting here (or escaping) is easier than it first appears.

How to get there:

By bus: Take bus to Troutneck Bridge, then follow signs ¾ mile up lane to hostel.

By car: From Windermere take A591 north 1 mile to Troutneck Bridge, make first right after gas station and go ¾ mile. Hostel is on left.

By train: From Windermere Station take shuttle bus to hostel.

WOOLER HOSTEL

30 Cheviot Street, Wooler, Northumberland NE71 6LW

Phone Number: 01668–81365

Fax: 01668–282368
Rates: £5.40–£8.00 per HI member (about $8.00–$12.00 US)
Beds: 52
Private/family rooms: Sometimes
Season: March 27 to October 31
Affiliation: HI-YHA
Extras: Dinner ($), laundry, bike storage
Lockout: 10:00 A.M.–5:00 P.M.
Curfew: 11:00 P.M.

Tucked in the Cheviot Hills—and right on that main auto route from London to Edinburgh—this hostel doesn't hurt for visitors. Lots of quads and nightly meals mean that families sink their teeth into the joint, possibly leaving you in the lurch; call ahead in summertime.

Two double rooms and a few six- to eight-bedded dorms are also available, but the quads make up the bulk of the accommodations here. The area's kinda boring, to be frank, but if you're crazy about fort ruins or Border castles, you'll certainly find something to do here.

Gestalt: Worsted Wooler

Party index:

How to get there:

By bus: Call hostel for transit route.

By car: Take A697 to Wooler turnoff, turn up Cheviot Street past Anchor pub. Hostel is on right.

By train: Call hostel for transit route.

YORK YOUTH HOTEL

11-13 Bishophill Senior, York YO1 1EF

Phone Number: 01904–625904

Rates: £9–£16.50 (about $14–$25 US) per person; doubles £24–£30 (about $36–$45 US)
Credit cards: Yes
Beds: 130
Office hours: Twenty-four hours
Affiliation: None
Extras: Laundry, bar, game room, bike rental, breakfast ($)

Gestalt:
York rinds

Party index:

This place is quite laid back but not always friendly. Also, the facilities are worn and not comfortable. The single advantage is that it's inside the city walls, as opposed to the HI joint's way-away positioning. And it's a bit cheaper. But not worth it—give it a miss.

How to get there:

By bus: Call hostel for transit route.

By car: Call hostel for directions.

By train: From York Station call hostel for directions.

YORK HOSTEL

Water End, Clifton, York, North Yorkshire YO3 6LY

Phone Number: 01904–653147

Fax: 01904–651230
Rates: £10.95–£14.40 per HI member (about $16–$22 US)
Credit cards: Yes
Beds: 150
Season: January 15 to December 5
Office hours: Twenty-four hours
Affiliation: HI-YHA
Extras: TV, restaurant, garden, laundry, breakfast

York's hostel is pretty good, and while it didn't exactly knock our socks off, it was certainly adequate, providing everything we needed in a hostel. Too bad you have to spend a few extra pounds than usual to stay here.

Best bet for a bite:
France

Insiders' tip:
Minster fills with song at 5:00 P.M.

Gestalt:
Minster mash

Hospitality:

Cleanliness: 

Party index:

The hostel's in a quiet neighborhood away from the tourist craziness that is downtown York. You can either walk a riverside footpath to get here from downtown, which is nicely green with lawns and fields, or else stroll down the city's main drag (watch out for the fast, mean drivers); either way is cool. (Bonus points: See if you can find poet W. H. Auden's birthplace along the way.)

Once here you're in a big Victorian house right off the river—we've heard rumors it was once the home of Brit chocolate barons the Rowntrees—about a half-hour jaunt from York Minster, one of the most awesome cathedrals you'll lay eyes on.

Start with small dorm rooms, mostly four to a room, plus some sixes and eights. A wide variety of really nice singles and doubles are also available, making this a good choice for the solo traveler or the couple—especially considering the B&B and hotel rates in this town—plus breakfast is always included with your night's sleep. They watch you like hawks to make sure you don't take too much food, though, which is annoying.

There's a garden, TV room, and laundry. Meals at the hostel restaurant are reputedly great, though we weren't impressed at all when we ate there.

How to get there:

By bus: Call hostel for transit route.

By car: From York center take A19 north and turn left at Clifton Green. From A1237 ring road turn south onto A19 (Shipton Road) and continue to Water End; turn right.

By train: From York Station go left on Station Road to Leeman; turn right, cross bridge, then turn left and walk 1 mile along river to hostel.

WALES

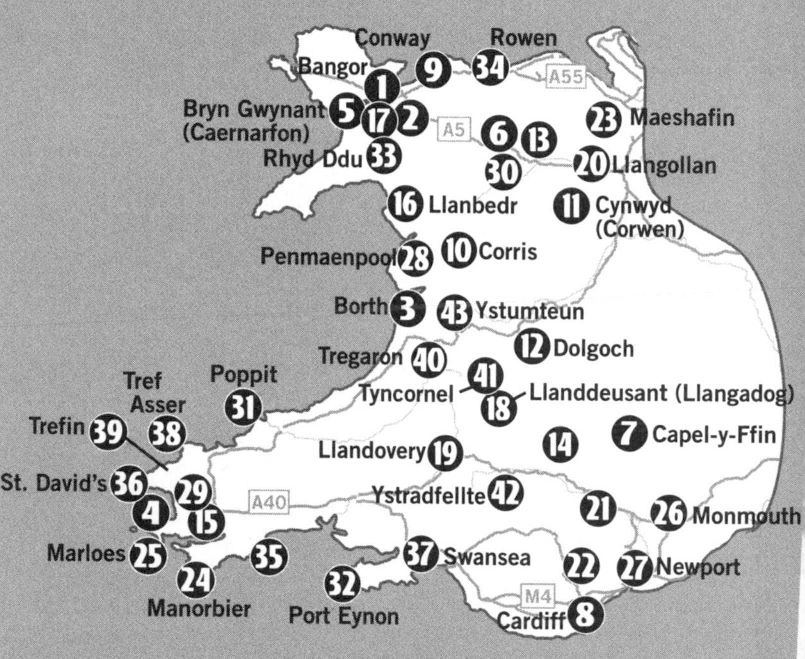

Numbers on map refer to towns numbered below.

1. Bangor
2. Bethesda
3. Borth
4. Broad Haven
5. Bryn Gwynant (Caernarfon)
6. Capel Curig
7. Capel-y-Ffin
8. Cardiff
9. Conway
10. Corris
11. Cynwyd (Corwen)
12. Dolgoch
13. Dolwyddelan
14. Groesffordd
15. Lawrenny
16. Llanbedr
17. Llanberis
18. Llanddeusant (Llangadog)
19. Llandovery
20. Llangollen
21. Llwyn-y-Celyn
22. Llwynypia
23. Maeshafn
24. Manorbier
25. Marloes
26. Monmouth
27. Newport
28. Penmaenpool
29. Penycwm (Solva)
30. Pen-y-Pass
31. Poppit
32. Port Eynon
33. Rhyd Ddu
34. Rowen
35. Saundersfoot
36. St. David's
37. Swansea
38. Tref Asser
39. Trefin
40. Tregaron
41. Tyncornel
42. Ystradfellte
43. Ystumtuen

WALES

Wales is the most mysterious, wildest part of the United Kingdom; its people speak Welsh, its identity is distinct from England's, and—although it probably won't ever push for secession like Scotland will—this is definitely a different land. Farms, quarries, mountains, and very few people make this the place to hike by yourself. Cardiff, the largest city, is the exception, a thriving (if not huge) metropolis with youthful energy.

Most Welsh hostels are extremely simple, but the legendary Welsh hospitality gives some of them an edge over some of their English and Scottish counterparts. We recommend more here than anywhere else in the Kingdom. Must be the air over here.

BANGOR HOSTEL

Tan-y-Bryn, Bangor, Gwynedd LL57 1PZ

Phone Number: 01248–353516

Fax: 01248–371176
Rates: £5.95–£8.80 per HI member (about $9.00–$13.00 US); doubles £20.50 (about $32 US)
Credit cards: Yes
Beds: 84
Season: January 1 to January 5; February 1 to November 30; December 27 to December 31
Affiliation: HI-YHA
Extras: Dinner ($), laundry, game room, bicycle shop, store

This hostel is better equipped than many of its Welsh sisters, and it has to be: It's in one of the only big cities in the whole of Wales. But the view of Penrhyn Castle is about the only reason to stay, unless you're craving a chance to wash your dirty clothes.

A Victorian house, it has medium to large dorm rooms that give it an occasional zoo feeling. Staff doesn't help matters any, though they are efficient at least. Bangor itself does have a university, so that's good.

Gestalt:
Bangor and mash

Hospitality: 

Party index:

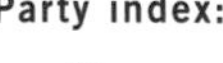

How to get there:

By bus: Call hostel for transit route.

By car: Hostel is on A5122, 50 yards before sharp left turn at sea on way into Bangor.

By train: From Bangor Station walk 1½ miles toward sea to hostel.

IDWAL COTTAGE HOSTEL

Nant Ffrancon, Bethesda, Bangor, Gwynedd LL57 3LZ

Phone Number: 01248–600225

Fax: 01248–602952
Rates: £4.95–£7.20 per HI member (about $7.00–$11.00 US)
Beds: 44
Season: Call ahead for open days
Affiliation: HI-YHA
Extras: Camping, store

This former cottage, in piney woods not far outside Bangor, features one big dorm and seven smaller ones. Facilities include a common room, dining room, kitchen, and hostel store with lotsa frozen meals. (Yum?) Hikers here attack the rugged Nany Ffrancon Valley; you can camp here, too.

Gestalt: Cottage industry

Party index:

How to get there:

By bus: From Bangor take 6 or 7 bus to Bethesda; walk 4 miles to hostel.

By car: From Bangor take A5. Four miles past Bethesda make right at Llyn Ogwen (body of water).

By train: From Bangor or Betsw-y-Coed stations, take 65 bus to Bethesda; walk 4 miles to hostel.

BORTH HOSTEL

Morlais, Borth, Dyfed SY24 5JS

Phone Number: 01970–871498

Fax: 01970–871827
Rates: £5.95–£8.80 per HI member (about $9.00–$13.00 US)
Beds: 60
Season: March 1 to October 31
Affiliation: HI-YHA
Extras: TV, bicycle shop, store
Lockout: 10:00 A.M.–5:00 P.M.
Curfew: 11:00 P.M.

This Edwardian house overlooks the sea and a beach just 10 miles from a hoppin' university town. Not to mention the adjacent golf links—a true links, hard by the salt water. The real key here, though, is closeness to CAT (the Center for Alternative Technology), a great showcase of alternative lifestyle done right.

Dorms come in quads, six-bed bunkrooms and eight-bed rooms. Facilities are adequate, and there's a TV for the bored as well as a hostel store for the unprepared. Sometimes the joint closes on a Sunday or Monday, though; call ahead in spring and fall to make sure it's open.

Gestalt: Borth sides now

Party index:

How to get there:

By bus: From Aberystwyth take 511, 512, 520, or 524 bus to Borth. Hostel is just north of village center, before golf course.

By car: Take A487 or B4353 to Borth; hostel is between central village and golf course.

By train: From Borth Station walk ¾ mile north to hostel.

BROAD HAVEN HOSTEL 

Broad Haven, Haverfordwest, Dyfed SA62 3JH

Phone Number: 01437–781688

Fax: 01437–781100
Rates: £6.55–£9.75 per HI member (about $10–$15 US); doubles £21 (about $32 US)
Beds: 75
Season: February 15 to October 31
Affiliation: HI-YHA
Extras: Laundry, dinner ($), TV, game room, bicycle shop
Lockout: 10:00 A.M.–1:00 P.M.
Curfew: 11:00 P.M.

This lovely one-story farmhouse, just 2 miles from the super destination of St. David's village, was a hit with our correspondents. They said it's big enough, it's smart enough, and—gosh darnit—people like it.

Most of the rooms are quads or bigger, though there's a double and a triple (£27.50, about $42 US) for lucky couples and families. We heard raves about the short lockout, which is mercifully only three hours; there's so much to do around here, though, that it might not matter. Further kudos for wheelchair accessibility and good meals. Looks like we have a winner.

Gestalt: Broad way

Party index:

How to get there:

By bus: From Haverfordwest take 311 bus to Broad Haven.

By car: Take B4341 to Broad Haven, then turn into parking lot at information center. Hostel is on left, beside information center.

By train: From Haverfordwest Station, 7 miles away, take 311 bus to Broad Haven.

BRYN GWYNANT HOSTEL 

Bryn Gwynant, Nantgwynant, Caernarfon, Gwynedd LL55 4NP

Phone Number: 01766–86251

Fax: 01766–890479
Rates: £5.95–£8.80 per HI member (about $9.00–$13.00 US)
Beds: 67
Season: March 1 to October 31
Affiliation: HI-YHA
Extras: Dinner ($), cycle shop

Located right in Snowdonia National Park, this stone mansion with an attached coach house is a good base for park exploration. Families—or anyone else—can rent entire triple or quad rooms for just £25–£32 (about $38–$48 US), a real deal.

Party index:

Dorms never get bigger than six beds, and there are many doubles, triples and quads—some with en-suite bathroom facilities. Wow! They serve dinner here, too, a welcome touch after weeks of rice and porridge or whatever else you've been cooking out on the hostel trail.

How to get there:

By bus: From Bangor or Llanberis take 96 bus to Beddgelert; walk 4 miles east on A498 to hostel.

By car: Drive A498 to hostel, which is 8 miles west of Capel Curig or 4 miles east of Beddgelert.

By train: From Bangor Station, 25 miles away, take 96 bus to Beddgelert; walk 4 miles east on A498 to hostel.

CAPEL CURIG HOSTEL

Plas Curig, Capel Curig, Betws-y-Coed, Gwynedd LL24 0EL

Phone Number: 01690–720225

Fax: 01690–720270
Rates: £5.95–£8.80 per HI member (about $9.00–$13.00 US); doubles £20 (about $30 US)
Credit cards: Yes
Beds: 52
Affiliation: HI-YHA
Extras: Dinner ($), store, bicycle shop
Lockout: 10:00 A.M.–5:00 P.M.
Curfew: 11:00 P.M.

A nice riverside location is the key to this hostel, which is thoughtfully outfitted with family quad bunkrooms (£31.50, about $47

US) and doubles. Dinner's served, there are two lounges, and a small store helps supply hostellers with chow.

Party index:

How to get there:

By bus: From Bangor or Llanberis take 96 bus.

By car: Take A5 to junction with A4086; turn away from A4086 and follow sign to hostel up steep driveway.

By train: From Betws-y-Coed Station, 5 miles away, take 96 bus or (in summer) 54 bus. From Bangor Station take 96 bus.

CAPEL-Y-FFIN HOSTEL

Capel-y-Ffin, Llanthony NP7 7NP

Phone Number: 01873–890650

Rates: £4.45–£6.50 per HI member (about $7.00–$10.00 US)
Credit cards: Yes
Beds: 40
Season: Call ahead for open days
Affiliation: HI-YHA
Extras: Camping, bicycle shop, store, horseback rides ($), dinner ($)
Lockout: 10:00 A.M.–5:00 P.M.
Curfew: 11:00 P.M.

A converted hill farm supplies the beds at this joint, to which most folks seem to have walked: A pair of walking trails converge at the hostel, including the popular Cambrian Way.

Set at the northeast edge of Brecon Beacons park, it consists of three smaller dorm rooms and one big twenty-bed sucker. Facilities are simple—kitchen, lounge—but they do have a hostel store and, surprisingly, serve dinner. Even more of a surprise, you can book horseback riding holidays here. It'll cost ya, but it is the classic English way of seeing the countryside.

Insiders' tip:
Bookshops in Hay-on-Wye

Gestalt:
Wye yes

Party index:

How to get there:

By bus: From Hereford take 40 bus to Hay-on-Wye. Walk 7 miles to hostel, or take taxi for about $10 US.

By car: Take A465 to Llanfihangel Crucorney; follow signs to Llanthony and then signs to Capel-y-Ffin. Hostel is 1 mile north of village center, on left.

By train: Closest Station is at Abergavenny, 16 miles away. From Hereford Station walk to 40 bus and take to Hay-on-Wye. Walk 7 miles to hostel, or take taxi for about $10 US.

CARDIFF INTERNATIONAL BACKPACKERS

96-98 Neville Street, Riverside, Cardiff CF1 8LS

Phone Number: 01222–345577

Rates: £12.50–£16 per person (about $19–$24 US); doubles £25–£29 (about $38–$45 US)
Credit cards: Yes
Beds: 45
Private/family rooms: Yes
Office hours: Call hostel for hours
Affiliation: None
Extras: Pub, TV, fax, e-mail, breakfast, travel agency, terrace, pool table

By far the more central of Cardiff's two hostels, this brand-new one's placed smack downtown—well, close enough, anyhow. It's housed in a hip purple building very close to the little Taff River that divides the city, and it's attached to a bar where most of the hostellers do their socializing. It didn't disappoint.

Best bet for a bite: Celtic Cauldron

Insiders' tip: Castle is worth it

Gestalt: Cardifferent

Party index:

Tremendous work seems to have gone into the facilities here, which include a fax, e-mail service, double and single rooms, newspaper subscriptions, a rooftop terrace, game room, and more. Recently added: a budget travel agency (albeit one geared toward Go Blue Banana's offerings).

You're not far from Cardiff's splendiforous castle, tons of pubs, and a big riverside park. A big thumbs-up from us for the nonsmoking policy, too.

How to get there:

By bus: From Cardiff bus station walk out to Wood Street and turn left. Cross river (street becomes Tudor) and turn right at Clare Street. Continue to corner of Neville Street; hostel is on left.

By car: Call hostel for directions.

By train: From Cardiff Central Station walk out to Wood Street and turn left. Cross river (street becomes Tudor) and turn right at Clare Street. Continue to corner of Neville Street; hostel is on left.

CARDIFF TY CROESO (WELCOME HOUSE) HOSTEL

2 Wedal Road, Roath Park, Cardiff CF2 5PG

Phone Number: 01222–462303

Fax: 01222–464751

Rates: £6.55–£9.75 per HI member (about $10–$15 US)
Beds: 68
Season: January 2 to November 30
Affiliation: HI-YHA
Extras: TV, laundry, bicycle shop, dinner ($), bar
Lockout: 10:00 A.M.–3:00 P.M.
Curfew: 11:00 P.M.

It's a couple miles outside the central city, yet Cardiff's hostel is still plagued by extremely busy surroundings. Bring some earplugs if you want some rest. Otherwise, it's a decent enough place, serving up good meals—and a beer on the side, if you like—to go with its plain dorm rooms. There are two lounges and a telly to occupy the little ones, plus a laundry to occupy the big ones.

While in town most visitors suck down a couple beers before quickly digging out for this beautiful country's rural parks. Cardiff's more interesting than you think, though. For one thing, there's a giant castle perched right at the head of downtown. Eyeball that baby while you're drinking a pint. (Pubs are scattered about.) Second, cheap and surprisingly diverse food options are everywhere. There's a bay. And you can get a bus or train from here to just about anywhere in Wales, it seems.

Best bet for a bite: Bella Pasta

Gestalt: Score Cardiff

Hospitality: 

Party index: 

Need direction? The local tourist office (located in the Cardiff Central train station) is great. We know. They once sent a free taxi to fetch our wayward credit card as we were waiting for a train to leave. Honest.

How to get there:

By bus: From downtown take 78, 80, or 82 bus to hostel.

By car: From M4 take A48M to roundabout; exit first left off roundabout, follow Whitchurch Road to Fairoak Road and make a left. Continue to smaller roundabout; hostel is at corner of Wedal Road and Fairoak.

By train: From Cardiff Central Station walk 2½ miles, or take 78, 80, or 82 bus to hostel.

CONWAY HOSTEL 

Larkhill, Sychnany Pass Road, Conway LL32 8AJ

Phone Number: 01492–593571

Fax: 01492–593580
Rates: £6.55–£9.75 per HI member (about $10–$15 US); doubles £21 (about $32 US)

Beds: 80
Affiliation: HI-YHA
Extras: TV, laundry, lockers, dinner ($), kids' room, bicycle shop

This big and relatively new hostel looked great to us—it had so many thoughtful touches that it might be the best bargain for your buck in Wales, amenities-wise at least.

Like what? Like a playroom for kids. Tons of double rooms and quads suited for couples and families. Several lounges, a television, lockers, washing machines . . . plus dinner. Did we mention that all those small rooms have en-suite bathrooms? You've got to be kidding!

Gestalt: Conwynner

Party index:

The location is good, too, just half a mile outside a cute, walled Welsh town with one of Europe's best towered walls and history galore. (Hit the fine castle, then top that off with the UK's smallest house for dessert.) As if all that weren't enough, this town's on the train line, too, and close to Snowdonia. If you're driving, it's 30 miles from a ferry in Holyhead that connects Wales with Ireland.

This one's a keeper, folks, even if it's somewhat sterile. Sometimes you just need a little comfort.

How to get there:

By bus: Call hostel for transit route.

By car: From Chester take A55 to second Conway exit (sign says A547). Follow into town; at town walls make a right into Mount Pleasant and another right at stop sign. Continue 150 yards to hostel on left.

By train: From Conway Station walk ½ mile west out of town to hostel.

CORRIS OLD SCHOOL HOSTEL

Canolfin Corris, Old School, Corris, Machynlleth, Powys SY20 9QT

Phone Number: 01654–761686

Fax: 01654–761686
Rates: £5.40–£8.00 per HI member (about $8.00–$12.00 US); doubles £18 (about $27 US)
Beds: 48
Season: Call ahead for open days
Affiliation: HI-YHA
Extras: Lockers, laundry, bicycle shop, globe, dinner ($)
Lockout: 10:00 A.M.–5:00 P.M.
Curfew: 11:00 P.M.

This building was once Corris's village schoolhouse. Now it's a super-eco-friendly hostel in a super location between a lake and a mountain—still serving its original purpose of educating the young, only in a slightly different way.

But this corner of green Wales has always moved to the beat of a slightly different drummer. Most people come here because it's just a hop from the great Center for Alternative Technology, an experiment in green living that has worked marvelously. As befits this location, the hostel itself won a Green Tourism Award.

Best bet for a bite: CAT's cafe

Gestalt: Cool CAT

Party index:

Dorms come in various shapes and sizes; there are a few triple and quad rooms for families, a fantastic bargain, and really inexpensive doubles. Then there are the bigger ones, all the way up to a room with twenty-two bunks. Hmmm. Guess this is communal living. Anyhow, dinner is served at 7:00 each night, and cyclists are encouraged and welcomed.

Really good.

How to get there:

By bus: From Machynlleth take 2 or 34 bus to Corris.

By car: Take A487 into Corris; at Slaters Arms pub make a left and drive 150 yards. Hostel is on right.

By train: From Machynlleth Station take 2 or 34 bus to Corris.

THE OLD MILL HOSTEL

The Old Mill, Cynwyd, Corwen, Denbighshire LL21 0LW

Phone Number: 01490–412814

Rates: £4.45–£6.50 per HI member (about $7.00–$10.00 US)
Beds: 30
Family/private rooms: Sometimes

Season: April 8 to April 14; May 2 to September 26
Affiliation: HI-YHA
Extras: Porch, camping, store, bicycle shop

A riverside setting draws hikers, cyclists, and other nature lovers here to the Old Mill, which was indeed once a woolen mill. Handsome wooden beams hold it up, and indoors you've got your standard-issue kitchen, dining room, and bathroom. The main attraction around here would be Pistyll Rhaeadr Falls, the very highest in Wales. Bala Lake is just 10 miles away, and camping is also allowed on the grounds.

Gestalt:
Run of the mill

Party index:

How to get there:

By bus: From Wrexham or Barmouth take 94 bus to Cynwyd; at Blue Lion crossroads turn east and go 100 yards to hostel.

By car: Take B4401 to Cynwyd village center; at Blue Lion crossroads turn east and go 100 yards to hostel.

By train: From Ruabon Station, 18 miles away, take 94 bus to Cynwyd; at Blue Lion crossroads turn east and go 100 yards to hostel.

DOLGOCH HOSTEL

Dolgoch, Tregaron, Dyfed SY25 6NR

Phone Number: 01222–396766

Rates: £4.00–£5.85 per HI member (about $6.00–$9.00 US)
Beds: 22
Season: Call ahead for open days
Affiliation: HI-YHA
Extras: Fireplace, store

Another bare-bones Welsh hostel, this one's a remote farmhouse without electricity. A fireplace keeps the place fairly warm, and gas lamps supply the light; three dorm rooms compete for your attention, containing four to twelve bunks apiece. There's a small kitchen/dining room, plus a tiny hostel store if you forgot some essentials.

Party index:

The setting is all quiet hills and fields, sheep crossing the road—in short, the Wales you dreamed of. Thrills around here would mostly consist of walking or biking, although they don't rent cycles here. Also, if you're driving in remember that the access road is extremely rough; don't bring that BMW in here.

How to get there:

By bus: Call hostel for directions.

By car: From Tregaron take Abergwesyn Mountain Road 9 miles to Dolgoch; hostel is ¾ mile south of bridge.

By train: Call hostel for transit route.

LLEDR VALLEY HOSTEL

Lledr House, Pont-y-Pant, Dolwyddelan, Conwy LL25 0DQ

Phone Number: 01690–750202

Fax: 01690–750410
Rates: £5.40–£8.00 per HI member (about $8.00–$12.00 US)
Credit cards: Yes
Beds: 60
Private/family rooms: Sometimes
Season: Call ahead for open days
Affiliation: HI-YHA
Extras: Camping, bicycle shop, dinner ($)
Lockout: 10:00 A.M.–5:00 P.M.
Curfew: 11:00 P.M.

This former quarry manager's home has tight quarters, to be sure, but a rustic location compensates. Dorms range from pretty big (ten and fifteen beds) to plenty of smaller ones, including quads and doubles. Camping is also allowed. Attractions include quarries, mills, and walks.

Party index:

How to get there:

By bus: Call hostel for transit route.

By car: Take A470 to 1 mile west of Dolwyddelan; hostel is on north side of highway.

By train: From Pont-y-Pant Station walk ¾ mile to A470, make a left, continue to hostel on right.

TY'N-Y-CAEAU HOSTEL

Groesffordd, Brecon, Powys LD3 7SW

Phone Number: 0187486–270

Fax: 01874–665278
Rates: £5.40–£8.00 per HI member (about $8.00–$12.00 US)
Beds: 54
Private/family rooms: Sometimes
Season: Call ahead for open days

Affiliation: HI-YHA
Extras: Dinner ($), TV, bicycle shop, porch
Lockout: 10:00 A.M.–5:00 P.M.
Curfew: 11:00 P.M.

Yet another old farmhouse on nice grounds, this hostel works as a low-comfort base to explore Brecon Beacons National Park. It has a television, a real rarity among Welsh hostels, plus a double room. Lots of free walks are run by the park staff during the warmer months, or you can tramp in from the park yourself if you're roughing it hut-to-hut style.

Things get busy around here in August, when a big international jazz festival books up rooms for miles around Brecon.

Gestalt: Brecon and eggs

Party index:

How to get there:

By bus: From Newport or Brecon take 21 bus to Llanfrynach turnoff and walk 1 mile to hostel; from Hereford take 39 or 40 bus to Llandew turnoff and walk ¾ mile to hostel.

By car: From A40 exit north at Llangorse turnoff. Go north to Groesffordd, then continue ¾ mile to hostel.

By foot: From Brecon walk 2 miles along bridle path east of town to hostel.

By train: From Hereford Station take 40 bus to Llandew turnoff and walk ¾ mile to hostel; from Abergavenny Station take 21 bus to Llanfrynach and walk 1 mile to hostel.

MILLENNIUM HOSTEL

Lawrenny, Kilgetty, Pembrokeshire SA68 0PN

Phone Number: 01646–651221

Rates: £4.45–£6.50 per HI member (about $7.00–$10.00 US)
Beds: 24
Season: Call ahead for open days
Affiliation: HI-YHA
Extras: Tours

How much darned simpler can it get? This schoolhouse has five dorm rooms, a kitchen, a lounge, showers. That's it: the key vitamins and minerals of hosteldom, nothing more.

In the area you might check out the Norman church or sign up for one of the hostel-run rock-climbing or canoeing expeditions.

Gestalt: Millennium falcon

Party index:

How to get there:

By bus: From Narberth take Postbus to Lawrenny.

By car: From Carmarthen take A40 west to Canaston, then take A4075 (Tenby Road) to CC 2000.

Turn right and follow signs 5 miles to Lawrenny. Hostel is in village, across from post office.

By train: Narberth Station is 10 miles away. From Narberth take Postbus to Lawrenny.

LLANBEDR HOSTEL

Plas Newydd, Llanbedr, Barmouth, Gwynedd LL45 2LE

Phone Number: 01341–241287

Fax: 01341–241389
Rates: £5.40–£8.00 per HI member (about $8.00–$12.00 US)
Beds: 47
Season: April 10 to October 31
Affiliation: HI-YHA
Extras: Garden, grill, bicycle shop, dinner ($)

Another plain hostel, situated near beaches and mountains in Snowdonia National Park. They've got the usual kitchen, common road, plus the bonus of a garden and grill for barbecueing. Triple rooms here are an exceptional bargain at just £24 (about $36 US), and it's all right on the rail and bus lines for easy access.

Insiders' tip:
Check out Portmeirion

Party index:

How to get there:

By bus: From Barmouth or Blaenau Ffestiniog, take 38 bus to Llanbedr.

By car: Take A496 to Llanbedr village center; hostel is beside stone bridge, at river.

By train: From Llanbedr Station walk ½ mile to hostel.

LLANBERIS HOSTEL

Llwyn Celyn, Llanberis, Caernarfon, Gwynedd LL55 4SR

Phone Number: 01286–870280

Fax: 01286–870936
Rates: £5.40–£8.00 per HI member (about $8.00–$12.00 US)
Credit cards: Yes
Beds: 67
Season: Call ahead for open days
Affiliation: HI-YHA
Extras: TV, bicycle shop, dinner ($), meeting room
Lockout: 10:00 A.M.–5:00 P.M.

This hilltop farm-style hostel has great views of Snowdon summit and offers two large dormitories as well as some smaller ones. This is a popular place in summer, and management has added nightly dinner service, a meeting room, and a television room to the usual kitchen/common room situation.

Gestalt:
Summit metting

Party index:

How to get there:

By bus: From Caernarfon take 88 bus to Llanberis. Walk ½ mile up High Street to Capel Coch Road, turn, continue through gate to hostel.

By car: From Llanberis take High Street to the Spar; turn onto Capel Coch Road, stay left at fork in road on hill, go through gate. Hostel is on left.

By train: From Bangor Station, 11 miles away, take 77 bus to Llanberis. Walk ½ mile up High Street to Capel Coch Road, turn, continue through gate to hostel.

LLANDDEUSANT HOSTEL

Llanddeusant, Llangadog, Dyfed SA19 6UL

Phone Number: 015504–634619

Rates: £4.45–£6.50 per HI member (about $7.00–$10.00 US)
Credit cards: Yes
Beds: 28
Season: April 3 to September 3
Affiliation: HI-YHA
Extras: Bicycle shop, camping, fireplace
Curfew: 11:00 P.M.

Four dorm rooms make up this former inn, which is simply furnished but does feature central heating and an open fire. It all makes for a very nice rural getaway; the only problem is, public transit doesn't come anywhere near here.

Party index:

Walking in the area among lakes and ruins is popular, and the fourteenth-century church next door provides something of a kick.

How to get there:

By bus: Bus stop 5 miles from hostel; call hostel for transit route.

By car: Take A40 to Trecastle, turn off main road, and go 9 miles to Cross Inn; turn left.

By train: Nearest station is Llangadog, 7 miles away; no public transit.

BRYN POETH UCHAF HOSTEL

Hafod-y-Pant, Cynghordy, Llandovery, Dyfed SA20 0NB

Phone Number: 015505–235

Rates: £4.00–£5.85 per HI member (about $6.00–$9.00 US)
Beds: 22
Season: April 3 to September 26
Affiliation: HI-YHA
Extras: Camping

Simple is as simple does: no electricity, gas lights, simple potty. But, hey, it's a converted farmhouse barn with four bunkrooms, including one precious double.

Remember that you're on the manager's farm, so respect the property—and if you drive in, you'll park there first, check in, and walk ¾ mile uphill to the place. (Bring a flashlight at night; you'll need it.) Stunning views of Brecon Beacons Park are the major positive here, unless you're into roughing it for hostel prices—in which case this is indeed roughing it.

Party index:

How to get there:

By bus: Call hostel for transit route.

By car: Call for directions. Small fee for parking.

By train: Cynghordy Station is 2 miles away; call hostel for directions.

LLANGOLLEN CENTRE HOSTEL

Tyndwr Hall, Llangollen, Denbighsire LL20 8AR

Phone Number: 01978–860330

Fax: 01978–861709
Rates: £5.95–£9.75 per HI member (about $9.00–$15.00 US); doubles £22 (about $33 US)
Beds: 130
Season: February 13 to October 31
Affiliation: HI-YHA
Extras: Dinner ($), lockers, bicycle shop, laundry

Very good hostel here, outfitted with perks like a laundry, lockers, and dinners. As a bonus they conduct lots of field programs—which could mean tons of shrieking schoolchildren, but could also mean you'll learn something about the flora and fauna of Snowdonia.

The place consists of a big Victorian house plus a coach house with nicer, slightly more expensive rooms. Dorm rooms are mostly huge, ten- to twenty-bed affairs, though there's also a goodly supply of doubles in the coach house. Plenty of attractions in the Dee Valley beyond, from an aqueduct to an abbey to walking tracks.

Gestalt: Field trip

Party index:

How to get there:

By bus: Call hostel for transit route.

By car: From Shrewsbury take A5 to sign; turn up Birch Hill, then go right at junction in ½ mile.

By train: From Ruabon Station take X5 bus to Llangollen; walk 1½ miles east on A5 to hostel. From Chirk Station walk 6 miles to hostel.

LLWYN-Y-CELYN HOSTEL

Llwyn-y-Celyn, Libanus, Brecon, Powys LD3 8NH

Phone Number: 01874–624261

Fax: 01874–625916
Rates: £4.95–£7.20 per HI member (about $7.00–$11.00 US)
Beds: 42
Season: Call ahead for open days
Affiliation: HI-YHA
Extras: Dinner ($), camping, bicycle shop, meeting rooms

This farmhouse is short on creature comforts but long on views. Just three dorm rooms in the whole joint, all of them big; plus there's a lounge, a kitchen, and some small meeting rooms for school classes and such. Nature trails run around the property's fifteen acres of grounds, many of them with knockout views of 3,000-foot Pen-y-Fan (which can also be climbed on a trail).

Gestalt: View finder

Party index:

How to get there:

By bus: From Brecon take bus toward Merthy Tydfil to hostel.

By car: On A470, hostel is on right 2 miles north of Storey Arms center and 7 miles south of Brecon.

By train: Merthyr Tydfil Station, 11 miles away, is closest. Call hostel for transit route.

GLYNCORNET CENTRE HOSTEL

Glyncornet Centre, Llwynypia, Rhondda, Mid Glamorgan CF40 2JF

Phone Number: 01443–430859

Fax: 01443–440232
Rates: £5.95–£8.80 per HI member (about $9.00–$13.00 US)

Beds: 62
Season: Call ahead for open days
Affiliation: HI-YHA
Extras: TV, porch

Whoever decided to put a hostel here at Llwynypia was smart: It boasts excellent position right on the train line and is attached to the Glyncoret Environmental Centre—which means amenities like a television, nature center, and museums usually absent from a Welsh hostel. All nine dorms are pretty big, which isn't pleasant, but it's still a good rural escape into the real Wales.

Remember, though: It is always closed weekends, so don't bother hauling that pack all the way from Cardiff on the train for nothing.

Gestalt: Green team

Party index:

How to get there:

By bus: From Cardiff take X9 bus to Rhondda.

By car: From M4 take Junction 34 and follow signs to Rhondda Valley and Glyncoret Centre. Hostel is attached to Centre.

By train: Llwynypia Station, walk ½ mile to hostel.

HOLT HOSTEL

Maeshafn, Mold, Denbighshire CH7 5LR

Phone Number: 01352–810320

Rates: £4.95–£7.20 per HI member (about $7.00–$11.00 US)
Beds: 31
Season: Call ahead for open days
Affiliation: HI-YHA
Extras: Bicycle shop

For some reason, this hostel closes five days a week in summer, making it an unlikely choice in high season. A Swiss chalet–style building among the Clwydian Hills, it also doesn't offer squat in the way of privacy: The only two dorms contain ten and twenty-one beds. Harumph! Best thing we can say here is that it's close to good bicycling lanes.

Gestalt: Holt it

Party index:

How to get there:

By bus: From Mold take B5 bus to Maeshafn Road; walk 1½ miles to village and then left to hostel.

By car: Take A494 to Gwernymynydd, turn off main road, and head toward Maeshafn. At village center, turn left and go ½ mile to hostel on left.

By train: From Flint or Chester Stations take B5 bus to Maeshafn Road; walk 1½ miles to village and then left to hostel.

MANORBIER HOSTEL

Skrinkle Haven, Manorbier, Pembrokeshire SA70 7TT

Phone Number: 01834–871803

Fax: 01834–871101
Rates: £6.55–£9.75 per HI member (about $10–$15 US)
Credit cards: Yes
Beds: 56
Season: February 13 to October 29
Affiliation: HI-YHA
Extras: Dinner ($), laundry, TV, store, bicycle shop, camping, porch
Lockout: 10:00 A.M.–5:00 P.M.
Curfew: 11:00 P.M.

Both ocean foam and beach sand can be reached with a Frisbee toss or two from this hostel's grounds. It's a pretty modern place—a welcome change from barracks-style schoolhouses, though it did in fact used to be a barracks!

Gestalt:
Skrinkle, skrinkle, little star

Party index:

The hostel includes eight dorms, most of them pretty big, but there's the added bonus of three separate apartments where a family could sleep five for about £40 (about $60 US). You'll probably spend most of your time beachcombing, anyway.

How to get there:

By bus: From Tenby take 358 or 359 bus to Skrinkle Haven; walk 1 mile to hostel.

By car: From Tenby take A4139 toward Pembroke 4 miles, then turn left onto B4585. Follow signs toward ocean to hostel; at playground, go straight and turn left at Artillery Range gates.

By train: Manorbier or Tenby Station, each 5 miles away, are closest stops. Walk to hostel. From Tenby take 358 or 359 bus to Skrinkle Haven and walk 1 mile to hostel.

MARLOES SANDS HOSTEL

Runwayskiln, Marloes, Haverfordwest, Pembrokeshire SA62 3BH

Phone Number: 01646–636667

Rates: £4.45–£6.50 per HI member (about $7.00–$10.00 US)
Beds: 30
Season: April 3 to October 31
Affiliation: HI-YHA

A bunch of farm buildings stand by the beach, protected by the National Trust; four dorm with four to ten beds supply the lodging. Views off the cliffs here are stunning, though the hostel itself is rather basic. At least there's access to a coastal path. The bird and marine reserves on Skomer Island can also be reached by ferry from nearby Martin Haven.

Gestalt: Sand castle

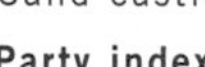

Party index:

How to get there:

By car: From Haverfordwest take B4327 for 11 miles, then make a right to Marloes. At church turn left to Marloes Sand parking area; hostel is down private lane, 200 yards.

By train: Milford Haven Station, 11 miles away, is closest. No public transit.

MONMOUTH HOSTEL

Priory Street School, Priory Street, Monmouth NP5 3NX

Phone Number: 01600–715116

Rates: £4.95–£7.20 per HI member (about $7.00–$11.00 US)
Beds: 30
Season: March 6 to October 24
Affiliation: HI-YHA

This former schoolhouse right smack on the English border isn't fancy at all. But there's good canoeing in the area, so it might be worth a look. Three dorms make up the place, which also has a kitchen and decent grounds. Two castles, Roman ruins, and other cool stuff can easily be reached, as well.

Party index:

How to get there:

By bus: From Hereford take 416 bus; from Chepstow take 65 or 69 bus; from Newport take 60 bus.

By car: Take A466 to Monmouth. Hostel is near center, where river runs along Priory Street.

By train: From Hereford Station, 16 miles away, take 416 bus; from Chepstow Station, 16 miles away, take 65 or 69 bus.

NEWPORT SANDS YOUTH HOSTEL

Lower St. Mary's Street, Newport, Pembrokeshire SA42 0TS

Phone Number: 01239–820080

Fax: 01239–820080
Rates: £5.40–£8.00 per HI member (about $8.00–$12.00 US); doubles £18 (about $27 US)
Beds: 28

Season: April 3 to October 31
Affiliation: HI-YHA

Don't confuse this new hostel's location with the big city of Newport, Wales; this Newport is a little beach town on the wild West Wales coast, not far from the Fishguard ferry that takes you to southeast Ireland.

It's basic, but nice in that it offers two double rooms and three quads. Families would find this a nice getaway. Pubs, shops, a bird sanctuary—it's all here, plus Iron Age ruins, walking hills, and, of course, the ocean. The place sometimes closes on Wednesdays and Thursdays during the shoulder seasons, so be aware.

Gestalt: Newport news

Party index:

How to get there:

By bus: Call hostel for transit route.

By car: From A487 turn off at Newport onto Lower St. Mary's Street. Hostel is in center of town, on right.

By foot: From Poppit Sands hostel follow coastal path 11 miles to hostel; from Pwll Deri hostel take coastal footpath 22 miles or coast road 13 miles.

By train: From Haverfordwest Station take 412 bus.

By ferry: Take ferry from Rosslare, Ireland, to Fishguard, Wales, then take two buses; call hostel for transit route.

KINGS DOLGELLAU HOSTEL

Kings, Penmaenpool, Dolgellau, Gwynedd LL40 1TB

Phone Number: 01341–422392

Fax: 01341–422477
Rates: £4.95–£7.20 per HI member (about $7.00–$11.00 US)
Credit cards: Yes
Beds: 56
Season: Call ahead for open days
Affiliation: HI-YHA
Extras: Dinner ($), bicycle shop

Party index:

This hostel's a country home with an annex set beside a river and looking up to Cader Idris. Seven dorms all have eight beds apiece, and in addition to the kitchen and common room there is dinner service each night at 7:00. Chief attractions include Celtica, a wildlife center; pony rides; and great lakes in the area.

How to get there:

By bus: From Dolgellau or Tywyn take 28 bus to Abergwynant Bridge; walk 1 mile to hostel.

By car: Take A493 toward Tywyn; go 1 mile west of Penmaenpool, turn up hill across from the Abergwynant Trekking Centre. Continue 1 mile along narrow lane to hostel.

By train: From Morfa Mawddach Station walk 5 miles to hostel. From Fairbourne Station take 28 bus to Abergwynant Bridge; walk 1 mile to hostel.

PENYCWM-SOLVA HOSTEL 

Whitehouse, Penycwm (Solva) Haverfordwest, Pembrokeshire SA61 6LA

Phone Number: 01437–720959

Fax: 01437–720959
Rates: £5.95–£8.80 per HI member (about $9.00–$13.00 US); doubles £21 (about $32 US)
Beds: 26
Affiliation: HI-YHA
Extras: TV, bicycle shop, dinner ($), bar

This hostel is a worthwhile detour for those walking the Pembrokeshire Coastal Path, otherwise it's a little removed from the main roads. Still, get this: Each and every one of its dorm rooms—which come in sizes of two to six beds—has en-suite bathrooms. This is remarkable. Pinch yourself. You won't get this amenity almost anywhere else in British Isles, we'd wager. To boot, they serve liquor with dinner. Okay, that officially clinches it: This is a good place for a layover.

Two local sights are worth checking out within a few miles of the hostel: the sand beach at Newgale if it's warm and sunny or the lovely harbor at Solva if it's not.

How to get there:

By car: Take A487 from Newgale to Solva Road at Penycwm; turn north off main road to Letterston/Mathry and follow signs to hostel.

PEN-Y-PASS HOSTEL 

Pen-y-Pass, Nantgwynant, Caernarfon, Gwynedd LL55 4NY

Phone Number: 01286–870428

Fax: 286–872434
Rates: £5.95–£8.80 per HI member (about $9.00–$13.00 US); doubles £20 (about $30 US)

Credit cards: Yes
Beds: 84
Family/private rooms: Yes
Season: January 1 to November 1
Affiliation: HI-YHA
Extras: TV, bicycle shop, game room, dinner ($), outings
Lockout: 10:00 A.M.–1:00 P.M.

$

Pretty well equipped for such a rustic hostel, this is a good spot to rest up before attempting the rugged trek up Mt. Snowdon. Pick up info and warnings at the national park office across the road from the hostel, then tackle either the Miners or Pyg trail.

The hostel itself has a great range of lodgings, including good doubles, triples (cheap at £25, about $38 US), quads (£32.50, about $49 US), and more. The staff is invariably composed of gearheads who won't hesitate on a sunny morning to head off for a day of rock-climbing and cliff-scaling. Go along if you dare. We also liked the short lockout—only three hours!—dinners and game room.

Gestalt: Forward pass

Party index:

How to get there:

By bus: From Llanberis take 96 bus to hostel.

By car: Take A4086 5 miles west of Capel Curig; hostel is north of highway, small parking area on south side.

By foot: From Idwal Cottage hostel in Nant Ffrancon Valley, walk 5 miles to hostel.

By train: From Bangor or Betws-y-Coed Stations, take 96 bus to hostel.

POPPIT SANDS HOSTEL

Sea View, Poppit, Cardigan, Dyfed SA43 3LP

Phone Number: 01239–612936

Fax: 01239–612936
Rates: £4.95–£7.20 per HI member (about $7.00–$11.00 US)
Beds: 30
Season: April 3 to October 31
Affiliation: HI-YHA
Extras: Porch, camping

The views of the Pembrokeshire coast don't get much better than they do right here, and a nice beach sits right below this hostel. Once an inn, the building has been divided into a number of dorm rooms, most manageably sized at four to six beds.

Most hostellers here want the scenery, or else they're beginning or ending a walk along the Pembrokeshire Coastal Path: This is the northerly end of that walking track.

Gestalt:
Sea urchin

Party index:

How to get there:

By bus: From Cardigan, July to August only, take 407 or 409 bus to Poppit Sands. Or take 407 or 409 bus to St. Dogmaels and walk 1½ miles to hostel.

By car: From Cardigan go west 1 mile to St. Dogmaels, then turn right onto B4546 and go 1½ miles to Poppit Sands. Hostel is on right, near lifeboat station.

By train: Fishguard Harbour Station, 20 miles away, is closest stop.

THE OLD LIFEBOAT HOUSE HOSTEL

Port Eynon, Swansea, West Glamorgan SA3 1NN

Phone Number: 01792–390706

Fax: 01792–390706
Rates: £4.95–£7.20 per HI member (about $7.00–$11.00 US)
Credit cards: Yes
Beds: 30
Season: April 3 to October 31
Affiliation: HI-YHA

This is a very good, if simple, hostel overlooking the ocean and providing great views of the extremely scenic Gower Peninsula. Seals can sometimes be seen, for instance, and sunrise (on nice days) is a good bet, too.

The hostel—obviously, it used to be a lifesaving station—is made up of three dorms, including a quad and two biggies. There's a kitchen and lounge, all capably run by nice management and staff.

Nature's the thing here, with many walking trails at hand around the peninsula. Port Eynon also supplies a pub and a few shops for whiling away the odd hour or two.

Gestalt:
Lifesaver

Hospitality:

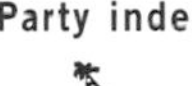

Party index:

How to get there:

By bus: From Swansea take 18A bus (except Sundays) to Port Eynon.

By car: From Swansea take A4118 to Port Eynon. Hostel is on water; park by ocean, walk ¼ mile to hostel.

By ferry: Take ferry from Cork, Ireland, to Swansea, Wales. From Swansea take 18A bus (except Sundays) to Port Eynon.

By train: Swansea Station, 16 miles away, is closest; from station take 18A bus (except Sundays) to Port Eynon.

SNOWDON RANGER HOSTEL

Rhyd Ddu, Caernarfon, Gwynedd LL54 7YS

Phone Number: 01286–650391

Fax: 01286–650093
Rates: £5.95–£8.80 per HI member (about $9.00–$13.00 US)
Beds: 66
Family/private rooms: Sometimes
Season: Call ahead for open days
Affiliation: HI-YHA
Extras: Dinner ($), game room, bicycle shop
Lockout: 10:00 A.M.–5:00 P.M.
Curfew: 11:00 P.M.

This former inn-turned-hostel is terrific: knockout scenery and quick access to trails running right from the base of Snowdon. There's even a lake here for swimming! An outdoorsperson's dream, that's what this is.

But wait. There's more.

Gestalt:
Ranger Rick

Party index:

You've also won great meals and access to a game room and—if you're very lucky—one of the twin-bedded rooms. Other dorms contain up to nine beds, but even these are okay. Did we mention the orienteering course? Simply put, this is a Welsh holiday sent by heaven. Not the fanciest place you can stay, not even for a hostel—but just great, great fun.

How to get there:

By bus: From Caernarfon or Beddgelert take 95 bus to hostel.

By car: Take A4085 8 miles south of Caernarfon or 5 miles north of Beddgelert; hostel is across road from lake.

By train: From Bangor or Porthmadog Stations, take 95 bus to hostel.

ROWEN HOSTEL

Rhiw Farm, Rowen, Conwy LL32 8YW

Phone Number: 01492–650089

Rates: £4.45–£6.50 per HI member (about $7.00–$10.00 US)
Beds: 24
Family/private rooms: Sometimes
Season: May 2 to September 5
Affiliation: HI-YHA
Extras: Bicycle shop

This Welsh farmhouse up a ste-e-e-ep hill (not all cars can make it) puts you in two- to ten-bedded dorm rooms only 5 miles from the coast. Common room, kitchen, bub; that's all you get. The ocean-side village of Llandudno is a popular sidetrip from here.

How to get there:

By bus: From Llanberis or Llandudno take 19A bus to Rowen; walk 1 mile to hostel.

By car: Take B5106 or A479 to turnoff for Rowen; turn, go through village ⅓ mile to hostel sign, drive up very steep hill. Continue ¾ mile; hostel is on left.

By train: From Tal-y-Cafn walk 3 miles to hostel. From Llandudno Station take 19A bus to Rowen and walk 1 mile to hostel.

PENTLEPOIR HOSTEL

The Old School, Saundersfoot, Dyfed SA69 9BJ

Phone Number: 01834–812333

Rates: £4.45–£6.50 per HI member (about $7.00–$10.00 US)
Credit cards: Yes
Beds: 34
Season: April 3 to October 31
Affiliation: HI-YHA
Extras: Dinner ($), bicyle shop
Lockout: 10:00 A.M.–5:00 P.M.
Curfew: 11:00 P.M.

This former schoolhouse, just inland from the beach towns of Tenby and Saundersfoot, features one small quad dorm room and two great big ones with ten and eighteen beds respectively. As a bonus, if you're driving it's on the way to the Pembroke ferry that brings you to southeast Ireland.

How to get there:

By bus: From Tenby take 350, 351, 352, or 361 bus to Saundersfoot.

By car: From Tenby take A478 to Saundersfoot; at crossroads with gas station, make a left. Hostel is on left.

By ferry: Ferry from Rosslare, Ireland, to Pembroke, Wales, 11 miles away.

By train: From Saundersfoot Station walk ¾ mile west to hostel.

ST. DAVID'S HOSTEL 

Llaethdy, St. David's, Haverfordwest, Pembrokeshire SA62 6PR

Phone Number: 01437–720345

Fax: 01437–721831

Rates: £4.45–£6.50 per HI member (about $7.00–$10.00 US)
Beds: 44
Season: April 3 to October 31
Affiliation: HI-YHA
Extras: Store

This old farmhouse couldn't be better placed, for our money: You've got the country (seaside views) and city (St. David's, one of our favorite Welsh towns). What else do you need?

Facilities are superbasic—hey, it's a farmhouse, not the Club Med—with three large dorms. The real gem here, though, is the separate four-bunk unit in an annex. And don't forget the stupendous sea views.

Gestalt:
Green jeans

Party index:

The town is interesting, featuring great architecture and a location on the tippy-top of a hill. The tourist draw here is a legitimate sight for the ages: St. Non's Well, a mile away, is the clifftop birthplace of St. David in A.D. 500. You won't see this at Disneyworld.

How to get there:

By bus: From Haverfordwest or Fishguard take 411 bus to St. David's and walk 2 miles out B4583 to hostel.

By car: From St. David's follow B4583 2 miles to Whitesands Bay. From golf course bear right and follow signs to hostel.

By train: From Haverfordwest or Fishguard Station take 411 bus to St. David's and walk 2 miles out B4583 to hostel.

STOUTHALL HOSTEL

Reynoldston, Gower, Swansea SA3 1AP

Phone Number: 01792–391086

Rates: £6.55–£9.75 per HI member (about $10–$15 US)
Beds: 60
Season: July 26 to August 30
Affiliation: HI-YHA
Extras: Game room, grill

This hostel's great location is offset somewhat by its incredibly short season—it's open for only a month! Bummer, because the place has everything you'd need for a rustic holiday by the sea. They've even got single, double, and quad rooms here, a real rarity in the UK. If you do get here in that slim window, though, all the Gower Peninsula's stark beauty is within your grasp from here.

Party index:

How to get there:

By bus: From Swansea take 18A bus to Reynoldston turnoff, then take next right. Walk 100 yards to hostel.

By car: From Swansea take A4118 to just past turnoff for Reynoldston. Take next right, pass over cattle grid, continue 100 yards to hostel parking lot.

By ferry: From Cork, Ireland, take ferry to Swansea, Wales. Take 18A bus to Reynoldston turnoff, then take next right; walk 100 yards to hostel.

By train: From Swansea Station, 13 miles away, take 18A bus to Reynoldston turnoff, then take next right and walk 100 yards to hostel.

PWLL DERI HOSTEL

Castell Mawr, Tref Asser, Goodwick, Pembrokeshire SA64 OLR

Phone Number: 01348–891233

Rates: £4.95–£7.20 per HI member (about $7.00–$11.00 US)
Beds: 32
Private/family rooms: Sometimes
Season: April 3 to October 31
Affiliation: HI-YHA
Extras: Bicycle shop

You've really got to want to get to this clifftop hostel, placed near Strumble Head in wild and wooly West Wales. (And try sayin' *that* five times fast.)

Dorms come in seven- to eight-bed sizes; there's also one double room. Kitchen and dining room are all you'll need to whip something up to eat, and the helpful staff keep things humming. It's so basic here that heating isn't a given. Come on a warm day or bring a sweater: You'll possibly be rewarded with seals, seabirds, and more. Or trek 4 miles to the Llagnloffan Farmhouse Cheese Center or the also-nearby woolen mill. And, lest we forget to mention it, this hostel is only 4½ miles from the ferry that takes you to Ireland.

Best bet for a bite: Bakery nearby

Hospitality: 

How to get there:

By bus: From Fishguard take 410 bus to Goodwick; walk 4 miles uphill to hostel.

By car: From Goodwick take Strumble Head road to Strumble Head, then follow signs to Pwll Deri.

By ferry: Take ferry from Rosslare, Ireland, to Fishguard, Wales; take 410 bus to Goodwick and walk 4 miles uphill to hostel.

By train: From Haverfordwest or Fishguard Station take 410 bus to Goodwick and walk 4 miles uphill to hostel.

TREFIN (TREVINE) HOSTEL

11 Ffordd-yr-Afon, Trefin, Haverfordwest, Pembrokeshire SA62 5AU

Phone Number: 01348–831414

Rates: £4.95–£7.20 per HI member (about $7.00–$11.00 US)
Beds: 26
Season: April 3 to October 31
Affiliation: HI-YHA
Extras: Bicyle shop

Simple City, yes, again. What can we say? It seems like all of these Wales hostels are just plain school buildings with kitchens, a lounge and/or a dining room, and group bathrooms.

This place is no different from the rest of them; six dorms sleep four to six hostellers each. Area attractions include a weaving center in the tiny village and the gorgeous Pembrokeshire Coastal Path for walking. You're only a day's walk from splendid hostelling in St. David's, Pwll Deri, and Solva, so you might as well lace 'em up and ease on down the path.

Note that the village's name is spelled two different ways—Trefin or Trevine—and might appear either way on various Welsh road signs. No matter; it's the same place.

How to get there:

By bus: From Fishguard take 411 or 412 bus to Trefin.

By car: Take A487 to Trevine turnoff; hostel is in village center.

By ferry: Take ferry from Rosslare Harbour, Ireland, to Fishguard, Wales. Then take 411 or 412 bus to Trefin.

By train: From Haverfordwest-Fishguard Station take 411 or 412 bus to Trefin.

BLAENCARON HOSTEL

Blaencaron, Tregaron, Dyfed SY25 6HL

Phone Number: 01974–298441

Rates: £4.00–£5.85 (about $6.00–$9.00 US)
Beds: 16
Season: April 3 to September 26
Affiliation: HI-YHA
Extras: Bicycle shop

This is in the sticks, all right, a very simple place on a farm property. There are just three dorm rooms, two quads and an eight-bed bunkroom, and not much else: A kitchen and a bathroom are about it. Even heat isn't a given, so remember that in spring or fall.

This is, however, a good spot for checking out lots of natural wonders, including Tregaron Bog. Birders are especially happy to find their way here.

Party index:

How to get there:

By bus: Call hostel for transit route.

By car: Take A485 or B4343 to Tregaron; at Red Lion Inn turn off main road. Continue 2 miles down lane to phone box; make right. Check in with hostel manager at first right, at farm; then proceed 1 mile to hostel.

By train: Call hostel for transit route.

TYNCORNEL HOSTEL

Tyncornel, Llanddewi-Brefi, Tregaron, Pembrokeshire SY25 6PH

Phone Number: 01222–222122 (regional office)

Fax: 01222–237817 (regional office)
Rates: £4.00–£5.85 per HI member (about $6.00–$9.00 US)
Beds: 16
Season: April 3 to September 26
Affiliation: HI-YHA
Extras: Fireplace

This mid-Wales farmhouse hostel is so basic it doesn't have a phone you can call, it doesn't have storage for bikes, and heat is supplied by an open fire instead of electricity. It's a 7-mile hike to the closest telephone or market. Peace and quiet, baby, that's what you've got here—in spades.

Two dorm rooms hold eight hostellers apiece. Miraculously, they did think to build in a shower, kitchen, and common room. That's it. Just you and the hill.

Gestalt: Hill yeah

Party index:

How to get there:

By bus: Call regional office for transit route.

By car: From Llanddewi-Brefi drive southeast up Brefi Valley almost 5 miles; bear left at fork, continue 1 more mile to signpost, get on rough lane, and drive 1 more mile.

By train: Call regional office for transit route.

YSTRADFELLTE HOSTEL

Ta'ir Heol, Ystradfellte, Aberdare, Mid Glamorgan CF44 9JF

Phone Number: 01639–720301

Rates: £4.45–£6.50 per HI member (about $7.00–$10.00 US)
Beds: 28
Family/private rooms: Sometimes
Season: Call ahead for open days
Affiliation: HI-YHA
Curfew: 11:00 P.M.

Cobbled together from two cottages, this hostel offers fresh air and proximity to Brecon Beacons Park's splendid sights—though not much in the way of creature comforts.

Four dorm rooms contain four to six beds apiece; there's one double room for the asking, too. During the daytime lockout you might take some really nice walks to the local waterfalls and natural swimming pool, or else hit Ystradfellte for a pint of ale.

Party index:

How to get there:

By bus: From Aberdare take bus to Penderyn; walk 3½ miles to hostel.

By car: Take A4059 to 1 mile north of Penderyn; turn west to Ystradfellte, then left again. Hostel is 1 mile farther, on right.

By train: From Aberdare Station, 10 miles away, take bus to Penderyn; walk 3½ miles to hostel.

YSTUMTUEN HOSTEL

Glantuen, Ystumtuen, Aberystwyth, Cardiganshire SY23 3AE

Phone Number: 0197085–693

Rates: £4.00–£5.85 per HI member (about $6.00–$9.00 US)
Credit cards: Yes
Beds: 24
Season: April 3 to September 26
Affiliation: HI-YHA
Extras: Store

About the only reasons you might end up here are (a) getting shut out of a bed in the college town of Aberystwyth, 13 miles distant, or (b) interest in Devil's Bridge, a set of three stacked bridges and waterfalls.

This hostel was a school once, when the lead-mining bloom was on this hamlet, but now it's just a mighty simple hostel of three dorm rooms with four to twelve bunks each. The small hostel store and credit card machine are surprises; the day-long lockout and usual kitchen aren't.

How to get there:

Party index:

By bus: From Aberystwyth take 501 bus to turnoff 1 mile west of Ponterwyd, then walk 1½ miles to hostel.

By car: From Aberystwyth take A44 and turn south 1 mile west of Ponterwyd; continue 1½ miles to hostel.

By train: From Aberystwyth Station, 12 miles away, take 501 bus to turnoff 1 mile west of Ponterwyd, then walk 1½ miles to hostel. From Vale of Rheidol narrow-gauge railway's Rhiwfron Station (summer only), walk 2 miles to hostel.

SOUTHERN SCOTLAND

Numbers on map refer to towns and islands numbered below.

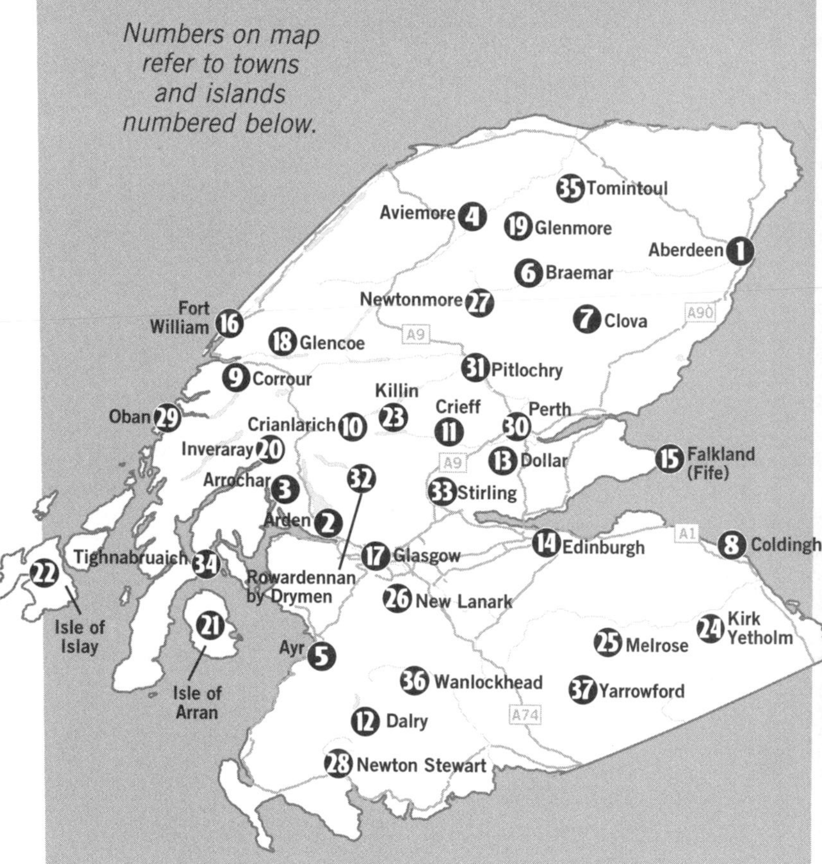

1. Aberdeen
2. Arden
3. Arrochar
4. Aviemore
5. Ayr
6. Braemar
7. Clova
8. Coldingham
9. Corrour
10. Crianlarich
11. Crieff
12. Dalry
13. Dollar
14. Edinburgh
15. Falkland (Fife)
16. Fort William
17. Glasgow
18. Glencoe
19. Glenmore
20. Inveraray
21. Isle of Arran
22. Isle of Islay
23. Killin
24. Kirk Yetholm
25. Melrose
26. New Lanark
27. Newtonmore
28. Newton Stewart
29. Oban
30. Perth
31. Pitlochry
32. Rowardennan by Drymen
33. Stirling
34. Tighnabruaich
35. Tomintoul
36. Wanlockhead
37. Yarrowford

Scotland can be summarized pretty quickly: bagpipes and beer. Stir in a little rain—make that a lot of rain in little bits—iffy food, and a huge dose of friendliness, and you've pretty much captured the essential Scottish experience.

And yet, there's so much more here. The scenery is always pastoral, and on the western coast it becomes some of Europe's most beautiful. The presence of castles, old men walking big shaggy dogs, and the omnipresent pubs doesn't hurt either. Locals often have a lot to say about politics, soccer, weather, and more.

Transit can be a problem, although good train lines do run to Edinburgh, Glasgow, Inverness, and the west coast. Buses fill in the gaps fairly well. Count on using your feet if you want to see the really remote and old-style bothies, croft houses, and other uniquely Scottish places that can be found here; they're worth it for the experience, not for the comfort.

That reminds us: Hostel quality here isn't always so great. SYHA places almost always suffer from terminal boredom, too many rules, and drab (and often cold) buildings; avoid them if you're here for a good time, except for our recommended joints like Glasgow and Pitlochry. The independent places are sometimes good, sometimes shabby.

Our call? Scotland: terrific. The hostels: horrific. Heh, heh. No, it's not quite that bad. In any case, let the hosteller beware.

KING GEORGE VI MEMORIAL HOSTEL

8 Queen's Road, Aberdeen AB1 6YT

Phone Number: 01224–646988

Rates: £7.10–£9.60 per HI member (about $10–$15 US)
Credit cards: Yes
Beds: 112
Private/family rooms: Yes
Office hours: 7:00 A.M. to 2:00 A.M.
Affiliation: HI-SYHA
Extras: Laundry, store, breakfast (summer only)
Lockout: 11:00 A.M.–1:00 P.M.
Curfew: 2:00 A.M.

Two miles outside downtown Aberdeen, this imposing granite hostel packs in more than a hundred beds with a combination of fifteen quad rooms and eight bigger dorm rooms. It's the usual SYHA drill (and we do mean drill)—efficient, lifeless rooms and common spaces.

Party index:

As a city, Aberdeen isn't much: kinda drab, famous as a hub of oil companies and not much else. It does contain a few historic attractions, though, and a university with active international programs brings the world to this corner of Scotland. Granite fishing villages along the coast can't be reached except by bike or car, but they're worth a detour. One, Pennan, is where they filmed part of the wonderful movie *Local Hero.*

How to get there:

By bus: From station walk 1 mile to hostel, or take 27 bus to Queen's Road. Or take 14 or 15 bus to Queen's Road.

By car: Call hostel for directions.

By train: From station walk 1 mile to hostel, or take 27 bus to Queen's Road.

LOCH LOMOND HOSTEL 

Arden, Alexandria, Dumbartonshire G83 8RB

Phone Number: 01389–850226

Rates: £7.10–£9.60 per HI member (about \$11–\$15 US)
Credit cards: Yes
Beds: 160
Private/family rooms: Sometimes
Office hours: 7:00 A.M. to 2:00 A.M.
Affiliation: HI-SYHA
Extras: Laundry, store, meals (\$), fireplace

This former hunting lodge really is a castle overlooking a beach and a lake—talk about location! Five quads are ideally suited for families; all private rooms disappear in summer, however, to handle the crush of hostellers. The remaining nineteen rooms are bigger.

Insiders' tip: Bagpipe factory nearby

Gestalt: Loch Nice

Party index:

In fact, this is one of the biggest hostels in Scotland, and yet it still sometimes fills at the height of summer, giving some idea how popular this piece of landscape can be. Loch Lomond is a big—and somewhat touristed—lake, but pretty nevertheless. You certainly won't be alone.

Other amenities here include a big hall with an open fireplace, nice grounds, and ornate decorations. I mean, where else are you gonna find a hostel with nine entrances, sixty-five rooms, and its own art gallery?

Only one question: Is it haunted by a friendly ghost? You decide.

How to get there:

By bus: Bus stops nearby; call hostel for transit route.

By car: From Glasgow take A82 1 mile north of Arden; hostel is on left, across from lake.

By ferry: Balloch ferry dock, 2 miles away.

By train: Balloch Station is 2 miles away.

ARDGARTAN HOSTEL

Ardgartan, Arrochar, Dunbartonshire G83 7AR

Phone Number: 01301–702362

Rates: £6.50–£7.75 per HI member (about $10–$12 US)
Credit cards: Yes
Beds: 60
Private/family rooms: Yes
Season: January 30 to December 31
Office hours: 7:00 A.M. to 11:45 P.M.
Affiliation: HI-SYHA
Extras: Store, laundry, meals ($), breakfast

This hostel, located in Argyll Forest Park on a loch (lake), looks like a two-story barracks from the outside. Inside, though, it's surprisingly well equipped if a bit frumpy. Accommodations consist of two quads and eight larger dorms, and they maintain a laundry and small store.

There's good rock climbing nearby, or—for less heart-palpitating fun—check out the tallest tree in Britain; hostel staff can direct you there.

Party index:

How to get there:

By bus: Bus stops ½ mile from hostel; call hostel for details.

By car: From Arrochar or Inverarary take A83 to Loch Long shore; turn in at hostel.

By train: Arrochar/Tarbert Station is 4 miles away.

AVIEMORE HOSTEL

25 Grampian Road, Aviemore, Inverness-shire PH22 1PR

Phone Number: 01479–810345

Rates: £7.10–£9.60 per HI member (about $11–$15 US)
Credit cards: Yes
Beds: 114
Private/family rooms: Yes
Office hours: 7:00 A.M. to 2:00 A.M.

Affiliation: HI-SYHA
Extras: Laundry, store, catered meals for groups

Not much to report at this joint, just fifteen quad rooms plus nine big dorms set in a birch grove beside a natural park. Nice location. There's a store nearby, too, for food purposes.

Insiders' tip: Great skiing

Gestalt: Aviemore is less

Party index:

The Strathspey region is well liked in Scotland for its outdoorsy pursuits, which include (among others) golf, skiing, ice skating, hiking, biking, fishing, canoeing, orienteering . . . you get the picture. Grab that tweed cap and go for it.

How to get there:

By bus: Bus stops ¼ mile from hostel; call hostel for details.

By car: Take B9152 to Aviemore.

By train: Aviemore Station is ¼ mile.

AYR HOSTEL

5 Craigweil Road, Ayr KA7 2XJ

Phone Number: 01292–262322

Rates: £6.50–£7.75 per HI member (about $10–$12 US)
Credit cards: Yes
Beds: 60
Private/family rooms: Yes
Season: February 27 to November 1
Office hours: 7:00 A.M. to 11:45 P.M.
Affiliation: HI-SYHA
Extras: Bike rentals, store, laundry, grill

This small castle boasts incredible views, is central to the west-coast town of Ayr, and sits close to a beach to boot. Great choice.

Gestalt: Air base

Party index:

Families love this place, as it's not as simple as most other Scottish hostels; a grill, laundry, and bicycle rentals are just some of the extra amenities. Three quad rooms and six larger dorm rooms handle the load; the strain of bagpipes reportedly wafts through the halls on occasion, too.

How to get there:

By bus: From station walk ¾ mile down Alloway Place to Blackburn Road, turn right, turn right again into Craigwell Road. Hostel is on left.

By car: Call hostel for directions.

By train: Ayr Station is ¾ mile.

BRAEMAR HOSTEL

Corrie Feragie, Braemar, Aberdeenshire AB3 5YQ

Phone Number: 013397–41659

Rates: £6.50–£7.75 per HI member (about $10–$12 US)
Credit cards: Yes
Beds: 62
Private/family rooms: None
Office hours: 7:00 A.M. to 11:45 P.M.
Affiliation: HI-SYHA
Extras: Laundry, store

A stolid looking stone building, Braemar's hostel consists of two quads, six larger dorms, and a kitchen and laundry. It's certainly adequate as a home base in this tiny town.

The Highland Games draw crowds here each September, so don't plan on dropping in then without a reservation booked well in advance. Interesting as heck if you can snag a bed, though. There's lots of walking and climbing around here, as well, and the Deeside region's whiskey is world-famous. Try to wangle a free taste.

How to get there:

By bus: Bus station is ¼ mile from hostel; call hostel for transit details.

By car: Take A93 to Braemar; hostel is just south of village center, uphill.

By train: Aberdeen Station, 56 miles away, is nearest.

Party index:

INVEREY HOSTEL

Inverey, (by Braemar), Aberdeenshire AB3 5YB

No phone (Call Central Reservation Service, 010541–55–32–55)

Rates: £3.85–£4.65 per HI member (about $6.00–$7.00 US)
Beds: 17
Private/family rooms: None
Season: May 15 to October 4
Office hours: 7:00 to 11:00 A.M.; 5:00 to 11:00 P.M.
Affiliation: HI-SYHA

This hostel is actually 5 miles outside Braemar and could serve as an option if the Braemar hostel's booked solid during Highland Games time. Three quad dorms and one larger bunkroom fill the tiny stone house.

Note that to book the place, you need to call Central Reservation; there's no phone here.

Gestalt:
Stone cold
Party index:

How to get there:

By bus: Postbus stops near hostel; call hostel for transit details.

By car: Call hostel for directions.

GLENDOLL HOSTEL

Clova, Kirriemuir, Angus DD8 4RD

Phone Number: 01575–550236

Rates: £4.95–£6.10 per HI member (about $7.00–$9.00 US)
Credit cards: Yes
Beds: 45
Private/family rooms: Yes
Season: March 20 to November 1
Office hours: 7:00 A.M. to 11:45 P.M.
Affiliation: HI-SYHA
Extras: Store, squash court

Gestalt: Glendollhouse

Party index:

This hostel's housed in a lovely building in remote country. It's got four large dorms, plus four quads that can be rented out as family units and a kitchen.

Unusually, it also has a squash court. If you're into that—and we are—it can be really fun to play on a rainy day. When the sun's shining, though, head for the Munros (local peaks) and hike away.

How to get there:

By bus: Postbus stops nearby; call hostel for details.

By car: Call hostel for directions.

By train: Dundee Station, 36 miles away, is closest stop.

COLDINGHAM HOSTEL

Coldingham Sands, Coldingham, Berwicks TD14 5PA

Phone Number: 01890–71298

Rates: £4.95–£6.10 per HI member (about $7.00–$9.00 US)
Beds: 54
Private/family rooms: Yes
Season: March 20 to November 1
Affiliation: HI-SYHA
Extras: Store, laundry

Set in a big house facing the sea, this hostel's the place for those seeking ocean views and not too many hostellers. It consists of two couples' rooms, plus five larger dorms and a kitchen.

Among the natural features of the area are seabird colonies and the nearby St. Abbs wildlife preserve. Or you might walk a footpath to the Eyemouth Museum.

Gestalt: Ocean in motion

Party index:

How to get there:

By bus: Bus stops ½ mile from hostel; call hostel for transit route.

By car: Take B6438 to Coldingham, bear right in village off main road and drive to water; hostel is on right.

By train: Berwick Station is 10 miles away.

LOCH OSSIAN HOSTEL

Corrour, By Fort William, Inverness-shire PH30 4AA

Phone Number: 01397–732207

Rates: £3.85–£4.65 per HI member (about $6.00–$7.00 US)
Credit cards: Yes
Beds: 20
Private/family rooms: None
Season: March 20 to November 1
Office hours: 7:00 to 11:00 A.M.; 5:00 to 11:00 P.M.
Affiliation: HI-SYHA

This place is really cool: a house you can only reach by train, then a 3-mile walk. Now this is Scotland!

The house, a hut set on a well-known loch, is surrounded on three sides by water. Bring your fishin' pole and some granola, though, since it's 20 miles to the nearest grocery shop and there really isn't a kitchen. Just two dorm rooms with ten spare bunks apiece and oodles of scenery.

Gestalt: Deer one

Party index:

Walking is the thing to do here, but you shouldn't do it from August through late October: That's when local hunters are out in full force stalking deer. The other popular thing to do around here is run around the lake, literally: If you can negotiate the 7½ mile distance in less than an hour (we didn't even come close), you're a hero. Can't do it? No worries. At least you'll be feeling no pain.

How to get there:

By bus: Postbus stops in Rannoch, 9 miles away

By train: From Corrour Station walk 1 mile on footpath to hostel.

CRIANLARICH HOSTEL

Station Road, Crianlarich, Perthshire FK20 8QN

Phone Number: 01838–300260

Rates: £6.50–£7.75 per HI member (about $10–$12 US)
Credit cards: Yes
Beds: 74
Private/family rooms: Sometimes
Season: January 30 to December 31
Office hours: 7:00 A.M. to 11:45 P.M.
Affiliation: HI-SYHA
Extras: Laundry, store

By the train station and near Loch Tay, this hostel consists of a simple but large complex of low buildings. It's really unimpressive from the outside. Inside, though, there are thirteen dorms of five to eight beds, some of them reserved for families except during the two busiest summertime months. A wheelchair ramp is a nice touch.

Gestalt: Tay awhile

Party index:

Plenty of hill walking in the area means you might not spend much time indoors here. In fact, it's at the halfway point of the popular West Highland Way. The village is teensie, and the only food shop is ¼ mile away; there's no bank, so strap on the walkin' shoes and have at the hills.

How to get there:

By bus: Bus stops ½ mile away; call hostel for transit details.
By car: From Glasgow or Fort William take A82 to Crianlarich.
By train: From Crianlarich Station walk less than ¼ mile to hostel.

BRAINCROFT BUNKHOUSE

By Comrie, Crieff, Perthshire PH7 4JZ

Phone Number: 01764–670140

Fax: 01764–670691
Rates: £7.00–£9.00 per person (about $12–$14 US)
Beds: 56
Private/family rooms: Yes
Affiliation: None
Extras: TV, VCR, laundry, store, bike rentals

This good independent hostel consists of a converted farm building in a small, authentically Scots village.

There are eleven rooms containing two to eight beds apiece; most have en-suite bathrooms, and extras like showers, sheets, tea, and coffee don't cost extra. A TV room with VCR, small hostel shop, and laundry facilities fill out the picture.

What to do? The area is known for Scotland's oldest whiskey distillery (Glenturret), plus gardens, golfing, fishing and more—a real Scottish holiday area, actually. There are some walking trails, of course. The managers also maintain a small fishpond with trout; salmon can be seen nearby, and the managers are experts on local fishing. But what they really recommend for you to do is stay close to home, renting a mountain bike from them and checking out their private course.

Party index:

How to get there:

By bus: Call hostel for transit route.
By car: Call hostel for directions.
By train: Call hostel for transit route.

KENDOON HOSTEL

Dalry, Castle Douglas DG7 3UD

Phone Number: 01644–460680

Rates: £3.85–£4.65 per HI member (about $6.00–$7.00 US)
Beds: 38
Private/family rooms: None
Season: March 20 to October 4
Office hours: 7:00 to 10:30 A.M.; 5:00 to 11:00 P.M.
Affiliation: HI-SYHA

Three miles off the Southern Upland Way walking trail, this plain building protected by a gate is made of big chunky stones. The beds come in six quad rooms and two larger ones; most hostellers opt to hang out nearby or else sightsee around the local lakes. This is quiet hostelling at its quietest.

Party index:

How to get there:

By bus: Bus stops 1 mile from hostel; call hostel for transit route.
By car: Call hostel for directions.

GLENDEVON HOSTEL

Glendevon, Dollar, Clackmannanshire FK14 7JY

Phone Number: 01259–781206

Rates: £3.85–£4.65 per HI member (about $6.00–$7.00 US)

Credit cards: Yes
Beds: 38
Private/family rooms: Yes
Season: March 20 to October 4
Office hours: 7:00 to 10:30 A.M.; 5:00 to 11:00 P.M.
Affiliation: HI-SYHA
Extras: Store, pony rides

Set in fields, this hostel has two great big dorm rooms, one merely big one, and a kitchen for fixing meals. Castle Campbell is a very popular stop, but many hostellers also opt for the hostel's own summertime pony trekking tours.

Gestalt: Bottom dollar

Party index:

How to get there:

By bus: Postbus stops 2 miles away; call hostel for details.

By car: From Crieff or Muckhart take A823 to Drove Road turnoff; make left to hostel.

By train: Gleneagles Station is 8 miles away.

EDINBURGH

You can't believe just how striking Edinburgh is until you've actually gotten there. Hop off the train and walk up the grueling Waverley Steps . . . hmm. A busy street, no big deal.

But then you turn around and see the castle up on its rock, symbol of Scotland . . . explore the Royal Mile's pubs and shops . . . check out how the other half lives in tony but nice New Town . . . and go for a long walk in the free and beautiful Botanic Gardens. If only the weather would cooperate more often.

Hostels here are generally decent, and most are concentrated close to downtown; all can be reached by a bus ride of up to half an hour. City buses, in fact, are generally excellent, though they do shut down late at night and run less frequently on Sundays. The bus and train stations are very convenient and close together.

Note that there are two train stations here; for downtown hostels, get off at Waverley. For suburban joints, hop off a stop earlier at Haymarket.

EDINBURGH HOSTELS at a glance

	RATING	COST	IN A WORD
Edinburgh Central	👍	£9.95–£12.50	nice
Bruntsfield Hostel		£7.10–£9.60	prim
Pleasance Hostel		£9.95–£12.50	boring
Eglinton Hostel		£9.95–£12.50	adequate
Castle Rock Hostel		£10.00–£13.00	good
Edinburgh Backpackers		£10.00–£12.50	big
High Street Hostel		£9.50–£9.90	small
Brodie's Hostel		£10.00	fun
Princes Street Backpackers		£10.00–£15.50	social
Belford Hostel		£9.50–£12	funkorama

BELFORD HOSTEL

6-8 Douglas Gardens, Edinburgh EH4 3DA

Phone Number: 0131–225–6209/221–0022

Fax: 0131–539–8695

Rates: £9.50–£12.00 per person (about $14–$18 US); doubles £27.50–£30.50 (about $42–$46 US)

Beds: 90

Private/family rooms: Yes

Affiliation: None

Extras: Laundry, pool table, bar

We've heard pretty mixed reports about this funky place housed in a former church: some good, some not-so-good.

Gestalt: Holy smokes

Hospitality: 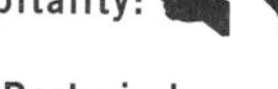

Party index: 

Yeah, it's a church. The windows still contain stained glass, and it's a bit of a creepy feeling if you're a heathen and you awaken to the sight of it. (Religious hostellers will probably faint with happiness, believing they've gone to heaven.)

Things are pretty noisy and lively here, and the pool table and bar keep it that way much of the time. There are five family rooms for those who seek a bit of extra quiet, and the location's good and central.

How to get there:

By bus: Call hostel for directions.
By car: Call hostel for directions.
By train: Call hostel for directions.

BRODIE'S BACKPACKERS HOSTEL

12 High Street, Edinburgh

Phone Number: 0131–556–6770

Rates: £10–£12 per person (about $15–$18 US)
Beds: 50
Office hours: Twenty-four hours
Affiliation: None
Extras: Laundry, stereo

Incredibly central, pretty happenin' and good, this new hostel is an offshoot of the Go Blue Banana bus folks downstairs. It's well managed as far as we can tell, supplying spacious bunks in mixed and coed dorm rooms. Bathrooms are a bit in short supply, and cleaning sometimes plays second, um, banana, but otherwise this is a fun place to hang your hat for a night or two.

Dorms are large, with three fourteen-bedded rooms and a single eight-bedded room. The big size is offset by cleanliness and wide spacing from neighbors. Also, they use hotel bunks here, a big plus. They do laundry for a small fee and will play your tapes on the hostel stereo if they like 'em.

Best bet for a bite: Tempting Tatties

Insiders' tip: Hit the Tass (pub)

Gestalt: Jekyll & Hide

Hospitality: 

Cleanliness: 

Party index:

It seemed much more fun that some of the other hostels (we're talking SYHA here) in town: People like playing music, hanging out in the small common room around the ying-yang table, and ducking out for a pint of ale or a stuffed baked potato around the corner.

But a warning: Some guests may be the dreaded "long-termers," folks who think the hostel is their home and pay by the month. Shame on management for allowing that. Otherwise, no complaints.

How to get there:

By bus: From bus station walk to Princes Street; cross street and turn right down South Bridge. Cross bridge and continue to High Street (Royal Mile). Turn left and walk down street to Go Blue Banana office on right-hand side; turn right at corner. Hostel is on right.

By car: Call hostel for directions.

Brodie's Backpackers Hostel
Edinburgh
(photo by Martha Coombs)

By train: From Waverley Station walk to Princes Street; turn right, then right again on South Bridge and cross bridge to High Street (Royal Mile). Turn left and walk down street to Go Blue Banana office on right-hand side; turn right at corner. Hostel is on right.

BRUNTSFIELD HOSTEL

7 Bruntsfield Crescent, Edinburgh EH10 4EZ

Phone Number: 0131–447–2994

Rates: £7.10–£9.60 per HI member (about $11–$15 US)
Beds: 150
Private/family rooms: None
Affiliation: HI-SYHA
Extras: Laundry
Curfew: 2:00 A.M.

This row of austere stone town houses is one of SYHA's two keystone hostels in Edinburgh. This one's in an okay residential neighborhood, a little far from the center and a little boring, however. If you're pressed for time, ring one of the independent joints instead. They're much closer to the key transit points.

Party index:

Management is strict and as devoid of personality as most other SYHA joints; at least the place overlooks the Bruntsfield Links park and area. A good choice for families and senior citizens; everyone else might not fancy it so much.

How to get there:

By bus: From bus station walk to Princes Street (Garden side) and take 11, 15, 16, or 17 bus to Forbes Road.

By car: Call hostel for directions.

By train: From train station take 11, 15, 16, or 17 bus to Forbes Road.

CASTLE ROCK HOSTEL

15 Johnston Terrace, Edinburgh EH1 2PW

Phone Number: 0131–225–9666

Rates: £10.00–£13.00 per person (about $15–$20 US)
Beds: 150
Affiliation: None
Extras: Internet access, breakfast ($)

A new, big hostel recently opened by the folks in the Scotland's Top Hostels chain, this place is okay—and dig the location! You're literally right beneath the famous castle that symbolizes all things Scottish, so start right here. Take a snapshot and send it home to your buds.

Just down a long set of stairs from the hostel, you're deep in the heart of student heaven. The University of Edinburgh and an art school make their homes around here, and the Grassmarket area is home to many a cool restaurant or other diversion. So, although this hostel is not on the main drag (i.e., Royal Tourist Trap), that means it's actually mostly immune to the hordes of wide-eyed American tourists dying to get their pictures taken next to the guy wheezing away on his bagpipes up on the Mile.

Best bet for a bite:
Helios Fountain

Gestalt:
No-hassle castle

Party index:

Nice view of that Castle, plus Internet access and a fun crowd. Not bad.

How to get there:

By bus: From bus station turn left and walk down to Princes Street; cross street, turn right and walk to Waverley Bridge; turn left and cross bridge. Climb up to Royal Mile (High Street), then turn right and walk uphill to Johnson Terrace on left. Bear left and walk downhill to hostel on left.

By car: Call hostel for directions.

By train: From Haymarket Station walk up ramp to Waverley Bridge and turn left; cross bridge, climb up to Royal Mile (High Street). Turn right on High Street and walk uphill to Johnson Terrace on left; bear left and walk downhill to hostel on left.

EDINBURGH BACKPACKERS HOSTEL

65 Cockburn Street, Edinburgh EH1 1BU

Phone Number: 0131–2210022

Fax: 0131–5398695
Rates: £10.00–£12.50 per person (about $15–$18 US)
Beds: 110
Family/private rooms: Yes
Affiliation: None
Extras: Meals ($)

This big hostel's located on too-hip-for-its-own-good Cockburn Street, which winds downhill from the famous Royal Mile. From the main train station, it's much easier to access from a ramp that ends at the Waverley Bridge than by the tortuous Waverley Steps.

Gestalt:
Hipper than thou

Party index:

Again, location is everything here if you're looking to get pierced or tattooed. The drill's the same as at the other indie hostels, a more lax attitude towards cleanliness and an emphasis on having a good time.

For all of you who thrive on the famous SYHA sterility, you'll not appreciate the vibes here. The building is standardly Victorian in architecture but wedged near the aforementioned tattoo parlor as well as an S&M shop, a hemp shop, and a half dozen pubs in which to wet your whistle.

How to get there:

By bus: Exit terminal and turn left. Walk downhill to Princes Street; cross over and walk towards Waverley Bridge. Turn left and cross bridge, then cross Market Street and walk uphill. Hostel is near top of the hill on left.

By car: Call hostel for directions.

By train: From Waverley Station follow signs uphill to Waverley Bridge. Follow ramp to bridge; turn left and walk to the end of the bridge. Cross Royal Mile at Market Street and walk uphill. Hostel is near top of street on left.

EDINBURGH CENTRAL YOUTH HOSTEL

Robertson Close, College Wynd, Cowgate, Edinburgh EH1 1LY

Phone Number: 0131–337–1120

Rates: £9.95–£12.50 per HI member (about $15–$19 US)
Beds: 121
Private/family rooms: Yes
Season: June 26 to September 7
Affiliation: HI-SYHA
Extras: Laundry

Believe it or not, this overflow annex to the HI hostels consists entirely of private rooms! That's great if you're traveling with a family. Not too hot if you want atmosphere or lotsa friends, 'cause you won't find them. At least you're in atmospheric digs, though.

It's only in summer, and you can only book it through the Bruntsfield or Eglinton hostels.

Gestalt:
Central perk

Party index:

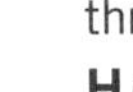

How to get there:

By bus: Call hostel for directions.

By car: Call hostel for directions.

By train: Call hostel for directions.

EGLINTON HOSTEL

18 Eglinton Crescent, Edinburgh EH12 5DD

Phone Number: 0131–337–1120

Rates: £9.95–£12.50 per HI member (about $15–$19 US)
Beds: 158
Private/family rooms: None
Affiliation: HI-SYHA
Extras: Laundry, store, breakfast, meals ($)
Curfew: 2:00 A.M.

Eglinton's the other SYHA hostel in Edinburgh, again placed far from the action and again plagued by sterility of location. There are seventeen dorm rooms here, most of them pretty large but with a few containing four to six beds per room.

As might be expected, this place is too popular with school groups. If you're looking to party on the Mile, keep on truckin' to a more relaxed option.

Gestalt: Good Eglinton

Party index:

How to get there:

By bus: From Princes Street (Garden side) take 3, 4, 12, 13, 22, 28, 31, 33, or 44 bus to Palmer Place. Walk to hostel.

By car: Call hostel for directions.

By train: From Haymarket Station walk ¼ mile to hostel.

HIGH STREET HOSTEL

105 High Street, Edinburgh EH11SG

Phone Number: 0131–557–6120

Fax: 0131–556–2981
Rates: £9.90–£10.50 per person (about $14–$15 US)
Credit cards: Yes
Beds: 38
Private/family rooms: None
Affiliation: None
Extras: Breakfast ($), laundry

Once an overflow hostel of sorts for the wildly popular High Street joint that closed in the fall of '98, this hostel is superbly placed—right *on* the Royal Mile, for gosh sakes.

Inside, dorms contain six beds each. Not the cleanest we've ever seen, and not dirtiest; people seem to have a really good time here, which is a good sign, and you're within a mile of more than a hundred pubs, we'd guess.

Gestalt: High times

Party index:

How to get there:

By bus: From bus station walk to Princes Street; cross street and turn right down South Bridge. Cross bridge and continue to High Street (Royal Mile). Turn left and walk down High Street. Hostel is on left, above cafe.

By car: Call hostel for directions.

By train: From Waverley Station walk to Princes Street; turn right, then right again on South Bridge and cross bridge to High Street (Royal Mile). Turn left and walk down High Street. Hostel is on left, above cafe.

EDINBURGH PLEASANCE HOSTEL

New Arthur Place, Edinburgh

Phone Number: 0131–337–1120

Rates: £9.95–£12.50 per HI member (about $15–$19 US)
Beds: 115
Private/family rooms: Yes
Season: June 26 to September 7
Affiliation: HI-SYHA
Extras: Laundry

Yes, it's another all-private-rooms overflow annex for the SYHA joints in Edinburgh—giving them a grand total of four (count 'em) hostels during the peak of summer season.

Once again, the digs are nice, but there's zero atmosphere or socializing going on. Book through the Eglinton or Bruntsfield hostels.

Gestalt: Summer camp

Party index: 🎉

How to get there:

By bus: Call hostel for directions.
By car: Call hostel for directions.
By train: Call hostel for directions.

PRINCES STREET BACKPACKERS

5 West Register Street, Edinburgh EH2 2AA

Phone Number: 0131–556–6894

Fax: 0131–558–9133
E-mail: hostelenvironment@cableinet.co.uk
Rates: £10–£15.50 per person (about $15–$23 US)
Credit cards: Yes
Beds: 110
Season: May 1 to September 30
Office hours: Twenty-four hours
Affiliation: None
Extras: Laundry, TV, VCR

Gestalt: Beer blast

Party index: 🎉🎉🎉🎉

This so-so hostel's tucked in a decidely unhip part of town. Still, it's not far from the pub action on Rose Street. In fact, there's really a pub just beneath it.

Dorms tend to include six beds to a room. Facilities aren't terrific, but it's fun, at least—the staff is okay, even if the guests were a wee bit strange—and there's a kitchen. Check out the interesting room-numbering (actually lettering) system, too.

How to get there:

By bus: From bus station walk down to Princes Street and make a right, then another immediate right onto West Register Street. Hostel is on right, above pub.

By car: Call hostel for directions.

By train: From Waverley Station walk across Princes Street to West Register and turn onto it. Hostel is on right, above pub.

FALKLAND HOSTEL

Back Wynd, Falkland, Fife KY7 7BX

Phone Number: 01337–857710

Rates: £3.85–£4.65 per HI member (about $6.00–$7.00 US)
Credit cards: Yes
Beds: 38
Private/family rooms: None
Season: March 20 to October 4
Office hours: 7:00 to 10:30 A.M.; 5:00 to 11:00 P.M.
Affiliation: HI-SYHA

A plain, two-story brick building, this hostel's smack in the middle of little Falkland. It contains three very large bunkrooms and a kitchen and little else. The town's known for its palace, and it isn't too far from much-more-famous St. Andrews, which is tremendously famous for guys in knickers flailing wood and metal clubs at little white balls.

Party index:

How to get there:

By bus: Bus stops nearby; call hostel for transit route.

By car: Take A912 to Falkland; hostel is in center of village.

By train: Ladybank and Markinch Stations are 5 miles away.

GLEN NEVIS HOSTEL

Glen Nevis, Fort William, Inverness-shire PH33 6ST

Phone Number: 01397–702336

Rates: £8.10–£9.60 per HI member (about $12–$15 US)
Credit cards: Yes
Beds: 119
Private/family rooms: Yes
Season: January 1 to October 27
Office hours: 7:00 A.M. to 2:00 A.M.
Affiliation: HI-SYHA
Extras: Store, laundry, meals ($)

Right across the road from the big, famous peak of the same name, the two-story Glen Nevis hostel is pretty well equipped—making it ideal for a family stay or a luuxrious night after one too many spare bunkrooms. There are six quad rooms at this fun place, plus eleven bigger dorms, a kitchen, and a laundry.

Party index:

Fort William's not much as a town, but it sure is stuck in the middle of some gorgeous territory; Glen Nevis is just the beginning. Catch a train to Mallaig for more jaw-dropping views, or take a bus to Glasgow or Edinburgh instead.

How to get there:

By bus: Bus stops in Fort William, 3 miles away.
By car: Call hostel for directions.
By train: Fort William Station is 3 miles away.

GLASGOW BACKPACKERS HOSTEL

8 Park Circus, Glasgow G3 6BY

Phone Number: 0141–332–5412

Rates: £8.90–£10.90 per person (about $13–$16 US)
Beds: 50
Private/family rooms: Yes
Season: June 29 to September 6
Affiliation: None
Extras: Laundry

Gestalt: Glasgow crazy

Hospitality: 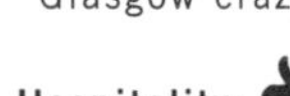

Cleanliness: 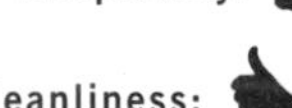 

Party index:

A big thumbs-up for this residence-hall-turned-summer hostel, which is staffed by great young folks and occupies a pretty neighborhood (the same street as the SYHA year-round hostel, in fact). Too bad it's only open during summer; this is among Scotland's best independently run hostels.

How to get there:

By bus: Call hostel for transit route.
By car: Call hostel for directions.
By train: Call hostel for directions.

GLASGOW HOSTEL

7-8 Park Terrace, Glasgow G3 6BY

Phone Number: 0141–332–3004

Rates: £9.95–£12.50 per HI member (about $15–$19 US)
Credit cards: Yes
Beds: 156
Private/family rooms: Yes

Affiliation: HI-SYHA
Extras: Store, laundry, meals ($)

A nice facility close to a green park, Glasgow's official Hostelling International joint gets the same thumbs-up as the next-door independent place, giving hostellers two solid options when visiting town. This historic building was recently renovated and features meals, a laundry, and more.

This university-area neighborhood's attractive and safe, a far cry from Glasgow's more industrial areas, and this working-class city is also enjoying a renaissance as a hotbed of the arts.

Gestalt:
Great Scot

Party index:

How to get there:

By bus: Bus station is 1 mile from hostel; walk to Cathedral Street and take 11 bus to Woodlands Road, walk to hostel. Local buses also available; call hostel for transit details.

By car: Call hostel for directions.

By train: From Queen Street Station walk to Cathedral Street and take 11 bus to Woodlands Road; walk to hostel. From Central Station take 44 or 59 bus to Woodlands Road and walk to hostel.

GLENCOE HOSTEL

Glencoe, Ballachulish, Argyll PA39 4HX

Phone Number: 01855–811219

Rates: £6.50–£7.75 per HI member (about $10–$12 US)
Credit cards: Yes
Beds: 62
Private/family rooms: Yes
Office hours: 7:00 A.M. to 11:45 P.M.
Affiliation: HI-SYHA
Extras: Laundry, store

It's a two-story brown building, but this hostel's blah exterior hides several amenities—like a laundry, for instance. Nine biggish dorms and one quad room, a kitchen, and a small store are the works here.

The Pass of Glencoe is a popular skiing area, and there are high mountains for walkers.

Party index:

How to get there:

By bus: Bus stops 1½ miles from hostel; call hostel for details.
By car: Call hostel for directions.
By foot: West Highland Way walkers can catch minibus at Ballachulish.
By train: Fort William Station, 19 miles away, is closest stop.

LOCH MORLICH HOSTEL

Glenmore, Aviemore, Inverness-shire PH22 1QY

Phone Number: 01479–861238

Rates: £6.50–£7.75 per HI member (about $10–$12 US)
Credit cards: Yes
Beds: 86
Private/family rooms: None
Office hours: 7:00 A.M. to 11:45 P.M.
Affiliation: HI-SYHA
Extras: Breakfast ($), meals ($), laundry, store, bike rentals

Seven miles outside Aviemore, this hostel contains four quad rooms and nine large dorms, plus a kitchen and laundry; they serve meals here, as well. Walking or biking in the Cairngorms is the usual pastime here, and—interestingly—there are orienteering trails in the woods near the hostel.

Party index:

How to get there:

By bus: Bus stops nearby; call hostel for transit route.

By car: Call hostel for directions.

By train: Aviemore Station is 7 miles away.

INVERARAY HOSTEL

Dalmally Road, Inveraray, Argyllshire PA32 8XD

Phone Number: 01499–2454

Rates: £4.95–£6.10 per HI member (about $7.00–$9.00 US)
Credit cards: Yes
Beds: 38
Private/family rooms: Yes
Season: March 20 to November 1
Office hours: 7:00 A.M. to 11:45 P.M.
Affiliation: HI-SYHA
Extras: Store

Insiders' tip:
Arctic Penguin museum

Party index:

This simple one-story home is outfitted with ten dorm rooms, all potential family rooms or relatively private bunks. There's a kitchen and a small hostel store to aid in meal preparation.

Fun in the area? Well, there are nice lawns on the hostel property. If you're a fisherperson, this is serious salmon country, and there's a new golf course nearby. The speck of a town at Inveraray is a place of whitewashed buildings on the shores of Loch Fyne. The local jail is said to be of some interest, though we didn't actually spend any time there, if you know what we mean.

How to get there:

By bus: Bus stops ¼ mile from hostel; call hostel for transit route.

By car: Take A83 or A819 to Inveraray. Hostel is 1 block away from pier, going away from the water.

By train: Arrochar Station, 16 miles away, is nearest.

LOCHRANZA HOSTEL 

Lochranza, Isle of Arran KA27 8HL

Phone Number: 01770–830631

Rates: £6.50–£7.75 per HI member (about $10–$12 US)
Credit cards: Yes
Beds: 68
Private/family rooms: Yes
Season: January 30 to December 31
Office hours: 7:00 A.M. to 11:45 P.M.
Affiliation: HI-SYHA
Extras: Store, laundry

You've got to do a little fancy footwork to get out here onto the Isle of Arran and over to Lochranza, but it's worth it: This simple three-story white building tucked beneath hills makes a good base for explorations. Eight quads here are often used as family rooms, plus there are six other large dorms. The hostel laundry and small supply store come in handy, too.

Arran is really quite a place, teeming with wildlife and interesting human characters who've landed here; it's become somewhat touristed, sure, but still worth a look. Goat Fell, a rugged 2,900-foot climb, is the place to go if you're wanting serious outdoors adventure.

Hospitality: 

Cleanliness: 

Party index:

How to get there:

By bus: Bus stops nearby; call hostel for transit route.

By car: Take A841 to Lochranza.

By ferry: Ferries at Claonaig (½ mile) and Brodick (14 miles).

WHITING BAY HOSTEL

Shore Road, Whiting Bay, Isle of Arran KA27 8QW

Phone Number: 017707–00339

Rates: £4.95–£6.10 per HI member (about $7.00–$9.00 US)

Credit cards: Yes
Beds: 52
Private/family rooms: Yes
Season: February 27 to November 1
Office hours: 7:00 A.M. to 11:45 P.M.
Affiliation: HI-SYHA
Extras: Store

This small castle-like building in a humdrum town is okay as a base on Arran, but fairly remote. Three quads are available, plus five rooms with five to eight beds each.

Gestalt:
Isle of view

Party index:

Only drawback here is that there's not very much to do within walking distance, so you'll need a car unless hanging out on the lawn all day is your idea of fun. Get yourself 8 miles over the Brodick (that's where the ferry dock is anyway) for a little culture, dancing, and the local castle.

How to get there:

By bus: Bus stops nearby; call hostel for transit route.

By car: Take ferry from Androssan to Brodick, then drive 8 miles south on A841.

By ferry: Ferry from Androssan lands in Brodick, 8 miles away.

ISLAY HOSTEL

Port Charlotte, Isle of Islay, Argyll PA48 7TX

Phone Number: 01496–850385

Rates: £4.95–£6.10 per HI member (about $7.00–$9.00 US)
Beds: 42
Private/family rooms: Yes
Season: March 20 to November 1
Office hours: 7:00 A.M. to 11:45 P.M.
Affiliation: HI-SYHA
Extras: Library, meeting room, slide shows, laundry, store

Check this out: a library, slide shows, a meeting room, cliffs, beaches—and it's near the ferry, too. This joint is right on the water, so the place has got its own rocky beach of sorts; otters and seals are often seen. It has three quads and five larger dorms. You just might stick around a day instead of hustling onward to Jura.

Party index:

How to get there:

By bus: Bus stops nearby; call hostel for details.

By car: Take A847 to Port Charlotte.

By ferry: Port Askaig, 13 miles; from Port Ellen, 20 miles.

KILLIN HOSTEL

Killin, Perthshire FK21 8TN

Phone Number: 01567–820546

Rates: £4.95–£6.10 per HI member (about $7.00–$9.00 US)
Credit cards: Yes
Beds: 46
Private/family rooms: None
Season: Call ahead for open days
Office hours: 7:00 A.M. to 11:45 P.M.
Affiliation: HI-SYHA
Extras: Store

On the main street of a small scenic town at the foot of Loch Tay, this handsome two-and-a-half-story stone building is simple but certainly adequate. It has one quad room, two rooms of five to eight beds each, and one larger dorm, plus a small store and kitchen.

Besides the nice town, this area is full of Celtic sites, and there are lots of big hills nearby for walkers. Gawkers, on the other hand, might check out the Falls of Dochart.

Gestalt:
Killin time

Party index:

How to get there:

By bus: Bus stops nearby; call hostel for transit route.
By car: From Crianlanich or Kenmore take A827 to Killin.
By train: Train stops 14 miles away; call hostel for transit route.

KIRK YETHOLM HOSTEL

Kirk Yetholm, Kelso, Roxburghshire TD5 8PG

Phone Number: 01573–420631

Rates: £4.95–£6.10 per HI member (about $7.00–$9.00 US)
Credit cards: Yes
Beds: 34
Private/family rooms: Yes
Season: March 20 to November 1
Office hours: 7:00 A.M. to 11:45 P.M.
Affiliation: HI-SYHA
Extras: Store

At the very end of England's Pennine Way, this hostel is coadministered by that country's YHA. It's yet another Scottish stone house, filled with two quads used as family rooms and three bigger dorm rooms—as well as a small store. What to do? This is shepherd country, not too culturally interesting but pastoral enough.

Gestalt:
End of the Road

Party index:

How to get there:

By bus: Bus stops ½ mile from hostel; call hostel for transit route.

By car: From Kelso or Coldstream take B6352 to Town Yetholm; turn off for signs to Kirk Yetholm, drive into village.

By train: Berwick Station, 24 miles away, is closest stop.

MELROSE HOSTEL 

Priorwood, Melrose, Roxburghshire TD6 9EF

Phone Number: 01896–822–521

Rates: £6.50–£7.75 per HI member (about $10–$12 US)
Credit cards: Yes
Beds: 76
Private/family rooms: Yes
Office hours: 7:00 A.M. to 11:45 P.M.
Affiliation: HI-SYHA
Extras: Meals ($), store, laundry

The stunning view of the local abbey is just the start here. This brick building is really nice, and staff come through by serving meals in summer season and maintaining a laundry. Rooms consist of ten quads and two larger dorms, plus there's a splendid lawn in front.

Gestalt:
Melrose place

Party index:

Hit the walking track that leads to town if you're wanting to enjoy small-town Scotland, checking out the Borders region up close and personal.

How to get there:

By bus: Bus stops nearby; call hostel for transit route.

By car: Take A6091 to Melrose, turn at signs to abbey, then immediately onto High Street. Hostel overlooks abbey.

NEW LANARK HOSTEL 

Wee Row, Rosedale Street, New Lanark ML11 9DL

Phone Number: 01555–666710

Rates: £8.50–£9.75 per HI member (about $13–$15 US)
Credit cards: Yes

Beds: 64
Private/family rooms: Yes
Season: January 1 to 13; January 30 to December 31
Office hours: 7:00 A.M. to 2:00 A.M.
Affiliation: HI-SYHA
Extras: Meals ($), store, laundry, breakfast

This stone hostel is special, paying tribute (in a way) to a Scotsman with a dream.

The extremely friendly and helpful staff doles out free continental breakfasts to all hostellers, who sleep in one of sixteen quad rooms—all of which could be a family room if you happen to be coming with your family. Laundry and meal service are also available for a charge.

Hospitality:

Party index:

The restored riverside village of New Lanark teaches visitors about Robert Owen, an industrialist who tried hard to build an ideal manufacturing community here around his cotton mill. It's been nicely restored and is worth a look as a day trip from Glasgow.

How to get there:

By bus: Bus stops nearby; call hostel for transit route.

By car: Take A73 to New Lanark; turn right into Rosedale Street. Hostel is on left.

By train: From Glasgow's Central Station take train to Lanark Station, 1½ miles away.

NEWTONMORE INDEPENDENT HOSTEL

Craigellachie House, Main Street, Newtonmore, Inverness-shire PH20 1DA

Phone Number: 01540–673360

Fax: 01540–673360
E-mail: hostel.newtonmore@dial.pipex.com
Rates: £6.67–£8.50 per person (about $10–$13 US)
Beds: 18
Affiliation: None
Extras: Woodstove, laundry, meals ($), e-mail, bike rentals

This hostel's in a teeny town in the central Highlands and scores points for local color. The hostel houses eighteen hostellers in three rooms: two eight-bed dorms and a single double room. Amenities such as laundry, meal service, e-mail, and mountain bikes for hire have been thoughtfully provided.

One of the owners is a former mountain guide, and he can point you to all sorts of outdoor pursuits in the surrounding mountains (which also contain wildcats, by the way).

Or just hang in the local village, soaking up the real Scotland. They make a big deal out of shinty around here: an old, old hockey-like game played by locals in fall, so try to catch a match.

Gestalt: Newtonmore of everything

Party index:

How to get there:

By bus: From Edinburgh or Inverness take bus to Newtonmore and walk 1 mile to hostel.

By car: From Edinburgh or Inverness drive A9 to Newtonmore; turn off onto Main Street and continue 1 mile to hostel.

By train: From Newtonmore Station walk 1 mile to hostel.

MINNIGAFF HOSTEL

Newton Stewart, Wigtownshire DG8 6PL

Phone Number: 01671–402211

Rates: £4.95–£6.10 per HI member (about $7.00–$9.00 US)
Credit cards: Yes
Beds: 36
Private/family rooms: None
Season: March 20 to November 1
Office hours: 7:00 A.M. to 11:45 P.M.
Affiliation: HI-SYHA

Three large dorms and a kitchen in a squat stone house: That's what you get here, plus access to tons of cycling, hiking, and horse riding opportunities in the area. Other potential trips could take you to a wild goat preserve or along the Southern Upland Way.

Party index:

How to get there:

By bus: Bus stops ½ mile from hostel; call hostel for transit route.

By car: Take A714 to Newton Stewart, turn onto B7079 and cross bridge; make a left into Minnigaff village. Hostel is on left.

By ferry: Stanraer ferry dock, 25 miles away.

By train: Barrhill Station is 16 miles away.

JEREMY INGLIS HOSTEL 

21 Airds Crescent, Oban, Argyll PA34 4BA

Phone Number: 01631–565065 or 01631–563064

Rates: £7.00–£7.50 per person (about $11–$12 US)

Beds: 14
Private/family rooms: Sometimes
Affiliation: None
Extras: Breakfast

This tiny place didn't grade out well at all with our snoops. Not at all. Sure, it's cheap, and they serve a bit of breakfast. But some hostellers told us it skanked, quite crowded and not so clean. Looks like we'll give it a miss, especially with other decent places in town.

Oban isn't really worth a stay anyway, unless you've missed the ferry or train and need to catch another first thing in the mornin'.

Gestalt: No hablo Inglis

Party index:

How to get there:

By bus: Call hostel for directions.
By car: Call hostel for directions.
By train: Call hostel for directions.

OBAN BACKPACKERS HOSTEL

Breadalbane Street, Oban, Argyll PA34 5NZ

Phone Number: 01631–562107

Rates: £9.50–£9.90 per person (about $13–$15 US)
Beds: 48
Private/family rooms: Yes
Office hours: 6:30 A.M. to 2:30 A.M.
Extras: Breakfast ($), bike rentals, pool table

This is not the cleanest hostel in the world; at least decent staff partly compensate. They rent bikes and maintain a pool table. Oban, as we've said, isn't terrific; it's only a way station, and this hostel feels that way, too.

How to get there:

By bus: Call hostel for transit route.
By car: Call hostel for directions.
By train: From Oban Station call hostel for directions.

OBAN HOSTEL

Corran Esplanade, Oban, Argyll PA34 5AF

Phone Number: 01631–562025

Rates: £7.10–£9.60 per HI member (about $11–$14 US)
Credit cards: Yes
Beds: 154

Private/family rooms: Yes
Season: January 1 to 13; January 30 to December 31
Office hours: 7:00 A.M. to 2:00 A.M.
Affiliation: HI-SYHA
Extras: Laundry, store, snack shop

Well decked-out and close to the train station, this three-story stone house has lots of windows. There are sixteen quad rooms best for families, plus ten larger dorms.

Gestalt: Mull sighter

Party index:

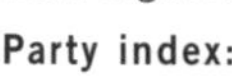

This is a gateway town, plain and simple, not so hot but a jumping-off point for Mull, Islay, and more. At least the place has good views of Mull. If you've gotta stay in town, might as well do it here.

How to get there:

By bus: Bus stops ¾ mile from hostel; call hostel for transit route.

By car: Take A85 to Oban; turn onto road for Oban Bay (Esplanade).

By ferry: Ferry dock to Mull, 1 mile.

By train: From Glasgow take train to Oban Station, ¾ mile from hostel.

PERTH HOSTEL

107 Glasgow Road, Perth, Tayside PH2 ONS

Phone Number: 01738–623658

Rates: £6.50–£7.75 per HI member (about $10–$12 US)
Credit cards: Yes
Beds: 62
Private/family rooms: Yes
Season: January 1 to 13; January 30 to December 31
Office hours: 5:00 A.M. to 11:45 P.M.
Affiliation: HI-SYHA
Extras: Store, laundry

Insiders' tip: Working water mill in town

Gestalt: Perthless

Sorry, gang, but this place is only so-so despite the nice three-story building it sits inside. Why? Well, it's drab and boring for starters. And the management blasts tunes each morning to roust you from bed. We've heard other complaints about the hospitality around here, as well.

Anyhow, if you're still going, there are three quads, two medium bunkrooms, and three pretty large ones. It's an uphill walk from the town, which isn't exactly the most exciting destination in Scotland, either.

Hospitality:

Party index:

How to get there:

By bus: From bus station walk ¾ mile to hostel.

By car: From Edinburgh take A9 to Perth. Hostel is on left, approaching town.

By train: From Perth Station walk ¾ mile to hostel.

PITLOCHRY HOSTEL

Knockard Road, Pitlochry PH16 5HJ

Phone Number: 01796–472308

Rates: £6.50–£7.75 per HI member (about $10–$12 US)
Office hours: 7:00 A.M. to 11:45 P.M.
Season: February 27 to November 1
Credit cards: Yes
Beds: 74
Private/family rooms: Yes
Affiliation: HI-SYHA
Extras: Meals ($), store, laundry

A hostel right at the heart of Scotland, this hotel-turned-hostel has eight quads plus seven with up to eight beds apiece. In summertime they serve meals. We'd say it's one of the better-run places in the SYHA chain, though it's pretty sterile. Your fellow guests will probably be older folks.

Each room has its own bathroom, a big plus—though their condition appears to be deteriorating, as this is an old hotel building. The kitchen's rather scary and gothic-looking, and you have to light the gas stoves; there's a sizable (if plain) dining room, too. Ah, well. The joint looks down on the town, so there are pretty views day and night. There's a supermarket and one of the best fish-and-chip shops in Scotland within a five-minute walk; take the shortcut through a gorgeous churchyard.

They kick you out early here—9:30 A.M. from your room, 10:30 A.M. from the hostel, but that's okay as long as it isn't raining too hard. Pitlochry's actually a nice country town to hang out in for a day, rightly famous for the local whiskey; take the in-town distillery tour, which everyone does, and you'll pay about five bucks. Or head a few miles out of town to a smaller one (Scotland's smallest, in fact) and sample for free.

Best bet for a bite:
Fish-and-chip shop nearby

Insiders' tip:
Scotland's Pub is cool

Gestalt:
Pit stop

Hospitality: 

Cleanliness: 

Party index:

For other fun, walk 4 miles to the Pass of Killiecrankie (no, we didn't make that name up) or check out the fish ladders, which the local fish use to paint rooftops. Naw, just kiddin'. Actually salmon occasionally—and we mean occasionally—pass through here on their difficult journeys upriver to spawn and spawn again.

How to get there:

By bus: Bus stops ½ mile from hostel.

By car: Take A9 to Pitlochry, turn left on Bonnethill Road, and then make an immediate right to Toberargan and next left onto Well Brae. Hostel is at corner of Knockard Road.

By train: Pitlochry Station is ½ mile.

ROWARDENNAN HOSTEL

Rowardennan by Drymen, Glasgow G63 0AR

Phone Number: 01360–870259

Rates: £6.50–£7.75 per HI member (about $10–$12 US)
Credit cards: Yes
Beds: 80
Private/family rooms: Yes
Season: January 30 to November 1
Office hours: 7:00 A.M. to 11:45 P.M.
Affiliation: HI-SYHA
Extras: Meals ($), laundry, outings, breakfast

This terrific hostel, a former hunting lodge, offers a super view over a lake and looks something like a little castle. The laid-back crowd is fun to hang with, and everyone's here for the outdoors pursuits like windsurfing, canoeing, and lounging around on the hostel's own beach. An activity center on premises offers still more outing possibilities.

Gestalt:
Muscle beach

Party index:

There are seven quad rooms here and eight larger ones, and all hostellers get continental breakfasts. All in all, as we said, the facilities are excellent—and they serve meals, too. Good thing; it's 12 miles to the nearest food!

To boot, this place is right at the foot of Ben Lomond, a two-hour climb—and the West Highland Way passes right by the front door, for gosh sake. Maybe the best outdoors-oriented hostel in Scotland.

How to get there:

By bus: Bus stops in Balmaha, 7 miles away; call hostel for transit route.

By car: Call hostel for directions.

By ferry: Ferry from Inverbeg Bay lands nearby.
By train: Balloch Station is 17 miles.

STIRLING HOSTEL

St. John Street, Stirling FK8 1EA

Phone Number: 01786–473442

Rates: £9.95–£12.50 per HI member (about $15–$19 US)
Credit cards: Yes
Beds: 126
Private/family rooms: Yes
Affiliation: HI-SYHA
Office hours: 7:00 A.M. to 2:00 A.M.
Extras: Meals ($), laundry, store

This could well be Scotland's top bunk, a superior hostel in a beautiful building that's literally a stone's throw away from Stirling's castle. Factor in the hilltop position—some of the double rooms have incredible views of the town, which looks like Hollywood (though it feels like Buffalo in daylight)—and you're talking a must-stay.

The hostel was built behind the facade of the historic Erskine Marykirk Church. You can walk around the corner and uphill to the castle: It's all right there, looming just above the hostel.

It's well equipped, wheelchair accessible, and almost all of the thirty-two rooms are quads or doubles, practically guaranteeing that you won't get that cattle-herd feeling. Get this: Every room has en-suite bathroom facilities, making this a great bet for famlies or anyone seeking a little extra privacy. Once you've sampled the spanking-new plumbing (meaning toilets actually flush when you flush them, for a change), you'll never settle for second-best again in a hostel.

Best bet for a bite: Good luck

Insiders' tip: Local "ghost walk"

Gestalt: Stirling effort

Party index:

But we heard a few complaints too; rooms were freezing, walls were paper-thin, and you needed to continuously push a button to ensure proper water flow (you get about thirty seconds of water per push). Also, we give the big thumbs down to SYHA's allowance of cigarette smoking inside the place. The smoke hits you in the face at check-in; the nasty habit is allowed in the TV/common room, which could obstruct some efforts at socializing.

The staff serves breakfast for free year-round and whips up other meals for a charge during the summertime. However, they also make blaring announcements over the loudspeaker at the strangest times to announce the ultra early 9:30 A.M. check/lockout. And they won't let you reserve a double room; you just show up and hope one's available. Sorry. That's the policy.

How to get there:

By bus: Bus stops nearby; call hostel for transit route.

By car: Call hostel for directions.

By train: From Stirling Station walk ahead toward Murray Place and turn left. Go right on King Street for 1 block, then turn left on Spittal. Go up hill until top; look for hostel signs.

STIRLING UNION STREET HOSTEL

Union Street Street, Stirling FK8 1NZ

Phone Number: 01786–473442

Rates: £9.95–£12.50 per HI member (about $15–$19 US)
Credit cards: Yes
Beds: 96
Private/family rooms: Yes
Season: June 20 to September 5
Office hours: 7:00 A.M. to 2:00 A.M.
Affiliation: HI-SYHA
Extras: Breakfast, laundry

Party index:

This overflow facility handles extra demand for the main Stirling hostel during summertime, but you can also book a bed here instead if you like even if they're not full. (Call the main Stirling hostel to book it.)

Every room here's a private room, so that's cool, but these buildings are incredibly lifeless—think cookie-cutter subdivision hell and you've got the idea. So the facility isn't thrilling, but if you're a family or you're sick and tired of socializing, this would be the pick in Stirling. Breakfast is included and there is a laundry.

How to get there:

By bus: From bus station walk ½ mile up Goosecroft Road to Union Street. Hostel is on right.

By car: Call hostel for directions.

By train: From Stirling Station walk ½ mile up Goosecroft Road to Union Street. Hostel is on right.

TIGHNABRUAICH HOSTEL

High Road, Tighnabruaich, Argyll PA21 2BD

Phone Number: 01700–811622

Rates: £4.95–£6.10 per HI member (about $7.00–$9.00 US)
Credit cards: Yes

Beds: 40
Private/family rooms: None
Season: March 20 to October 4
Office hours: 7:00 A.M. to 11:45 P.M.
Affiliation: HI-SYHA
Extras: Store, bike rentals

Blessed with superior location on a hillside, this homey hostel comes with views galore. It's got one quad room, three rooms of five to eight beds each, and one still larger dormitory. You can get a few supplies at the hostel store, or head for the market half a mile away in the village.

The area is known for attracting artists and birds. You might also check out the windsurfing and sailing school.

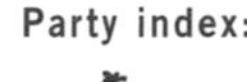

Party index:

How to get there:

By bus: Bus stops ½ mile from hostel; call hostel for transit details.

By car: Take A8003 to Tighnabruaich.

By ferry: Dunoon ferry dock is 24 miles away.

TOMINTOUL HOSTEL

Main Street, Tomintoul, Ballindalloch, Banffshire AB3 9HA

Phone Number: 01807–580282

Rates: £3.85–£4.65 per HI member (about $6.00–$7.00 US)
Beds: 38
Private/family rooms: None
Season: May 15 to November 1
Office hours: 7:00 to 11:00 A.M.; 5:00 to 11:00 P.M.
Affiliation: HI-SYHA

A rather simple place in a rather small village, Tomintoul's hostel at least sits near the beginning of the Speyside Way walking trail. There are just two dorm rooms here and a kitchen. The top draw, we'd say, would be the 6-mile walk to some standing stones, but plenty of other outdoorsy stuff can be done here, too.

Gestalt:
I Speyside

Party index:

How to get there:

By bus: Bus stops nearby; call hostel for transit route.

By car: Take A939 to Tomintoul.

LOTUS LODGE HOSTEL

Lotus Lodge, Wanlockhead, Lanarkshire ML12 6UT

Phone Number: 01659–74252

Rates: £4.95–£6.10 per person (about $7.00–$9.00 US)
Credit cards: Yes
Beds: 28
Private/family rooms: None
Season: March 20 to November 1
Office hours: 7:00 A.M. to 11:45 P.M.
Affiliation: None
Extras: Store

There's gold in them thar hostels! Well, not exactly, but this is gold country and the highest-elevation village in Scotland. The facilities consists of one quad dorm, two dormitories with five to eight beds each, and one large bunkroom, plus a kitchen and small hostel store. No lotuses in sight, though, as far as we could tell. Nor a party scene.

Gestalt: Lotus eaters

Party index:

How to get there:

By bus: Bus stops ½ mile from hostel; call hostel for details.

By car: Take B797

By train: Sanquar Station is 8 miles away.

BROADMEADOWS HOSTEL

Old Broadmeadows, Yarrowford, Selkirk TD7 5LZ

Phone Number: 01750–76262

Rates: £3.85–£4.65 per HI member (about $6.00–$7.00 US)
Credit cards: Yes
Beds: 28
Private/family rooms: None
Season: March 20 to October 4
Office hours: 7:00 to 10:30 A.M.; 5:00 to 11:00 P.M.
Affiliation: HI-SYHA
Extras: Store, garden

This was Scotland's first hostel, opened way back in 1931, and it's still going strong by the look of things. Then as now basically just a house in the fields, it's outfitted with four bunkrooms averaging seven beds each.

The joint is wheelchair accessible and close to the Southern Upland Way walking track; there's a decent museum and some castle ruins nearby as well.

Insiders' tip:
Brewery nearby

Party index:

How to get there:

By bus: Bus stops nearby three times weekly; call hostel for transit details.

By car: From Selkirk take A708 to Yarrowford; turn off main road and continue to hostel at end.

ORTHERN SCOTLA D

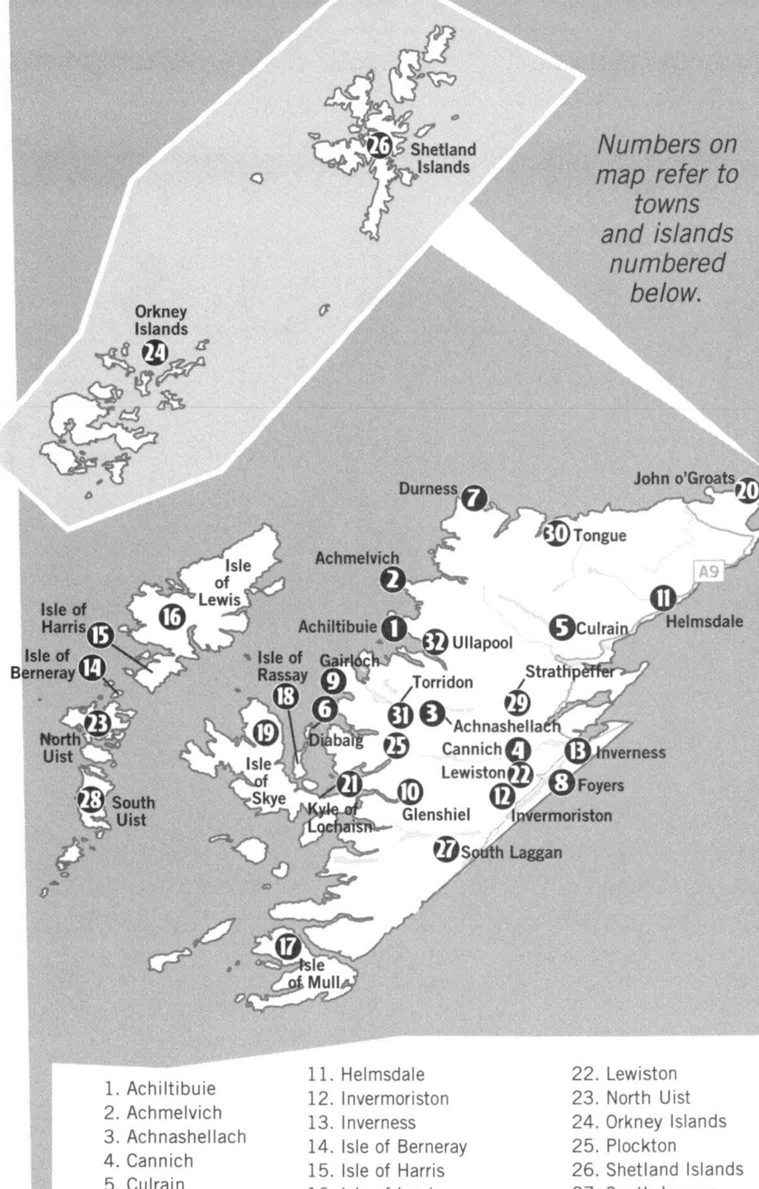

1. Achiltibuie
2. Achmelvich
3. Achnashellach
4. Cannich
5. Culrain
6. Diabaig
7. Durness
8. Foyers
9. Gairloch
10. Glenshiel
11. Helmsdale
12. Invermoriston
13. Inverness
14. Isle of Berneray
15. Isle of Harris
16. Isle of Lewis
17. Isle of Mull
18. Isle of Raasay
19. Isle of Skye
20. John O'Groats (Canisbay)
21. Kyle of Lochalsh
22. Lewiston
23. North Uist
24. Orkney Islands
25. Plockton
26. Shetland Islands
27. South Laggan
28. South Uist
29. Strathpeffer
30. Tongue
31. Torridon
32. Ullapool

NORTHERN SCOTLAND

Northern Scotland is incredibly beautiful, and there are plenty of hostels here to help you see it. Most are simple, just as in the rest of Scotland, but you do run across the occasional oddball place with spirit, character, and good facilities out in the middle of absolutely nowhere.

Interestingly, the Gatliff Hebridean Hostels Trust works with SYHA to outfit some simple hostels, charging a pittance per bed. But you've gotta bring your own sleeping bag and expect nothing, not even a kitchen in some cases.

ACHININVER HOSTEL

Achiltibuie, Ullapool, Ross-shire IV26 2YL

Phone Number: 01854–622254

Rates: £3.85–£4.65 per HI member (about $6.00–$7.00 US)
Credit cards: Yes
Beds: 20
Private/family rooms: Sometimes
Season: May 15 to October 4
Office hours: 7:00 to 10:30 A.M.; 5:00 to 11:00 P.M.
Affiliation: HI-SYHA
Extras: None

A quiet Highlands hostel, this one features its own beach and is also positioned near some big hills and ferries to the so-called Summer Isles. Three dorms fill a simple white house in rugged countryside. For fun, hit the nearby Hydroponicum, an indoor tropical garden.

Gestalt: Highlander

Party index:

How to get there:

By bus: Bus station, ½ mile; call hostel for transit route.

By car: Call hostel for directions.

By foot: Footpath from Ullapool; call hostel for details.

ACHMELVICH HOSTEL

Achmelvich, Recharn, Lairg, Sutherland IV27 4JB

Phone Number: 01571–844–480

Rates: £3.85–£4.65 per HI member (about $6.00–$7.00 US)
Credit cards: Yes
Beds: 38
Private/family rooms: Yes
Season: March 20 to October 4
Office hours: 7:00 to 10:30 A.M.; 5:00 to 11:00 P.M.
Affiliation: HI-SYHA
Extras: Store

Think remote beachside, and you'll get the picture of this hostel's location. The place consists of two buildings filled with one great big dorm, three smaller ones, and a lone quad room. You'll likely stick around if you get here, as it's 4 miles to the nearest food. Swimming is said to be excellent here.

Party index:

How to get there:

By bus: Postbus stops 1½ miles from hostel; call hostel for details.

By car: From Lochinver take B869 to Feaden; turn off, drive to end of road. Hostel is on right.

By train: Lairg Station, 40 miles away, is closest; call hostel for transit route.

GERRY'S ACHNASHELLACH HOSTEL

Achnashellach, Strathcarron, Wester Ross IV54 8YU

Phone Number: 01520–766232

Rates: £8.00 per person (about $12 US)
Beds: 24
Affiliation: None
Extras: Stereo, fireplace, library

Just 2 miles east of Achnashellach's train station, this was Scotland's first independent hostel (at least according to Gerry). It's a long, stucco-like building in a town situated amidst gorgeous countryside on the way from Inverness to the pleasures of the west coast.

Gestalt:
Gerry's Kid

Party index:

Among the comforts here: a library, a fireplace, a stereo, and a strict nonsmoking policy. Still a decent place, although Gerry rules the roost.

How to get there:

By car: Call hostel for directions.

By train: From Inverness take train to Achnashellach Station; walk 2 miles east to hostel.

CANNICH HOSTEL

Cannich, Beauly, Inverness-shire IV4 7IT

Phone Number: 01456–415244

Rates: £4.95–£6.10 per HI member (about $7.00–$9.00 US)
Credit cards: Yes
Beds: 66
Private/family rooms: Yes
Season: March 20 to November 1
Office hours: 5:00 to 11:45 P.M.
Affiliation: HI-SYHA

A rather long and rather brown building, this hostel surprises by packing in ten dorm rooms and one family unit. It's wheelchair accessible, too, and well located if you're wanting to see Loch Ness and (yeah, right) the famous monster. Nearby Glen Affric contains some of Scotland's most beloved pine groves—an aromatic hike in summer.

Party index:

How to get there:

By bus: From Inverness take bus to Cannich; call hostel for transit route.

By car: From Beauly or Loch Ness take A831 to Cannich village.

By train: From Inverness Station take bus to Cannich; call hostel for transit details.

GLEN AFFRIC HOSTEL

Allt Beithe, Glen Affric, Cannich, Beauly, Inverness-shire IV4 7ND

No phone (Call Central Reservation Service, 010541–55–32–55)

Rates: £4.85–£5.65 per HI member (about $7.00–$9.00 US)
Beds: 26
Private/family rooms: None
Season: March 20 to November 1
Office hours: 7:00 to 11:00 A.M.; 5:00 to 11:00 P.M.
Affiliation: HI-SYHA

Not in Cannich at all, but in fact 21 miles away by a footpath, this place is exceedingly simple and remote. (Better to drive to Cluanie, if you're doing that, and hike in from there: It's a shorter, gentler hike.)

No matter what, you have to hike 10 miles up a valley to get here, there's no hot water or electricity or linens, the bathrooms are outhouses, and only one room is heated. But ya know what? We loved it. There's something invigorating about this much

Gestalt:
Whispering pines

Party index:

raw wilderness and effort, something primal, and other hostellers who took the time to get here were interesting too. Bring a thick sleeping bag, though, 'cause it can get cold up here at night.

Glen Affric is one of Scotland's prettiest valleys, famous throughout the land as home to an ancient grove of Caledonia pine trees.

How to get there:

By bus: Cannich, 21 miles away by foot, is nearest bus stop.

By car: From Kyle or Invergary drive A87 to Cluanie; park at trailhead, near Cluanie Inn, and hike 10 miles up river valley to hostel.

CARBISDALE CASTLE HOSTEL 

Carbisdale Castle, Culrain, Ross-shire IV24 3DP

Phone Number: 01549–421–232

Rates: £9.95–£12.50 per HI member (about $15–$19 US)
Credit cards: Yes
Beds: 195
Private/family rooms: Yes
Season: February 27 to May 4; May 14 to November 1
Office hours: 7:00 A.M. to 2:00 A.M.
Affiliation: HI-SYHA
Extras: Breakfast, meals ($), store, laundry

Hostellers love this place, which is sort of a castle overlooking the Kyle of Sutherlands, an inlet of water. It's either tacky or amazing, depending on your perspective.

Statues lurking everywhere, music, dancing, huge rooms, rumors of ghosts . . . it's all very head-spinning and quite unusual for an English hostel. Altogether there are twenty-six dorm rooms here, most pretty large; they do have six quad rooms that families like, but they go fast. It's a reasonably fun place—witness the ceilidh (kay'-lee) dances in summertime—but the enormous size makes it a little harder to get to know people.

Gestalt: Crazy castle

Party index:

How to get there:

By bus: Bus stops at Ardgay, 4½ miles away; call hostel for details.

By car: From Dornoch take A836 to Ardgay turnoff; turn left, cross bridge and bear right toward Culrain. Continue 4 miles; hostel is on left, just after train station.

By train: Culrain Station is less than ¼ mile.

CRAIG HOSTEL

Diabaig, Achnasheen, Ross-shire IV22 2HE

No phone (Call Central Reservation Service, 010541–55–32–55)

Rates: £3.85–£4.65 per HI member (about $6.00–$7.00 US)
Beds: 16
Private/family rooms: None
Season: May 15 to October 4
Office hours: 7:00 to 10:30 A.M.; 5:00 to 11:00 P.M.
Affiliation: HI-SYHA

Wow, the hostels just keep getting wilder and more remote. This rural cottage has no phone, you can't drive here, and it's so far off the beaten track you need to bring your own food and sleeping bag. (It's 3 miles to any semblance of a village, 12 miles to actual civilization.)

Two eight-bed dorms make up the place, and thankfully there is a kitchen, too. Views over the moors and out to the Isle of Skye are breathtaking when it's not raining. This is about as much peace and quiet as you'll get at a hostel, and that we like.

Party index:

How to get there:

By bus: Take Postbus to Diabaig or Red Point; walk 3 miles to hostel.

By car: From Torridon drive 9 miles west to Diabaig or Red Point; park car; walk 3 miles to hostel.

By train: Achnasheen Station, 30 miles away, is closest stop.

DURNESS HOSTEL

Smoo, Durness, Lairg, Sutherland IV27 4QA

Phone Number: 01971–511244

Rates: £3.85–£4.65 per HI member (about $6.00–$7.00 US)
Credit cards: Yes
Beds: 40
Private/family rooms: None
Season: March 20 to October 4
Office hours: 7:00 to 10:30 A.M.; 5:00 to 11:00 P.M.
Affiliation: HI-SYHA
Extras: Store

Two words here: super simple. Okay, two more: great views. This small building, actually in the whimsically named village of Smoo, has four dorms and a kitchen plus a small hostel store.

Fun options around here include a boat trip to Smoo Cave, lots of beaches, and the annual Highland Gathering in late July.

Gestalt: Smoopy

Party index:

How to get there:

By bus: Bus stops 1 mile from hostel; call for transit details.

By car: From Tongue take AA838 to just before Durness; hostel is on right, in Smoo.

By train: Lairg Station, 56 miles away, is nearest.

FOYERS HOUSE HOSTEL

Foyers, Inverness-shire IV1 2XU

Phone Number: 01456–486405

Rates: £8–£12 per person (about $12–$18 US)
Beds: 10
Private/family rooms: None
Affiliation: None

Gestalt: Nessential

Hospitality: 

Cleanliness:

Party index:

Right by the shore of Loch Ness, in a tiny town, this is a good little independent joint, very homey. Not superluxurious, no, but this is by far the best part of Loch Ness, the quiet southern shore—well worth a detour, although it's very hard to get here without a car.

How to get there:

By bus: Call hostel for transit route.
By car: Call hostel for directions.
By train: Call hostel for transit route.

CARN DEARG HOSTEL

Carn Dearg, Gairloch, Ross-shire IV21 2DJ

Phone Number: 01445–712219

Rates: £4.95–£6.10 per HI member (about $7.00–$9.00 US)
Credit cards: Yes
Beds: 50
Private/family rooms: None
Season: May 16 to October 4
Office hours: 7:00 A.M. to 11:45 P.M.
Affiliation: HI-SYHA

Extras: Store

Right on the brink of Loch Gairloch, this is a good outdoor hostel: Cliffs, walking paths, sea caves, and gardens abound in the area. Five dorm rooms are all pretty big—they average ten beds apiece—plus there's a kitchen and a few food staples for sale. Check out the mural of Winnie the Pooh, too.

Party index:

How to get there:

By bus: Bus stop at Strath, 3 miles away; call hostel for transit route.

By car: Take B8021 to Gairloch. Hostel is on right, overlooking loch.

RATAGAN HOSTEL

Glenshiel, Kyle, Ross-shire IV40 8HP

Phone Number: 01599–511–243

Rates: £6.50–£7.75 per HI member (about $10–$12 US)
Credit cards: Yes
Beds: 44
Private/family rooms: None
Season: January 30 to December 31
Office hours: 7:00 A.M. to 11:45 P.M.
Affiliation: HI-SYHA
Extras: Laundry, store

Here's another Scottish lakeside hostel, near the 3,300-foot-high Saddle, equipped with one quad room, two bunkrooms of five to eight beds each, and three bigger ones. They maintain a laundry and small store.

Party index:

How to get there:

By bus: Bus stops 1¼ miles from hostel; call hostel for transit details.

By car: From Kyle take A87 for 18 miles to hostel.

By ferry: Glenelg ferry, 10 miles.

By train: Kyle of Lochalsh Station, 18 miles.

HELMSDALE HOSTEL

Helmsdale, Sutherland KW8 6JR

Phone Number: 01431–821577

Rates: £3.85–£4.65 per HI member (about $6.00–$7.00 US)

Beds: 38
Private/family rooms: None
Season: May 15 to October 4
Office hours: 7:00 to 11:00 A.M.; 5:00 to 11:00 P.M.
Affiliation: HI-SYHA

Right on the train line north of Inverness, this plain gets high marks despite the two really huge dorm rooms. (Try to snag the lone quad room instead if you can.) A nice alternative base to walk the highland hills if Inverness is full or you're wanting more quietude.

Gestalt: At the Helmsdale

Party index:

How to get there:

By bus: Bus stops ¼ mile from hostel; call hostel for transit route.

By car: Take A9 to Helmsdale.

By train: From Helmsdale Station cross bridge and walk ½ mile to hostel.

LOCH NESS HOSTEL

Glenmoriston, Invermoriston, Inverness-shire IV3 6YD

Phone Number: 01320–351274

Rates: £4.95–£6.10 per HI member (about $7.00–$9.00 US)
Credit cards: Yes
Beds: 57
Private/family rooms: Yes
Season: March 20 to November 1
Office hours: 7:00 A.M. to 11:45 P.M.
Affiliation: HI-SYHA
Extras: Store

This two-story white building sits by famous Loch Ness and includes nine quad rooms plus three big dorms. A small hostel store doles out some food supplies, and that's good because you're more than 3 miles from the nearest market. Keep in mind, though, that the Nessie exhibits are a good long way off.

Party index:

How to get there:

By bus: Bus stops nearby; call hostel for transit route.

By car: Call hostel for directions.

By train: Inverness Station, 24 miles away.

INVERNESS HOSTELS at a glance

	RATING	COST	IN A WORD
Bazpackers Hostel		£7.50–£9.00	friendly
Eastgate Hostel		£8.90	decent
Inverness Millburn Hostel		£9.95–£12.50	military
Inverness Student Hotel		£9.50–£9.90	iffy
Ho Ho Hostel		£8.50–£9.50	chaotic

BAZPACKERS BACKPACKERS HOSTEL

4 Culduthel Road, Inverness IV2 4AB

Phone Number: 01463–717663

Rates: £7.50–£9.00 (about $10–$13 US); doubles £24 (about $36 US)
Beds: 28
Affiliation: None

This place gets the thumbs up from everyone: A laid-back and much more central hostel than the SYHA joint, it should probably be your first choice when bunking up in Inverness. They thoughtfully maintain double rooms in addition to the bunks; everyone agrees they're tops in friendliness, too.

Gestalt: Baz room

Hospitality: 

Cleanliness: 

Party index:

How to get there:

By bus: Call hostel for directions.
By car: Call hostel for directions.
By train: Call hostel for directions.

EASTGATE HOSTEL

38 Eastgate, Inverness IV2 3NA

Phone Number: 01463–718756

Fax: 01463–718756
Rates: £8.90 per person (about $13 US)
Beds: 47

Family/private rooms: Yes
Office hours: 7:00 A.M. to 12 midnight
Affiliation: None
Extras: Grill, coffee, bike rentals, breakfast ($)

This is the only hostel that advertises at the train station tourist bureau, so you might get suckered into thinking it's the only game in town. Not so, but it's still pretty decent.

Best bet for a bite: Takeaways

Gestalt: East of Eden

Party index:

Bunkrooms contain six bunks each, and there are three family rooms for couples or families with at least two beds apiece. A grill is maintained, bikes are for rent, and the usual no-rules independent spirit prevails here. Definitely an option.

How to get there:

By bus: Call hostel for directions.
By car: Call hostel for directions.
By train: Call hostel for directions.

HO HO HOSTEL

23A High Street, Inverness IV1 1HY

Phone Number: 01463–221225

Fax: 01463–221225
Rates: £8.50–£9.50 per person (about $13–$14 US)
Beds: 85
Affiliation: None

This place is well named: It's basically a ho-ho kinda place for the Go Blue Banana folks. What that means for you really depends on your idea of a good time: If you're wanting a quiet, social experience, forget it. Beer cans and late-night groping are the rule. On the other hand, if that sounds good to you, it's probably the most fun hostel in Inverness.

And it's the most central, too, occupying a beautiful second-floor location above the main row of shops.

Best bet for a bite: Safeway

Insiders' tip: Get yer e-mail at Invernet

Gestalt: Ho Hum

Hospitality:

Cleanliness:

Party index:

How to get there:

By bus: Walk ¼ mile from bus station down High Street.
By car: Call hostel for directions.
By train: Walk ¼ mile from train station down High Street.

INVERNESS MILLBURN HOSTEL

Victoria Drive, Inverness IV2 3QB

Phone Number: 01463–231771

Rates: £9.95–£12.50 per HI member (about $15–$19 US)
Credit cards: Yes
Beds: 166
Private/family rooms: Yes
Office hours: 7:00 A.M. to 2:00 A.M.
Affiliation: HI-SYHA
Extras: Laundry, cafeteria ($), breakfast, conference rooms

Gestalt: Invermess

Hospitality:

Cleanliness:

Party index:

Incredibly bland and resembling a prison, this is nevertheless a fairly well equipped hostel in the Highland capital of Inverness. It ought to be: SYHA and others recently poured the equivalent of $3 million US into renovations.

They didn't get everything right, however. The hostel sits in a really poor location, wedged between the airport, a private school (off-limits to hostellers), and a super-rich neighborhood. You pick from ten quad rooms and twenty-five bigger ones, each with sink and mirror and some with en-suite toilets and/or showers.

A big, institutional dining room holds the cafeteria, where the lousy breakfast is free and meals cost. Thumbs up for the good kitchen, secure key-card entry system, free lockers (you bring the lock), conference rooms, and laundry. Rooms are very roomy and modern, so that was nice, too.

Big thumbs down, though, for the characterless digs, the super-heavy doors that sucked our will to live, and poorly kept-up bathrooms. The heat wasn't working at all when we slept here, and we stayed an extra night to see if things would improve. They didn't. We also hated the smoke-filled reception area: You get smoked out while you're checking in!

Staff is so-so, and school groups and older folks run rampant here, too. Bottom line? Not a place to party, or to have fun.

How to get there:

By bus: Bus stops in Inverness; from station, turn left and walk through to main road. Turn immediately right and then left again onto Crown Drive. Continue uphill to Victoria Drive, turn left; hostel is on right, up driveway.

By car: Call hostel for directions.

By train: From Inverness Station turn left on main road; immediately turn right and then left again onto Crown Drive. Continue uphill to Victoria Drive, turn left; hostel is on right, up driveway.

INVERNESS STUDENT HOTEL HOSTEL

8 Culduthel Road, Inverness IV2 4AB

Phone Number: 01463–236556

Fax: 0131–556–2981
Rates: £9.50–£9.90
Beds: 57
Private/family rooms: None
Office hours: 6:30 A.M. to 2:30 A.M.
Extras: Coffee

This place is so-so, an option but not the top bunk in town. It's pretty fun, though. Facilities are basic bunks, centrally located for traipsing into the compact downtown with its seemingly endless string of pubs and other diversions.

Gestalt: Inverted

Hospitality: 

Cleanliness: 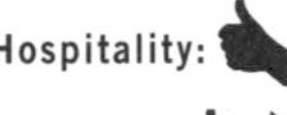

Party index:

How to get there:

By bus: From bus station walk onto main road (Academy) and turn left. Cross street and continue to third right, turn, continue to High Street and turn right. Walk to Castle Street and turn left; walk down Castle (which becomes Culduthel). Hostel is on right.

By car: Call hostel for directions.

By train: From train station walk onto main road (Academy) and turn left. Cross street and continue to second right, turn, continue to High Street and turn right. Walk to Castle Street and turn left; walk down Castle (which becomes Culduthel). Hostel is on right.

BERNERAY HOSTEL

Isle of Berneray, North Uist HS6 5BQ

No phone

Rates: £3.85–£4.65 per HI member (about $6.00–$7.00 US)
Beds: 16
Office hours: Vary
Private/family rooms: None
Affiliation: HI-SYHA

You can't get much simpler than this one, a whitewashed croft house turned into a hostel set on its own tiny island and beach. How simple is it? Bring sheets—there aren't any here. And don't bother booking in advance; they don't take reservations. Might as well leave those credit cards behind, too . . .

Three dorm rooms split up the sixteen beds, which you reach by ferry from North Uist. Berneray Island is only 8 miles around, so it's an obvious bike ride or walk; also, the island's two little villages hold an annual festival week in July. For food, you haven't got much choice: A village market half a mile away is about it. But that's okay; this is a unique experience anyway.

Gestalt:
Seals and croft

Party index:

How to get there:

By ferry: From North Uist take ferry to Berneray.

RHENIGIDALE HOSTEL

Rhenigidale, Isle of Harris, Western Isles HS3 3BD

No phone

Rates: £3.85–£4.65 per HI member (about $6.00–$7.00 US)
Beds: 11
Private/family rooms: None
Office hours: 7:00 A.M. to 11:45 P.M.
Affiliation: HI-SYHA

This ultrasimple, whitewashed croft house is no-frills all the way. You can't even book in advance, and there are no linens or kitchen; just three small dorm rooms.

But the location! Positioned on wild, unspoiled Harris, this place overlooks the Minch. You can walk a coastal path and check out the barren landscape of stone fields and empty beaches. Come for the scenery, not the comfort.

Gestalt:
Harris tweed

Party index:

How to get there:

By bus: Bus stops in Maaruig, 5 miles away.
By car: Write hostel for directions.
By ferry: Tarbert ferry, 6 miles.

STOCKINISH HOSTEL

Kyles, Stockinish, Isle of Harris HS3 3EN

Phone Number: 01859–530–373

Rates: £3.85–£4.65 per HI member (about $6.00–$7.00 US)
Beds: 32
Private/family rooms: None
Season: March 20 to October 4
Office hours: 7:00 to 11:00 A.M.; 5:00 to 11:00 P.M.

Affiliation: HI-SYHA

Set among the stones and green, green grass of Harris Island, this converted school consists of three dorm rooms. We can't repeat it enough times: There are some amazing beaches and scenery on this island, and you'll likely be all alone, or nearly so.

Gestalt: Rising stockinish

Party index:

How to get there:

By bus: Bus from Tarbert stops nearby; call hostel for transit route.

By car: Call hostel for directions.

By ferry: Dock in Tarbert, 7 miles away.

GARENIN HOSTEL

Carloway, Isle of Lewis HS2 9AL

Rates: £3.85–£4.65 per HI member (about $6.00–$7.00 US)

Beds: 14

Private/family rooms: None

Office hours: 7:00 to 11:00 A.M.; 5:00 to 11:00 P.M.

Affiliation: HI-SYHA

This gets one of our awards for best location in Scotland: It's a thatched-roof beauty of a hostel, on a little secluded cove. (The structure is actually what's known as a "Black house" in these parts, for the stone used in its walls.) It is, of course, quite simple—just two dorm rooms and a kitchen, no sheets or advance bookings.

But you can get a really authentic feel for Scotland here. Explore the little village where it's located, or truck it 8 miles to Callinish and the famous, evocative standing stones. There's a beach close by, plus a good folk museum.

Party index:

How to get there:

By bus: Bus stops 1½ miles from hostel; call hostel for details.

By ferry: Ferry to Stornaway, 24 miles

KERSHADER HOSTEL

Ravenspoint, Kershader, South Lochs, Isle of Lewis HS2 9QA

Phone Number: 01851–880236

Rates: £6.50–£7.75 per HI member (about $12–$14 US)

Beds: 14
Private/family rooms: None
Office hours: Call hostel for hours
Affiliation: HI-SYHA
Extras: Store

This joint's a plain building with two quad rooms and one bigger dorm, and that's about it. Next door, a cafe sells local treats, and an attached store sells local crafts and knitwear; a bigger food market sits 4 miles away. This part of Lewis Island is, as usual, rich with bird-watching and hills to climb.

Party index:

How to get there:

By bus: Bus stops nearby; call hostel for transit route.
By car: Call hostel for directions.
By ferry: From ferry, 23 miles

TOBERMORY HOSTEL

Main Street, Tobermory, Argyll, Isle of Mull PA75 6NU

Phone Number: 01688–302481

Rates: £4.95–£6.10 per HI member (about $7.00–$9.00 US)
Credit cards: Yes
Beds: 41
Private/family rooms: None
Season: February 27 to November 1
Office hours: 7:00 A.M. to 11:45 P.M.
Affiliation: HI-SYHA
Extras: Store, bike rentals

This hostel's so rustic there's no hot water or even a shower. At least they do bike rentals. Eight dorms, all the same size, provide your bunk; the real attraction here isn't the hostel at all, of course, but rather the colorful main street and harbor of Tobermory village.

Insider's tip:
Tiny theater in Dervaig

Gestalt:
Mull house

Party index:

How to get there:

By bus: Bus stops ¼ mile from hostel; call hostel for transit route.
By car: Take A848 to Tobermory.
By train: Take train to Oban, switch to ferry for Tobermory. Walk to hostel near dock.

RAASAY HOSTEL

Creachan Cottage, Isle of Raasay, Kyle IV40 8NT

Phone Number: 01478–660240

Rates: £3.85–£4.65 per HI member (about $6.00–$7.00 US)
Beds: 30
Private/family rooms: None
Season: March 20 to November 1
Office hours: 7:00 to 11:00 A.M.; 5:00 to 11:00 P.M.
Affiliation: HI-SYHA

Four dorms of roughly equal size occupy this stone building set on a peaceful little island nestled within the Isle of Skye; it's as wild and beautiful as Skye, and equally little-populated. There is also a kitchen. While on the island, kick back and check out the nature—especially nice on two wheels.

Party index:

How to get there:

By ferry: Take ferry to dock, then walk 3 miles to hostel (except Sundays).

ISLE OF SKYE

Skye has rightly been called "Scotland in a thimble" (or something like that): a short course in everything that is wonderful about this land—enough cliffs, castles, white-capped peaks, green hills, and gray ocean that you wouldn't need to go anywhere else and you'd still get a staggering eyeful of scenery.

A controversial bridge was recently installed to connect the island to the "mainland," but the island hasn't changed too much yet. It's still an incredibly wild land.

Hostels are sprouting left and right here, too, to take advantage of increasing numbers of visitors—most of them really excellent places, a cut above Scotland's usually fairly drab digs.

Bus service is the only way to go here, but it's darned expensive. Oh, well, you've got no choice; renting a car is even more pricey, and a bike won't get you everywhere on this up-and-down, surprisingly huge island.

SKYE HOSTELS at a glance

	RATING	COST	IN A WORD
Kyleakin Hostel	👍	£7.10–£9.60	comfy
Portree Backpackers	👍	£7.50–£9.00	good
Dun Flodigarry	👍	£7.50–£8.50	okay
Skye Backpackers	👍	£8.90–£9.90	cheery
Skyewalker Hostel		£7.00	rustic
Croft Bunkhouse		£6.00	simple
Broadford Hostel		£6.50–£7.75	typical
Armadale Hostel		£4.95–£6.10	scenic
Glenbrittle		£4.95–£6.10	plain
Uig Hostel		£4.95–£6.10	big
Portree Independent		£7.50–£8.50	worn
Portree Harbour		£7.50	spartan

ARMADALE HOSTEL

Armadale, Sleat, Isle of Skye

Phone Number: 01471–844260

Rates: £4.95–£6.10 per HI member (about $7.00–$9.00 US)
Credit cards: Yes
Beds: 40
Private/family rooms: None
Season: March 20 to November 1
Office hours: 7:00 A.M. to 11:45 P.M.
Affiliation: HI-SYHA

A simple place to crash overlooking Armadale Bay, this hostel has a view of boats below. The hostel—equipped with six quad rooms and five larger bunkrooms—is positioned just half a mile from the ferry to Mallaig on the Scottish mainland. Good if you're exhausted and don't wanna walk far.

A couple of problems we noticed here, though: The hostel's a ways from anything besides a convenience store. And the dorms got

Armadale Hostel entrance

Armadale, Isle of Skye, Scotland

(photo by Martha Coombs)

quite cramped, especially in the larger ten-person rooms; the ceiling is peaked and quite low, so top-bunk denizens better watch their heads.

Couldn't ask for a better setting, though, right on the water in some of Scotland's most beautiful country. The Sleat area's known for its otters, deer, eagles, flowers, castle, and a local Gaelic college; sample it all, but be prepared to walk. Buses run only occasionally (and hardly at all on Sunday). A bike is a near necessity.

Insiders' tip:
Hike to castle costs money

Party index:

How to get there:

By bus: Bus stops ¼ mile from hostel; call hostel for transit route.

By car: From Broadford take A851, or from Ardvasar take A853 to Armadale Bay. Hostel is marked by sign, near Armadale pier.

By train: From Mallaig Station take ferry to island; walk ½ mile to hostel.

BROADFORD HOSTEL

Broadford, Isle of Skye IV49 9AA

Phone Number: 01471–822442

Rates: £6.50–£7.75 per HI member (about $10–$12 US)
Credit cards: Yes
Beds: 65
Private/family rooms: None
Season: January 30 to December 31
Office hours: 7:00 A.M. to 11:45 P.M.
Affiliation: HI-SYHA
Extras: Store, laundry

Right near Broadford Bay on the spectacular Isle of Skye, this hostel's a big house with fourteen dorm rooms of four to eight beds apiece. They're small and slightly cramped rooms, yeah, but at least the place was sparkling clean when we came through.

The hostel maintains a laundry, hostel store, and kitchen as well. Don't miss the scenery or the seal sanctuary near the hostel. Broadford itself is nothing but a place to crash, a base for cycling miles out into the gorgeous west Skye countryside.

Insiders' tip:
Serpentarium nearby

Gestalt:
Broadford tough

Party index:

How to get there:

By bus: Bus stops ½ mile from hostel; call hostel for transit route.

By car: Take A850 to Broadford, turn north on A854. Hostel is on left.

GLENBRITTLE HOSTEL

Glenbrittle, Carbost, Isle of Skye IV47 8TA

Phone Number: 01478–640278

Rates: £4.95–£6.10 per HI member (about $7.00–$9.00 US)
Credit cards: Yes
Beds: 46
Private/family rooms: None
Season: March 20 to November 1
Office hours: 7:00 A.M. to 11:45 P.M.
Affiliation: HI-SYHA
Extras: Store

This place is best used as a base for climbers or hikers. There are four big dorm rooms for you, although schoolkids sometimes come

Party index:

here to study local flora and fauna and pack 'em up.

A small store and kitchen are also included. For historical buffs, there are some slight Viking remains in the area. This is definitely off-the-beaten-track Skye, which might appeal to you after a couple days in the major towns of the island.

How to get there:

By bus: Bus stops 7 miles from hostel; call hostel for transit route.

By car: Call hostel for directions.

KYLEAKIN HOSTEL

Kyleakin, Isle of Skye IV41 8PL

Phone Number: 01599–534–585

Rates: £7.10–£9.60 per HI member (about $11–$15 US)
Credit cards: Yes
Beds: 108
Private/family rooms: Yes
Office hours: 7:00 A.M. to 2:00 A.M.
Affiliation: HI-SYHA
Extras: Meals ($), laundry, store, breakfast

This good hostel, located in a blah building with cute awnings, has a country-inn feel to it.

Almost all the thirty-eight rooms here are quads (though there are three big bunkroooms if you're into that sort of thing); indeed, you can pay extras for nice doubles with light breakfast included—a rare treat on the hostelling highway. Meals here are pretty good, too. Other niceties include a store, laundry, and wheelchair accessibility.

Gestalt: Big Skye

Party index:

In the area, check out the Viking-era castle ruins just above the village—pretty cool—or maybe take a seal-watching cruise. That's about all there is to do. Oh, and by all means take a local bus (which doesn't run Sundays) about 10 miles inland to Eilean Donan castle, a spectacular ruin featured in the film *Highlander* and on zillions of Scottish postcards.

How to get there:

By bus: From Inverness take bus to Kyleakin. Hostel is across street from bus stop.

By car: Take A87 across toll bridge and into Kyleakin; hostel is on right, across street from bus stop and next to church.

By train: From Inverness take train to Kyle of Lochalsh; walk 1 mile to hostel or take bus. Hostel is across street from bus stop.

SKYE BACKPACKERS 

Benmhor, Kyleakin, Isle of Skye IV41 8PH

Phone Number: 01599–534510

Fax: 01599–534510
Rates: £8.90–£9.90 (about $13–$15 US) per person
Beds: 35
Private/family rooms: Yes
Office hours: 7:00 A.M. to 2:00 A.M.
Affiliation: None
Extras: Breakfast ($), bike rentals, fireplace

Skye Backpackers is a fun hostel located right at the entranceway village on the Isle of Skye. It's a little more expensive than the others on the island, and cleanliness isn't the top priority, but a really international crowd supplies maximum socializing before you jump onto Skye. The place gives off a cheery, cozy, inviting vibe. The comfy common room's a hit, and sometimes fires in the fireplace make it even more so.

Dorm rooms here are separated by sex, which was nice to see. The bathrooms were separated as well, another definite plus. One private room is actually romantic, although—as with the rest of the place—the physical condition could use some work.

People here are really friendly, though, and the kitchen is nicely decorated; you get free coffee and cocoa, are welcome to use the kitchen to store food and make meals, and a nice breakfast is prepared each morning for a small charge.

Given a choice, we'd never base ourselves in Kyleakin (say Kyle-ahk'-in)—it's too far from all the natural wonders of Skye and doesn't have anything besides a couple pubs and restaurants for fueling up tourists. But this hostel's so much fun that if you're starving for contact, it is definitely recommendable, and if you're heading on or off early in the morning, it's a good bet.

Best bet for a bite:
Wholefoods restaurant across bridge

What hostellers say:
Duuuuude!

Gestalt:
Skye opener

Hospitality: 

Party index:

How to get there:

By bus: Hostel is across street from Kyleakin bus stop.

By car: Take A87 to Kyle of Lochalsh; cross toll bridge to Isle of Skye, turn left, then turn right to hostel.

By train: Take train from Inverness to Kyle of Lochalsh, then take local bus across bridge to Kyleakin. Hostel is across street from bus stop.

CROFT BUNKHOUSE AND BOTHIES

Portnalong, Isle of Skye IV47 8SL

Phone Number: 01478–640254

Fax: 01478–640254
Rates: £6.00 (about $9.00 US) per person
Credit cards: Yes
Beds: 30
Affiliation: None
Extras: Camping, laundry, table tennis, darts

This croft farm-turned-hostel wonderfully preserves the feisty spirit of independent hostelling. Owner Pete Thomas coordinates a network of northern Scotland hostels, bothies, and other rustic accommodations and also finds time to run this place—a combination of all three, really.

Gestalt: Arts and crofts

Party index:

The main bunkhouse holds fourteen on foam mattresses, the bothy (a primitive barnlike structure made of stone) holds six, a new unit sleeps four and adds a private kitchen and bathroom, and a cabin facing the sea functions as simple but homey love nest.

How to get there:

By bus: Call hostel for transit route.
By car: Call hostel for directions.

SKYEWALKER INDEPENDENT HOSTEL

Old School Fiskavaig Road, Portnalong, Isle of Skye IV47 8SL

Phone Number: 01478–640250

Fax: 01478–640440
E-mail: skyewalker@easynet.co.uk
Beds: 34
Rates: £7.00 per person (about $11 US)
Affiliation: None
Extras: Cafe, TV, laundry

This whimsically named hostel, located in the same building as the Portnalong post office and practically beside the village pub, offers a genuine look at the real Skye; this town isn't on the tour bus itinerary, not at all.

It's a basic bunk, sure, but includes a good restaurant on premises as well as decent kitchen facilities. Dorms come in three eight-bedded rooms and one bigger ten-bedded room; a laundry and television lounge complete the picture.

How to get there:

By bus: Call hostel for transit route.
By car: Call hostel for directions.

PORTREE BACKPACKERS HOSTEL

6 Woodpark, Dunvegan Road, Portree, Isle of Skye IV51 9HQ

Phone Number: 01478–613641

Fax: 01478–613641
Rates: £7.50–£9.00 per person (about $12–$14 US)
Beds: 26
Season: March 1 to October 1
Affiliation: None

A good place that's sometimes booked up with lucky groups, this is the best of Portree's three hostels. It's also the only one that isn't right in town, but it's only a short walk to get here.

Gestalt:
Portreehouse

Hospitality:

Cleanliness:

Party index:

How to get there:

By bus: From Kyleakin take bus to Portree; call hostel for directions.
By car: Call hostel for directions.
By train: From Kyle of Lochalsh Station, take bus to Portree; call hostel for directions.

PORTREE HARBOUR BACKPACKERS

The Pier, Portree, Isle of Skye IV51 9DD

Phone Number: 01478–613332

Rates: £7.50 per person (about $13 US); doubles £17 (about $25 US)
Beds: 11

You can't get any more basic than this. Located on the second floor above a fish-and-chips shop, the hostel consists of five singles in one room and three double mattresses. On the floor. There are a couple of pubs nearby, a great view of Portree Harbor out the window, and that's it. The kitchen and bathroom are adequate.

Best bet for a bite: Chip shop below

Gestalt: Piss-Portree

Party index:

Strangely, staff are never around; things work somewhat on the honor system here. We're not even sure if they lock the doors at night. At any rate, it's a bed if everything else is full, but we wouldn't go out of the way to stay here.

How to get there:

By bus: From Kyleakin take bus to Portree; walk to harbor and down steps. Hostel is on right, just past fish-and-chips shop.

By car: Call hostel for directions.

By train: From Kyle of Lochalsh Station, take bus to Portree; walk to harbor and down steps. Hostel is on right, just past fish-and-chips shop.

PORTREE INDEPENDENT HOSTEL

Old Post Office, The Green, Portree, Isle of Skye IV51 9BT

Phone Number: 01478–613737

Rates: £7.50–£8.50 per person (about $12–$15 US); doubles £17–£19 (about $25–$30 US)
Beds: 60
Family/private rooms: Yes
Season: March 1 to October 31
Office hours: 7:30 A.M. to 10:00 P.M.
Extras: Laundry, breakfast

Right off the main square of workaday Portree, this hostel's conveniently placed and is practically the first thing you see when you get off the bus. As a hostel, it's so-so; with some improvement, it could be really good.

Best bet for a bite: Ben Tianavaig (veggie)

Insiders' tip: Ceilidhs on weekends in area

Gestalt: Postal service

Hospitality: 

Cleanliness: 

Party index:

Beds come in rooms of four to ten bunks each, plus there's a double room and a number of quad rooms on the top floor that work as family rooms in a pinch. The enormous kitchen is terrific, and staff were very friendly when we passed through.

However, this is a quite worn building (it used to be the town post office, by the way), and cleaning is not scrupulous. Don't be surprised if the lights don't work sometimes. Laundry and breakfast are also offered here.

How to get there:

By bus: Call hostel for transit route.

By car: Call hostel for directions.

Portree Independent Hostel
Portree, Isle of Skye, Scotland
(photo by Paul Karr)

DUN FLODIGARRY HOSTEL

Staffin, Isle of Skye IV51 9HZ0

Phone Number: 01470–552212

Fax: 01470–552212
Rates: £7.50–£9.00 per person (about $12–$13 US)
Beds: 66
Private/family rooms: Sometimes
Affiliation: None
Extras: Breakfast ($), laundry

This good hostel near Staffin, north of Portree on the Isle of Skye, is worth figuring out the confusing local bus routes. You'll pay a small charge for breakfast; otherwise they supply everything you'll need.

You're near pretty Staffin Bay, the towering Old Man of Storr (a rock), and other coastal treasures; hostellers reported good experiences here. Note that you might need to take a postbus—basically, pay a few pounds to ride along with the mail carrier—to get here, and you can't get here at all Sundays by public transit.

Gestalt:
Dun deal

Party index:

How to get there:

By bus: Take bus from Inverness to Portree or to Kyleakin and transfer for local bus to Portree. Then take a local bus to Staffin.

By car: Call hostel for directions.

UIG HOSTEL

Uig, Isle of Skye IV51 9YD

Phone Number: 01470–542–211

Rates: £4.95–£6.10 per HI member (about $7.00–$9.00 US)
Credit cards: Yes
Beds: 62
Private/family rooms: Yes
Season: March 20 to November 1
Office hours: 7:00 A.M. to 11:45 P.M.
Affiliation: HI-SYHA
Extras: Store

Gestalt: Uigwam

Hospitality:

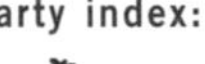

Party index:

A whitewashed but surprisingly big building, this hostel's 2 miles from a ferry boat to Harris Island. It's quite a friendly place, stocked with seven dorm rooms, a store, and a kitchen. Fun stuff in the area includes a July music festival and the August Highland Games.

How to get there:

By bus: Bus stops nearby; call hostel for transit route.

By car: Take A586 to Uig Bay.

JOHN O' GROATS (CANISBAY) HOSTEL

Canisbay (John O' Groats), Wick, Caithness KW1 4YH

Phone Number: 01955–611424

Rates: £4.95–£6.10 per HI member (about $7.00–$9.00 US)
Credit cards: Yes
Beds: 40
Private/family rooms: None
Season: March 20 to November 1
Office hours: 7:00 A.M. to 11:45 P.M.
Affiliation: HI-SYHA

Party index:

This solid-as-a-rock house contains two quad hostel rooms and five bigger ones. It's 3 miles to food, but at least you can eat the scenery along the way. You're a couple miles from the famous northern tip of Scotland, as well as ferries to Orkney.

How to get there:

By bus: Bus stops nearby; call hostel for transit route.

By car: Take A836 to Canisbay turnoff.

By ferry: Orkney passenger ferry, 3 miles; Orkney car ferry, 21 miles.

By train: Wick Station, 17 miles away, is closest.

CUCHULAINN'S BACKPACKERS HOSTEL

Station Road, Kyle of Lochalsh, Ross-shire IV40 8AF

Phone Number: 01599–534492

Rates: £8.00–£9.50 per person (about $12–$14 US)
Beds: 12
Affiliation: None
Extras: Laundry, bar, restaurant

This hostel is just as well situated as the other three hostels that lie in Kyleakin across the hotly debated bridge to the Isle of Skye. Though small, it's nicely outfitted with a twin (two people can sleep here), a quad, and a small dorm with six beds. Toilets and showers, unfortunately, are on the ground floor and not near the rooms. A tidy and well-equipped kitchen rounds out the accommodations.

For social life, you can't ask for much more than a pub/restaurant combo adjacent to the hostel—it serves up everything from Mexican to vegetarian to pub grub, plus local beers on tap! Truly excellent food choices.

Insiders' tip:
Toilets cost at bus stop, free at train station

Gestalt:
Skye's the limit

Party index:

If you're traveling with a big group, it would be advantageous to book out the entire hostel; you'll end up having the entire place to yourself and will be steps away from regular buses going to the Isle of Skye one way and the amazing Eilean Donan Castle in the other direction. The train station back to Inverness is just a short walk away.

How to get there:

By bus: Take bus from Inverness to Kyle of Lochalsh. From bus station walk up to main road (A87). Cross street to hostel, above pub.

By car: Drive A87 to Kyle of Lochalsh; hostel is on right, just before Skye Bridge.

By train: Take train from Inverness to Kyle of Lochalsh. From station walk up inclined road to main road (A87). Turn left and walk 1 block; hostel is on left.

LOCH NESS BACKPACKERS LODGE

Coiltie Farmhouse, Lewiston, Drumnadrochit, Inverness-shire IV3 6UT

Phone Number: 01456–450–807

Beds: 32
Rates: £8.50–£9.00 per person (about $13–$14 US); doubles £22–£24 (about $33–$36 US)
Office hours: 7:30 A.M. to 11:30 P.M.
Extras: Bike rentals, breakfast, tours, TV, VCR, garden, grill

Having a choice between a remote and sterile SYHA hostel or this one, ensconced in a wildly stereotypical quaint little Scots village, you'd do slightly better to pick this one, though we're not giving it a wholehearted recommendation.

How come? Well, management is a little forgetful about reservations, and the quarters are ultracramped. More emphasis is placed on the outward appearance of the hostel than on the actual comfort of the guests, but it's still okay.

Best bet for a bite: Lewiston Arms

Insiders' tip: Hostellers have sighted "something"

What hostellers say: "I felt something slither against my leg . . ."

Gestalt: Loch on wood

Hospitality: 

Cleanliness: 

Party index:

The hostel is divvied up between a nice little farmhouse and a purpose-built addition in the back that is usually reserved for groups. Seven beds and a tiny double as well as a common room occupy the main house. For couch potatoes, a moist cold TV room with a confounding TV/VCR and sagging couches awaits with lots of videos with a Scots theme; i.e., *Braveheart, Rob Roy,* and *Highlander III* (skip it, it sucks). Sadly, though, the ultimate Scots movie, *Local Hero,* is missing from the lineup.

We found the bunkroom where we were stuffed to be really unpleasant, though. A freezing room that should be a private room, it's crammed with three sets of bunks. If you can count, that means six adult-sized people have to share a room that, by fire code standards, should only fit two. To add insult to injury, you have to go outside to access the toilets (void of loo rolls) and scalding hot showers.

Despite the negatives, you are well located here. The town of Lewiston is picture-perfect and ultrapastoral (verdant hills, hairy coos, and purple thistles border the hostel). You can do your Nessie stalking (staff and hostelers have claimed sightings) either by foot (a dangerous road with not a lot of shoulder) or by

Loch Ness Backpackers Lodge

Lewiston, Scotland

(photo by Paul Karr)

a boat tour that you can book through the desk. Urquhart Castle (or what's left of it) is also accessible by this road or by boat.

There's a small supermarket up the road a piece with lots of refined and superprocessed foods; you'd do better to stock up in Inverness before you arrive. Otherwise, take a chance on pub food. Buses run rather infrequently to and from Inverness. Make sure you get correct timetables and bus stop instructions from the hostel; the bus drivers are sticklers about time and place. You can also take buses from here to the Isle of Skye.

How to get there:

By bus: From Inverness take bus to Drumnadrochit; stay on bus and ask driver for drop-off at Backpackers in Lewiston, 1 mile farther along. Walk down lane to hostel on left.

By car: From Inverness drive south to Drumnadrochit, then continue south 1 mile. Turn left at sign; hostel is on left.

By train: From Inverness Station take bus to Drumnadrochit; stay on bus and ask driver for drop-off at Backpackers in Lewiston, 1 mile farther along. Walk down lane to hostel on left.

LOCHMADDY HOSTEL

Ostram House, Lochmaddy, North Uist PA82 5AE

Phone Number: 01876–500–368

Rates: £4.95–£6.10 per HI member (about $7.00–$9.00 US)
Credit cards: Yes
Beds: 36
Private/family rooms: None
Season: May 15 to October 1
Office hours: 7:00 A.M. to 11:45 P.M.
Affiliation: HI-SYHA

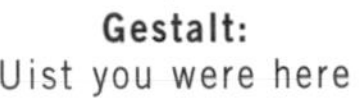

Gestalt:
Uist you were here

Party index:

Five dorm rooms in a handsome big house at the center of tiny Lochmaddy village on North Uist island: That's all she wrote here. There is a kitchen, too, and everything you need—village market, ferry dock—is within a couple minutes' walk.

How to get there:

By bus: Bus stops ¼ mile from hostel; call hostel for details.

By car: Take A865 to Lochmaddy turnoff; hostel is in village.

By ferry: Ferry dock, ½ mile.

EDAY HOSTEL

London Bay, Eday, Orkney Islands KW17 2AB

Phone Number: 01857–622283

Rates: £3.85–£4.65 per HI member (about $6.00–$7.00 US)
Beds: 24
Private/family rooms: None
Season: April 1 to September 30
Office hours: 7:00 to 11:00 A.M.; 5:00 to 11:00 P.M.
Affiliation: HI-SYHA

Gestalt:
East of Eday

Party index:

This is definitely getting away from it all: a plain brown-and-green building on lightly visited Eday island outfitted with two dorm rooms of twelve beds apiece . . . yeah, that's about it. It's about a mile and a half to a shop with food.

How to get there:

By ferry: Take ferry to Eday landing, 4 miles away.

HOY HOSTEL

Hoy, Stromness, Orkney Islands KW16 3NJ

Rates: £4.95–£6.10 per HI member (about $7.00–$9.00 US)
Beds: 26
Private/family rooms: None
Season: May 2 to September 12
Office hours: 7:00 A.M. to 11:45 P.M.
Affiliation: HI-SYHA

Hoy, the second largest of the Orkneys, has this simple but intriguing hostel. All six dorm rooms are about the same size, there's a simple kitchen, and the place is wheelchair accessible. It's 10 miles to the nearest market, however.

At least you're near the Old Man of Hoy, a sandstone pillar that's justifiably famous to gawkers and nutso rock-climbers alike.

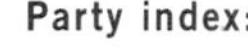

Party index:

How to get there:

By ferry: Ferry from Stromness lands 1½ miles away.

RACKWICK HOSTEL

Hoy, Stromness, Orkney Islands KW16 3NJ

Phone Number: 01856–873535, extension 2404

Rates: £4.95–£6.10 per HI member (about $7.00–$9.00 US)
Beds: 8
Private/family rooms: None
Season: March 14 to September 12
Office hours: 7:00 A.M. to 11:45 P.M.
Affiliation: HI-SYHA

Another Hostelling International hostel on the Isle of Hoy, this one's the closer of the two to the Old Man of Hoy. It's just two quad rooms in a simple cottage, and there are no sheets or kitchen. You're probably here for the Old Man, which is 2 miles away—and a serious and dangerous climb for experts only.

Party index:

How to get there:

By ferry: From Stromness take ferry to Hoy; dock is 6 miles from hostel.

KIRKWALL HOSTEL 

Old Scapa Road, Kirkwall, Orkney Islands KW15 1BB

Phone Number: 01856–872243

Rates: £6.50–£7.75 per HI member (about $10–$12 US)
Credit cards: Yes
Beds: 83
Private/family rooms: Yes
Season: February 27 to November 1
Office hours: 7:00 A.M. to 11:45 P.M.
Affiliation: HI-SYHA
Extras: Store, laundry

Thumbs up to the staff here, who run a low-slung building in the capital island (and town) of the Orkneys. This hostel is spacious and never loud; all rooms are quads, and the nearby attractions include a twelfth-century cathedral. Extra thumbs-up for thinking to include a laundry and kitchen, as well as making the place accessible to wheelchairs.

Gestalt: Noah's Orkney

Hospitality:

Party index:

How to get there:

By bus: Bus stops ½ mile from hostel; call hostel for transit route.

By ferry: Fifteen miles to Stromness ferry, ½ mile to island ferry

PAPA WESTRAY HOSTEL

Beltane House, Papa Westray, Orkney Islands KW17 2BU

Phone Number: 01857–644–267

Rates: £6.50–£7.75 per HI member (about $10–$12 US)
Beds: 16
Private/family rooms: Sometimes
Office hours: 7:00 A.M. to 11:45 P.M.
Affiliation: HI-SYHA
Extras: Store, pickups from ferry

Gestalt: Papa bear

Party index:

Just two dorms here in a low stone building, but if they're empty—which is fairly often—they'll let you use them for your family or sweetie. There's no kitchen, but a nearby shop sells staples.

"Papay," as the island of Papa Westray is locally known, is a small and less-visited island with an old, old history: An archaeological site dating from 5,500 years ago near the hostel called the Knap of Howar may be the oldest structure in northwest Europe. Coooooool!

How to get there:

By ferry: Ferry to Kirkwall, 2 miles away.

STROMNESS HOSTEL

Hellihole Road, Stromness, Orkney Islands KW16 3DE

Phone Number: 01856–850589

Rates: £4.95–£6.10 per HI member (about $7.00–$9.00 US)
Credit cards: Yes
Beds: 40
Private/family rooms: None
Season: March 20 to November 1
Office hours: 7:00 A.M. to 11:45 P.M.
Affiliation: HI-SYHA

In the mainland village of the Orkneys, not far from the ferry pier to the islands, this place is okay if you're stuck for the night—though, given a choice, we'd definitely jump a boat and head out to sea. Five dorm rooms are available here.

Insiders' tip: Great folk festival in May

Party index:

How to get there:

By bus: Bus stop nearby; call hostel for transit route.

By car: Call hostel for directions.

PLOCKTON STATION BUNKHOUSE

Plockton, Ross-shire IV52 8TF

Phone Number: 01599–544235

Rates: £10 per person (about $15 US)
Beds: 20
Affiliation: None

This place is pretty basic, set in a bunkhouse next to Plockton Station (in case you couldn't figure that out). That location's a bummer, as you're eyeball to eyeball with the trains—unless you like trains, in which case you'll be in heaven.

Gestalt: Stationary

Party index:

This is the last stop on the North Highland train line before the Isle of Skye, and it's a little hard to figure out at first glance why anyone in his or her right mind would get off here. However, a number of pretty walks can start in Plockton—and they go where the tourists aren't, as opposed to Skye, where they definitely are. Plockton itself's a cute little lochhead town that doubles as the town in a Scottish soap opera. Worth a visit? Maybe. Check out the palm trees by the water, too.

How to get there:

By car: Call hostel for directions.

By train: Take train from Inverness or Kyle of Lochalsh to Plockton. Hostel is next to train platform.

LERWICK HOSTEL

Isleburgh House, King Harald Street, Lerwick, Shetland Islands ZE1 0EQ

Phone Number: 01595–692114

Rates: £6.50–£7.75 per HI member (about $10–$12 US)
Beds: 64
Private/family rooms: Yes
Season: April 3 to October 2
Office hours: 7:00 A.M. to 11:45 P.M.
Affiliation: HI-SYHA
Extras: Meals ($), store, laundry

This grand renovated two-story house on a peninsula has six quads for family rooms, plus five bigger dorms. They also have a kitchen, store, and laundry and do meal service.

Party index:

This is a small but surprisingly hip town, too, with Deadhead and granola types abounding. Maybe it's hip because it's so accessible for such a remote place: You can take a ferry here from Bergen (that's in Norway!), Aberdeen, or the Orkneys.

How to get there:

By bus: Bus stops ½ mile from hostel.

By car: From Scalloway take A970 to Shetland; make a left onto King Harald Street. Hostel is on left.

By ferry: One mile.

LOCH LOCHY HOSTEL

South Laggan, Spean Bridge, Inverness-shire PH34 4EA

Phone Number: 01809–501–239

Rates: £4.95–£6.10 per HI member (about $7.00–$9.00 US)
Credit cards: Yes
Beds: 60
Private/family rooms: None
Season: March 20 to November 1
Office hours: 7:00 A.M. to 11:45 P.M.
Affiliation: HI-SYHA

Extras: Store

This hostel is inside a two-story stone house beside a canal. It consists of eight dorms with five to eight bunks each and one still larger dorm. Invergary Castle's ruins are just 2½ miles away if you don't mind the walk, or hang out in the shade of the fir trees.

Party index:

How to get there:

By bus: Bus stops neaby; call hostel for transit route.

By car: From Fort William or Inverness, take A82 to Loch Lochy.

By train: Spean Bridge Station, 11 miles.

HOWMORE HOSTEL

Howmore, South Uist HS8 5SH

No phone

Rates: £3.85–£4.65 per HI member (about $6.00–$7.00 US)
Beds: 17
Private/family rooms: None
Office hours: Vary
Affiliation: HI-SYHA

It's another whitewashed croft house hostel, and therefore extremely simple: Bring a heavy sleeping bag, don't try to make an advance booking, and just enjoy the peace and quiet of the place. Wild and lonely beaches abound in the area.

Party index:

How to get there:

By bus: Bus stops ¾ mile from hostel; write hostel for transit route.

By ferry: Ferry lands at Lochboisdale, 28 miles away.

STRATHPEFFER HOSTEL

Strathpeffer, Ross-shire IV14 9BT

Phone Number: 01997–421532

Rates: £4.95–£6.10 per HI member (about $7.00–$9.00 US)
Credit cards: Yes
Beds: 62
Private/family rooms: None
Season: February 27 to November 1
Office hours: 7:00 A.M. to 11:45 P.M.
Affiliation: HI-SYHA

Extras: Store

In a famous spa town, this tall house contains seven dorms plus food supply depot and kitchen. The best thing to do in this tiny town is go to the square on Saturday nights and listen to bagpipe music. Cool. Or head to Kinellin Loch nearby for a dose of nature.

Party index:

How to get there:

By bus: Bus stops nearby; call hostel for transit route.

By car: Take A834 to Strathpeffer.

By train: Dingwall Station is 5 miles away.

TONGUE HOSTEL

Tongue, By Lairg, Sutherland IV27 4XH

Phone Number: 01847–611301

Rates: £4.95–£6.10 per HI member (about $7.00–$9.00 US)
Credit cards: Yes
Beds: 40
Private/family rooms: None
Season: March 20 to November 1
Office hours: 7:00 A.M. to 11:45 P.M.
Affiliation: HI-SYHA
Extras: Store

A two-story building with impressive chimneys, this place has five dorm rooms. It's a mile to market, or you can get basic supplies in the hostel shop. There's good bird-watching at hand in the area.

Insiders' tip: Tongue bath

Party index:

How to get there:

By bus: Bus and Postbus stop nearby; call hostel for transit route.

By car: Take A836 to Tongue; hostel is just outside village, near A838 causeway to Durness.

By train: Lairg Station, 37 miles away, is nearest stop.

TORRIDON HOSTEL

Torridon, Ross-shire IV22 2EZ

Phone Number: 01445–791284

Rates: £6.50–£7.75 per HI member (about $10–$12 US)
Credit cards: Yes
Beds: 80
Private/family rooms: Yes

Season: January 30 to November 1
Office hours: 7:00 A.M. to 11:45 P.M.
Affiliation: HI-SYHA
Extras: Store, laundry

This hostel's grim-looking, but it's in an amazing location right at the shore of Loch Torridon and at the base of huge rugged hills. Climbing opportunities abound.

The facility itself has two quad rooms, eight dorms of five to eight beds each and one even larger bunkroom, as well as a kitchen, laundry, and hostel store.

How to get there:

By bus: Bus stops nearby; call hostel for transit route.
By car: Take A896 to Torridon.
By train: Achnasheen Station is 19 miles away.

ULLAPOOL HOSTEL

Shore Street, Ullapool, Ross-shire IV26 2UJ

Phone Number: 01854–612254

Rates: £6.50–£7.75 per HI member (about $10–$12 US)
Credit cards: Yes
Beds: 62
Private/family rooms: None
Season: January 30 to December 31
Office hours: 7:00 A.M. to 11:45 P.M.
Affiliation: HI-SYHA
Extras: Store, laundry

Central in the village of Ullapool, this hostel's got two quads and seven larger dorms, plus good facilities including a laundry, store, and kitchen.

The ferry to Lewis Island is close by, and that's where most arrivals are going. Frankly, Lewis is probably more interesting than this town, but you might try out the indoor swimming pool in the area. Also check out the interesting mix of folks who wind up in Ullapool: It's not just Scots!

Gestalt:
Ullapool party

Party index:

How to get there:

By bus: Bus stops ¼ mile from hostel; call hostel for transit route.
By car: Take A835 to Ullapool. Hostel is on right, entering village.

NORTHERN IRELAND

Numbers on map refer to towns numbered below.

1. Armagh
2. Ballintoy
3. Ballycastle
4. Belfast
5. Cushendall
6. Derrylane
7. Irvinestown
8. Londonderry (Derry)
9. Newcastle
10. Omagh
11. Portaferry
12. Portstewart

NORTHERN IRELAND

You'll hear good and bad stuff about Northern Ireland. The bad, of course, you've seen on the evening news. The good, well, that's less publicized—but this in an incredibly gorgeous land of sea cliffs, farms, and nice squares in small, manageable cities. The hostels here are almost all uniformly good, the people are very friendly, and the roads—well, if you've just come from Ireland, you'll be in for a pleasant treat.

To get here, you can take a ferry from Scotland or Wales. Or board a special bus that includes your ferry fare with the cost of the ticket.

ARMAGH HOSTEL

39 Abbey Street, Armagh BT61 1EB

Phone Number: 011861–511800

Fax: 011861–511801
Rates: £7.00–£13 per HI member (about $11–$20 US)
Credit cards: Yes
Beds: 64
Affiliation: HI-YHANI
Extras: TV, bureau de change, bike rental

This hostel is so brand-spankin'-new that we couldn't get there by press time, but we're hearing good early reports. All the rooms are doubles or quads, which is terrific news, and all apparently contain en-suite bathrooms, too. Other services include bikes for rent and a money exchanging desk; the common room, of course, has a television.

Gestalt:
Call to Armagh

Party index:

Armagh itself, though troubled in recent decades because it's on the border of Ireland and Northern Ireland, is a decent place to stop over. The city has a beautiful mall—not the kind where you shop, but rather a beautiful green area surrounded by trees, perfect for Frisbee playing or sitting or whatever else.

How to get there:

By bus: Bus station is 250 yards from hostel.
By car: Call hostel for directions.
By train: Call hostel for transit route.

SHEEP ISLAND VIEW HOSTEL

42A Main Street, Ballintoy, Ballycastle, County Antrim BT546 LX

Phone Number: 012657–69391 or 012657–62470

Rates: £8.00–£9.00 per person (about $12–$14 US); double £16–18 (about $24–$27 US)
Beds: 38
Private/family rooms: Yes
Affiliation: IHH
Extras: Meals ($), camping, laundry, bike rentals

This IHH-affiliated joint is pretty new, but it's well placed on the wild northern coast of Northern Ireland, and early reports say it's a decent place.

Gestalt: Sheepish

Party index:

Besides the dorms, there's one private room here, a campground, a laundry, and some bikes for hire.

How to get there:

By bus: Call hostel for pickup.
By car: Call hostel for directions.
By train: Call hostel for transit route.

WHITEPARK BAY HOSTEL 

157 Whitepark Road, Ballintoy, Ballycastle, County Antrim BT54 6NH

Phone Number: 012657–31745

Fax: 012657–32034
Rates: £7–£13 per person (about $11–$20 US)
Credit cards: Yes
Beds: 62
Family/private rooms: Yes
Affiliation: HI-YHANI
Extras: Bike rentals, meals ($), conference room, TV, bureau de change, tours, activities

This newly fixed up facility is the creme de la creme of Northern Irish hostelling. If you're bringing the family or are just starting out as a hosteller, it's a good place to get your feet wet—about as luxurious as a hostel can be, though predictably bland.

Rooms consists of ten quad rooms, four doubles, and one six-bedded dorm—all of which have en-suite bathroom facilities. The private rooms even have televisions in them. Coming with a group? Check out the conference rooms. Short of cash? There's a currency exchange desk here, too.

For fun, the staff sometimes organizes pub crawls and pony rides in the area and always rents out bicycles. Nearby, there's a great mile-long sandy beach that's rarely used. All in all, it's hard to go wrong.

Gestalt: Great Whitepark

Party index:

How to get there:

By bus: Bus stops 200 yards from hostel; call hostel for transit route.

By car: Take A2 6 miles west of Ballycastle; turn off at sign for Whitepark Bay, continue 150 yards to hostel.

By train: Portrush Station (12 miles away) and Coleraine Station (17 miles) are closest.

CASTLE HOSTEL

62 Quay Road, Ballycastle, County Antrim BT546 LX

Phone Number: 012657–62337

Fax: 012657–69822
Rates: £6.00 per person (about $9.00 US); doubles £15 (about $23 US)
Beds: 30
Private/family rooms: Yes
Affiliation: IHH
Extras: Laundry facilities

Plenty of room here in Ballycastle, where this thirty-bed facility doesn't ever seem to fill up. It's spic-'n'-span clean, has two private rooms and a laundry, and is wheelchair accessible.

Gestalt: Bally up

Cleanliness: 

Party index:

How to get there:

By bus: Call hostel for transit route.
By car: Call hostel for directions.
By train: Call hostel for transit route.

KEY TO ICONS

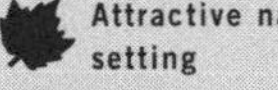

Attractive natural setting

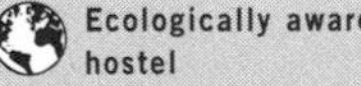

Ecologically aware hostel

Superior kitchen facilities or cafe

Offbeat or eccentric place

Superior bathroom facilities

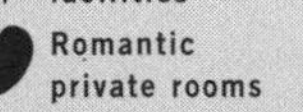

Romantic private rooms

Comfortable beds

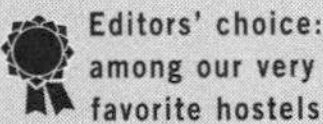

Editors' choice: among our very favorite hostels

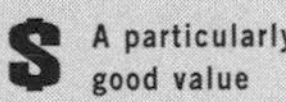

A particularly good value

Wheelchair accessible

Good for business travelers

Especially well suited for families

Good for active travelers

Visual arts at hostel or nearby

Music at hostel or nearby

Great hostel for skiers

Bar or pub at hostel or nearby

BELFAST

Despite a recent resurgence of "the Troubles," Belfast remains a fascinating visit—a peek into the real character of Northern Ireland. Just take good care to avoid a certain few neighborhoods where violence has periodically erupted.

ARNIE'S BACKPACKERS HOSTEL

63 Fitzwilliam Street, Belfast, County Antrim BT9 6AX

Phone Number: 01232–24867

Fax: 01232–24867
Rates: £7.50 per person (about $11 US)
Beds: 22
Private/family rooms: None
Affiliation: IHH
Extras: TV, fireplace, laundry

Popular, sociable, small and comfortable: That describes Arnie's, which is less ragamuffin and more tasteful than you might have expected. Dormitories are good, there's a fireplace and television in the common room, and the kitchen's kept surprisingly orderly. Queen's University is nearby, if you need the culture. There are no private rooms here, however.

Gestalt: Arnie's Army

Party index:

How to get there:

By bus: Take 70 or 71 bus to hostel.
By car: Call hostel for directions.
By ferry: Call hostel for transit route.
By train: Call hostel for transit route.

THE ARK HOSTEL

18 University Street, Belfast, County Antrim BT71 F2

Phone Number: 01232–329626

Rates: £7.50–£9.50 per person (about $12–$14 US); doubles £28 (about $42 US)
Beds: 24
Private/family rooms: Yes
Affiliation: IHH
Extras: Laundry, bike rentals

BELFAST HOSTELS at a glance

	RATING	COST	IN A WORD
Arnie's Backpackers		£7.50	comfy
The Ark		£7.50–£9.50	new
Belfast International		£12–£13	iffy

This newest Belfast joint is an unknown quantity to us. Accommodations include bunks plus three private rooms, and the hostel staff maintains a laundry and rents out bikes. Worth checking into.

Gestalt: Central Ark

Party index:

How to get there:

By bus: Call hostel for transit route.
By car: Call hostel for directions.
By ferry: Call hostel for transit route.
By train: Call hostel for transit route.

BELFAST INTERNATIONAL HOSTEL

22-32 Donegall Road, Belfast, County Antrim BT12 5JN

Phone Number: 01232–315435

Fax: 01232–439699
Rates: £12–13 per HI member (about $18–$20 US)
Credit cards: Yes
Beds: 124
Family/private rooms: Yes
Office hours: Twenty-four hours
Affiliation: HI-YHANI
Extras: Laundry, meals ($), TV, bike rentals, car rental discounts, bike storage

This An Oige hostel is a big concrete block of a building—generally blah and not in the best neighborhood of downtown, so we'd look at the two smaller places in town as possible alternatives. Also, there's no kitchen. Say what?? You gotta be kidding. We appreciate the fact that this hostel was purpose-built, but geeez.

Anyway, the place is as institutional and sterile as a hospital, though most rooms are doubles (16 of 'em) or quads (19 of those), so that's cool. It's quite clean, of course, and has a decent cafeteria and laundry. The huge common room is dominated by the TV, unfortunately.

Insiders' tip: Good bus tours of city

Gestalt: Not so Belfast

Cleanliness: 

Party index:

The area can be dodgy at night—actually, violence has occurred here during the daytime, too. It's a touchy place during summertime parades that flare the tension between Protestants and Catholics, and hostellers could come into the line of fire. That's not exactly the kind of culture we were wanting to get.

How to get there:

By bus: From bus station take 89 or 90 bus to hostel; from downtown take 69, 70, or 71 bus to hostel.

By car: Call hostel for directions.

By train: Central Station is 3 miles away.

CUSHENDALL HOSTEL

42 Layde Road, Cushendall, County Antrim BT44 0NQ

Phone Number: 012667–71344

Fax: 012667–72042
Rates: £6.50–£7.50 per HI member (about $10–$12 US)
Beds: 56
Family/private rooms: Yes
Season: March 1 to December 23
Affiliation: HI-YHANI
Extras: TV, nature center, bike rental

Interesting, um, collection of folks find their ways to this old house filled with three quad rooms, an eight-bedded dorm, and two even larger ones. There's an on-site nature center, they rent bikes, and the common room has the dreaded television—don't know how many stations they get up here, but still.

Party index:

How to get there:

By bus: Call hostel for transit route.
By car: Call hostel for directions.
By train: Call hostel for transit route.

FLAX-MILL HOSTEL 

Mill Lane, Derrylane, Dungiven, County Derry BT47

Phone Number: 015047–42655

Rates: £5.00 per person (about $8.00 US); doubles £10 (about

$15 US)
Beds: 16
Private/family rooms: Yes
Extras: Camping, laundry, bike rentals, fireplace

This old stone cottage—tucked in the woods not far from Derry City—is something else: It's powered by gas, candles, open fireplace, and a peat-fired boiler instead of electricity and offers a throwback from modern living.

The wonderful owners used to serve delicious meals, but check ahead—that practice may have been discontinued. There are still two nice private rooms, however, and a friendly pub nearby. A great place to kick back from frantic traveling.

Gestalt: Millicious

Hospitality: 

Party index:

How to get there:

By bus: Call hostel for pickup.
By car: Call hostel for directions.
By train: Call hostel for transit route.

CASTLE ARCHDALE HOSTEL

Irvinestown, County Fermanagh BT94 1PP

Phone Number: 013656–28118

Rates: £6.50–£7.50 per HI member (about $10–$12 US)
Beds: 55
Family/private rooms: Yes
Season: March 1 to December 23
Affiliation: HI-YHANI
Extras: Bike rental, TV

About 10 miles north of pretty Enniskillen, this hostel sits in a county park fronting the shores of quiet Lough Erne (and, no, that's not Lough Ernie).

Accommodations consist of one quad room, one six-bedded dorm room, and two huge dorms in an eighteenth-century house. They'll rent you a bike for trolling around, and there's a television in the common room if you really need one.

Gestalt: Arch angel

Party index: 

How to get there:

By bus: From Enniskillen take Pettigo bus to Lisnarick and walk 2 miles to hostel. Or take 194 bus to park.
By car: From Enniskillen take B82 for 11 miles north. Hostel is in park.
By train: Kesh Station is 2 miles away.

DERRY CITY HOSTEL

Oakgrove Manor, 4–6 Magazine Street, Londonderry BT48 6HJ

Phone Number: 01504–372273

Fax: 01504–372409
Rates: £8.00–£17.50 per HI member (about $12–$27 US)
Credit cards: Yes
Beds: 120
Family/private rooms: Yes
Affiliation: HI-YHANI
Extras: Breakfast, bureau de change, bike rental, laundry, fax, copier, TV
Curfew: 2:00 A.M.

Right inside the impressive city walls of Derry, this new four-story hostel with murals painted on the side looks good—dorms are roomy, there's plenty of tourist information, and a host of professional services like a fax, photocopier, and laundry should you happen to need them. A big, heavy breakfast is free, too.

Gestalt: Derry good

Party index:

The rooms come in four doubles, twelve six-bedded dorms and three fourteen-bedded dorms.

How to get there:

By bus: From bus station walk 100 yards to hostel.
By car: Call hostel for directions.
By train: From station walk 1 mile across bridge into city.

ABERFOYLE INDEPENDENT HOSTEL

29 Aberfoyle Terrace, Strand Road, Derry City (Londonderry), County Derry BT48 6HJ

Phone Number: 01504–370011

Fax: 01504–353675
Rates: £7.50 per person (about $11 US); doubles £15 (about $23 US)
Beds: 12
Season: May 15 to September 30
Affiliation: IHH
Extras: Laundry

Gestalt: Aberfoyled again

This place didn't cut it with our snoops, who judged it poorly managed and equipped. If you're still coming, though, there are just twelve beds—those include one private room—and a laundry. A bed, sure, but there are others in town, too.

How to get there:

By bus: From bus station call hostel for directions.
By car: Call hostel for directions.
By train: From train station call hostel for directions.

Party index:

NEWCASTLE HOSTEL

30 Downs Road, Newcastle, County Down BT33 0AG

Phone Number: 013967–22133

Fax: 013967–22133
Rates: £6.50–£7.50 per HI member (about $10–$12 US)
Beds: 40
Family/private rooms: Yes
Season: March 1 to December 23
Affiliation: HI-YHANI
Extras: Laundry, TV

This hostel, located on the ocean in the "other" Newcastle, is a strangely decorated old home, but it's nice to see a little change after all the drab hostels throughout the U.K. and Ireland. (Our only question: Was the wackily retro look here intentional or borne of necessity? You decide.)

Gestalt:
New order

Party index:

How to get there:

By bus: From bus station walk 150 yards to hostel.
By car: Call hostel for directions.
By train: From train station walk 1 mile to hostel.

OMAGH INDEPENDENT HOSTEL 

9A Waterworks Road, Omagh, County Tyrone BT79 7JS

Phone Number: 01662–241973

Fax: 01662–241973
Rates: £6.50 per person (about $10 US); double £15 (about $23 US)
Beds: 29
Private/family rooms: Yes
Season: January 6 to December 21
Affiliation: IHH
Extras: Camping, laundry, bike rentals

Nice place here, with an emphasis on getting out into the fresh Northern Irish air—even when that air's a little soggy. They rent bikes here, maintain a campground and laundry, and have one private room.

Gestalt:
Omagh goodness

Party index:

How to get there:

By bus: From station walk along Mountjoy Road to Killybrack Road; turn right, continue to hostel. Or call hostel for pickup.

By car: Call hostel for directions.

By train: Call hostel for transit route.

BARHOLM HOSTEL

11 The Strand, Portaferry, County Down BT22 1PS

Phone Number: 012477–29598

Fax: 012477–29598
Rates: £7.75–£8.95 per person (about $12–$13 US)
Beds: 42
Family/private rooms: Yes
Affiliation: HI-YHANI
Extras: Laundry, meeting room

This Hostelling International joint is pretty good: an old house with lake views, equipped with two dining rooms and a conference center. There are thirteen dorms in all sizes, including singles, doubles, and family rooms; some have their own en-suite bathrooms.

Gestalt:
Portaferry tale

Party index:

How to get there:

By bus: Bus stop 100 yards from hostel; from Belfast take 10 bus to Portaferry.

By car: Call hostel for directions.

By train: Belfast Central Station, 30 miles away, is closest stop; call hostel for transit route.

CAUSEWAY COAST HOSTEL

4 Victoria Terrace, Atlantic Circle, Portstewart, County Derry BT55

Phone Number: 01265–833789

Rates: £6.00 per person (about $9.00 US); doubles £15 (about $23 US)

Beds: 30
Private/family rooms: Yes
Affiliation: IHH
Extras: Fireplace, laundry

Another YHANI winner, this place is so well designed that it actually has baths and fireplaces. There's a laundry for your convenience, too, and the three private rooms are also nice.

Insiders' tip:
Morelli's for ice cream

Gestalt:
Toast of the coast

Party index:

How to get there:

By bus: Call hostel for transit route.
By car: Call hostel for directions.
By train: Call hostel for transit route.

THE TEN BEST HOSTELS IN THE U.K.

A DOZEN CLASSIC BRIT, SCOT, AND NORTHERN IRISH HOSTELS

ABOUT THE AUTHORS

Paul Karr, 32, is an award-winning writer, writing coach and author or co-author of six travel guidebooks. He contributes regularly to magazines such as *Sierra, New Age,* and *Spa,* and writes screenplays when he's not traveling. He has twice been named a writer-in-residence by the National Parks Service. You can contact him directly by e-mailing him at the following address:

Atomev@aol.com

Martha Coombs, 32, works as a translator, writer and photographer. During the past two years she has worked on location in England, France, Italy, Canada and the United States.